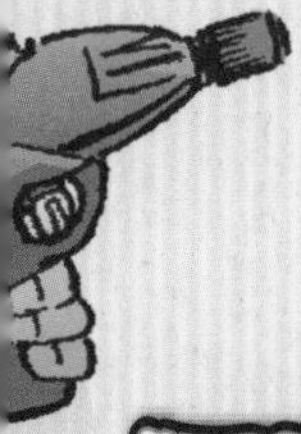

JACK of FABLES

THE FULMINATE BLADE

Bill Willingham
& Matthew Sturges
Writers

Tony Akins
Jim Fern
Pencillers

Andrew Pepoy
Joe Rubinstein
Inkers

Daniel Vozzo
Colorist

Todd Klein
Letterer

Brian Bolland
Cover Art &
Original Series Covers

Jack of Fables created by
Bill Willingham

Logo design by JAMES JEAN

JACK OF FABLES: THE FULMINATE BLADE

JACK of FABLES

THE FULMINATE BLADE

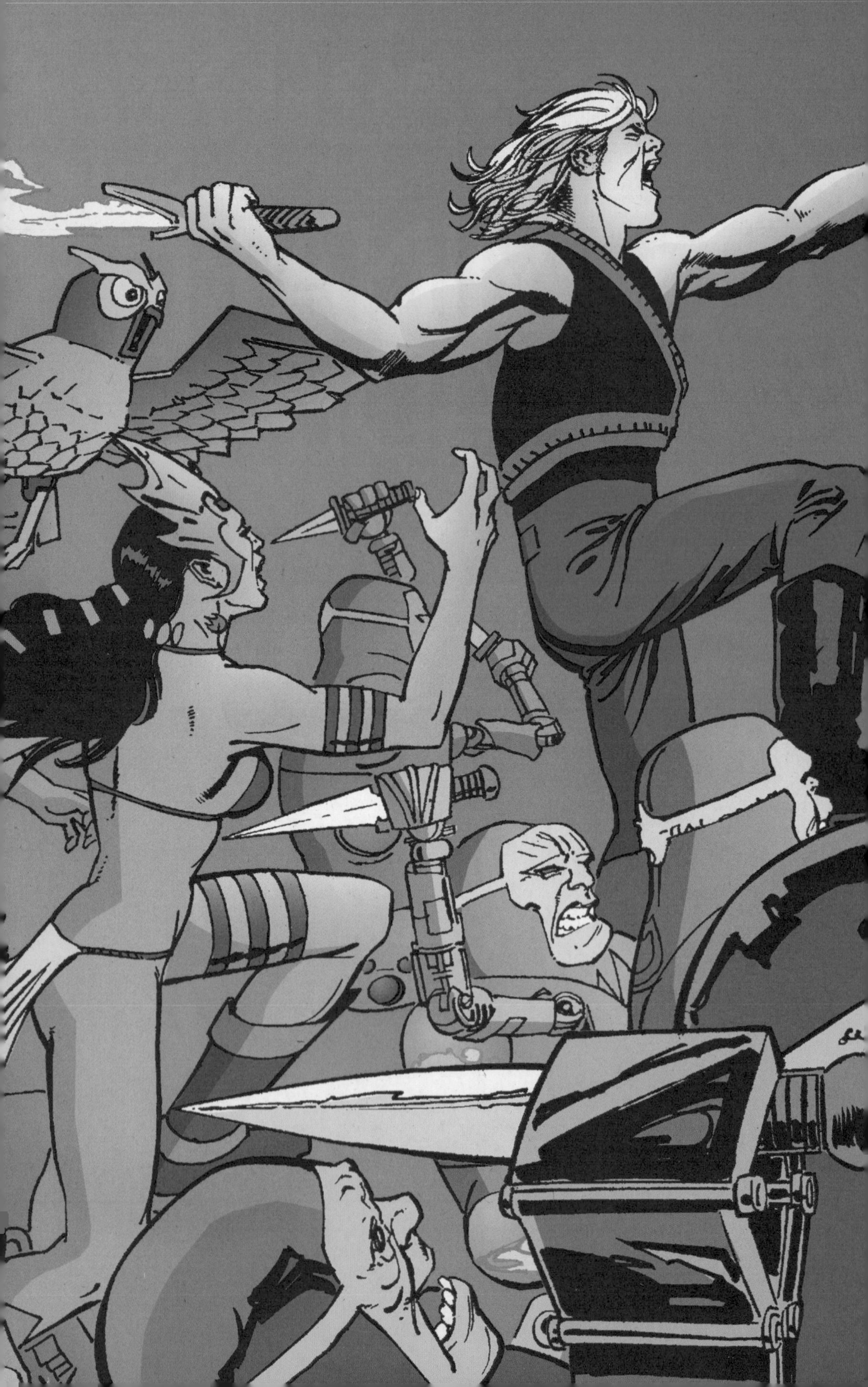

TABLE OF CONTENTS

DRAMATIS PERSONAE

JACK OF THE TALES

Ostensibly the star of the series, he couldn't be bothered to even make an appearance in this book. He's only showing up here to remind everyone how important he is.

JACK FROST

Jack's son, now grown to manhood and making a name for himself in the high-stakes game of freelance heroism.

MACDUFF

Jack Frost's companion and advisor, fashioned out of wood from Geppetto's Sacred Grove.

BABE

A blue ox whose flights of fancy seem to know no limit.

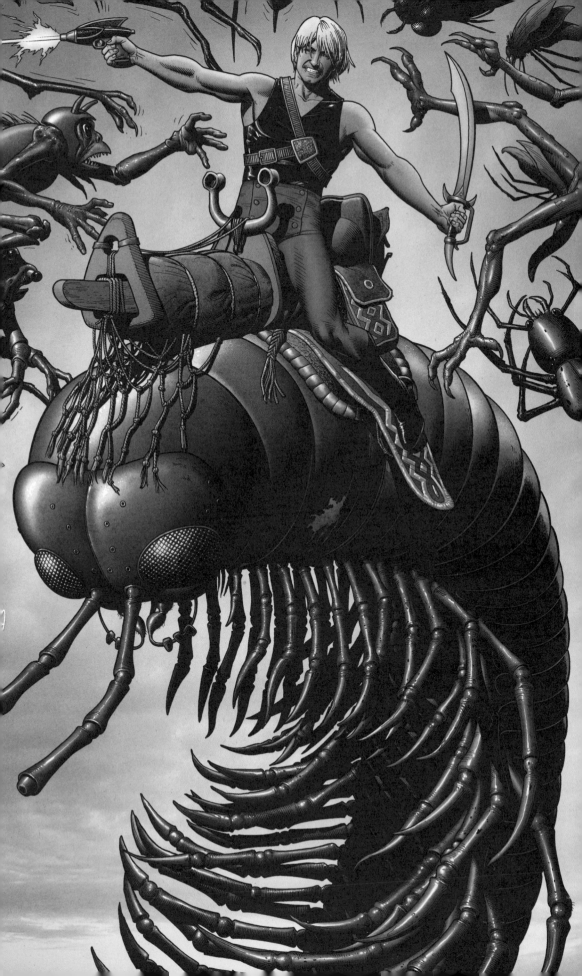

*"I've been around a long time,
my friend, and I haven't
ever seen much evidence
that life is fair."*

he events related here take place relatively early in the career of Jack Frost. Some scholars place the tale ere days after the loss of his wintry powers and his befriending of the wooden owl called MacDuff. thers insist that Jack's encounter with the Sub-People occurred prior to this. Most agree, however, that ck's ill-fated first encounter with the Lady Cerise was still months – if not years – in the future.
From: "A Probable Outline of Jack Frost's Life and Adventures" by Wulf Alondair Lathe

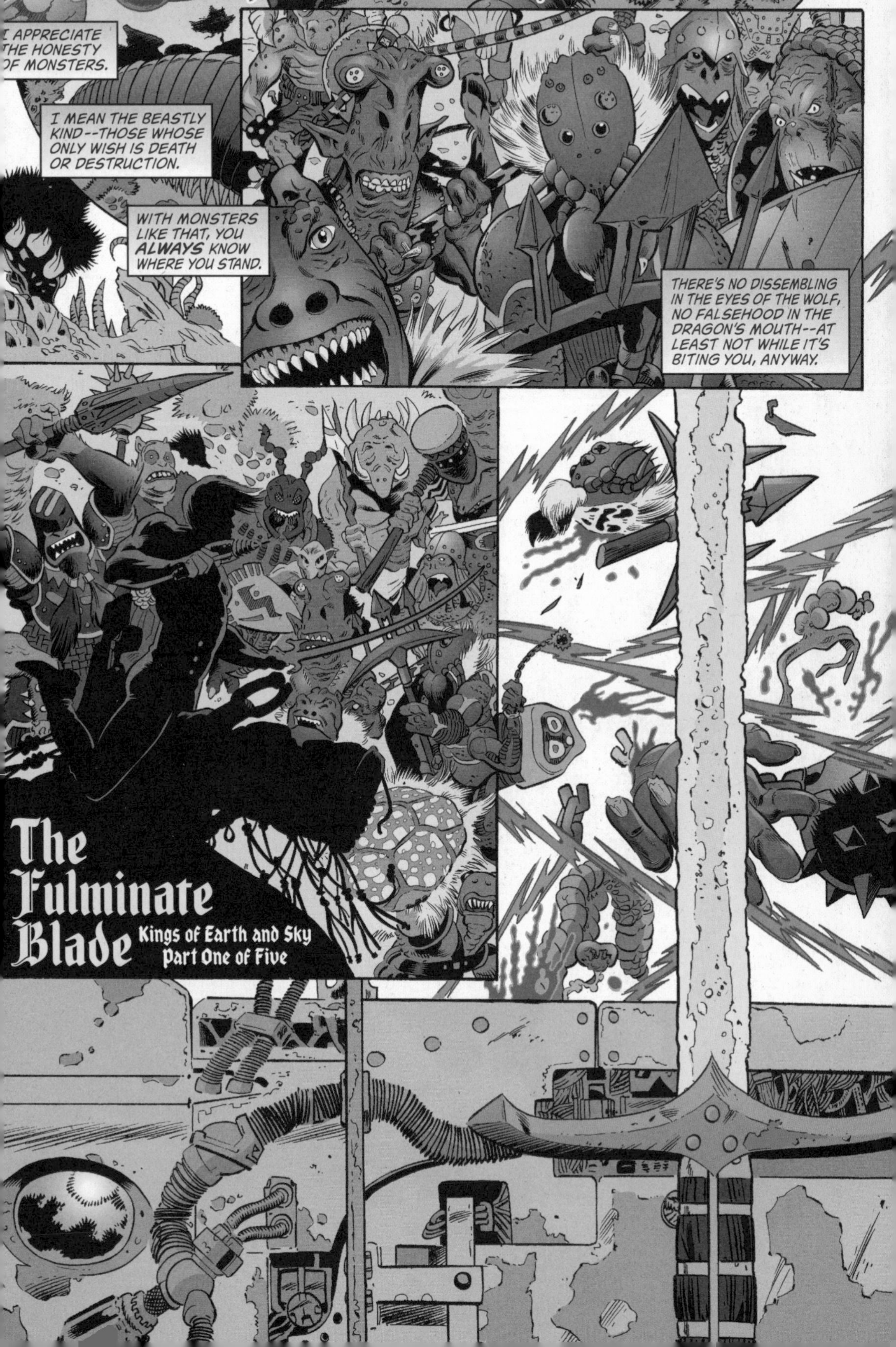

I APPRECIATE THE HONESTY OF MONSTERS.
I MEAN THE BEASTLY KIND--THOSE WHOSE ONLY WISH IS DEATH OR DESTRUCTION.
WITH MONSTERS LIKE THAT, YOU ALWAYS KNOW WHERE YOU STAND.
THERE'S NO DISSEMBLING IN THE EYES OF THE WOLF, NO FALSEHOOD IN THE DRAGON'S MOUTH--AT LEAST NOT WHILE IT'S BITING YOU, ANYWAY.
The Fulminate Blade
Kings of Earth and Sky
Part One of Five

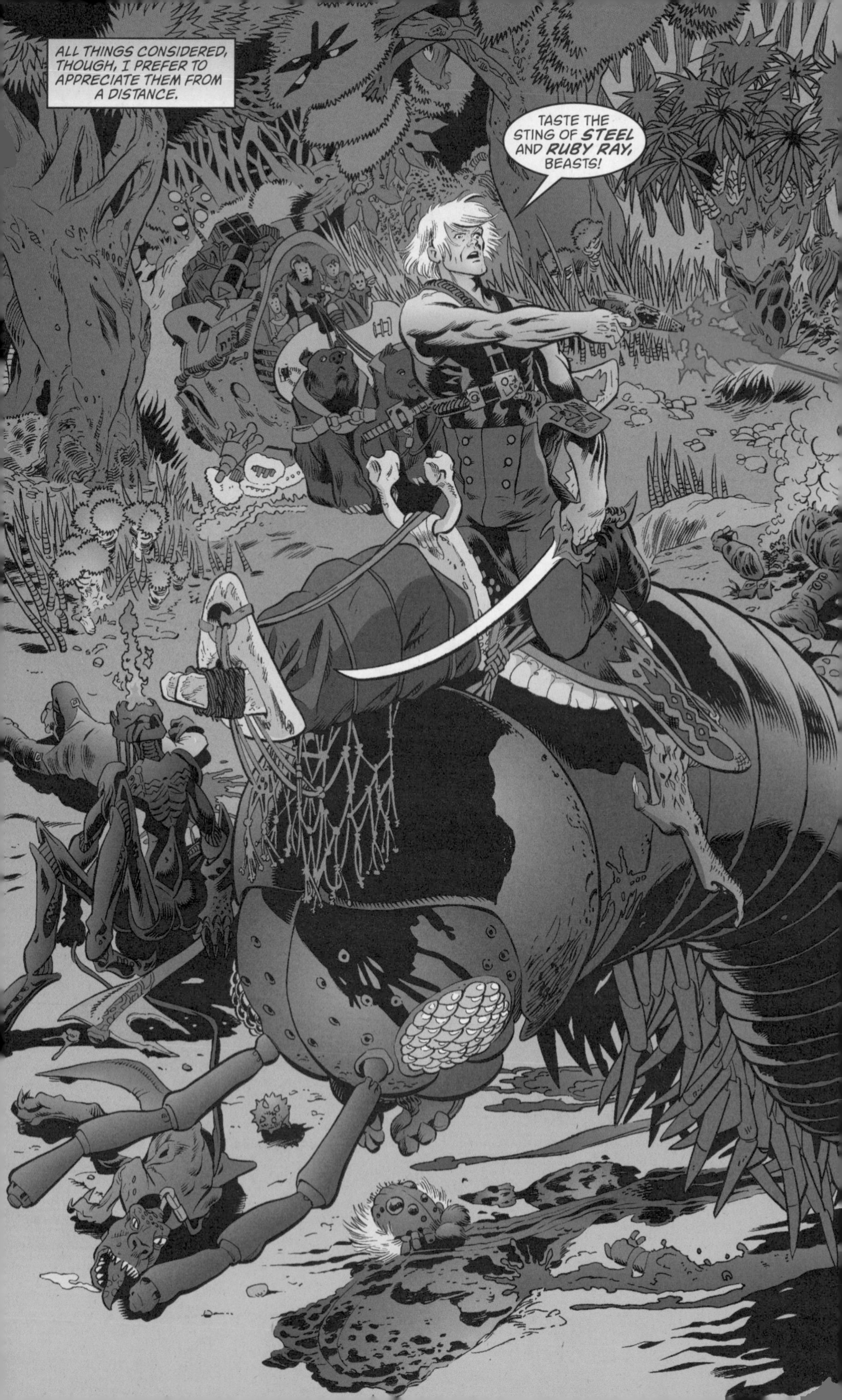
ALL THINGS CONSIDERED, THOUGH, I PREFER TO APPRECIATE THEM FROM A DISTANCE.
TASTE THE STING OF STEEL AND RUBY RAY, BEASTS!

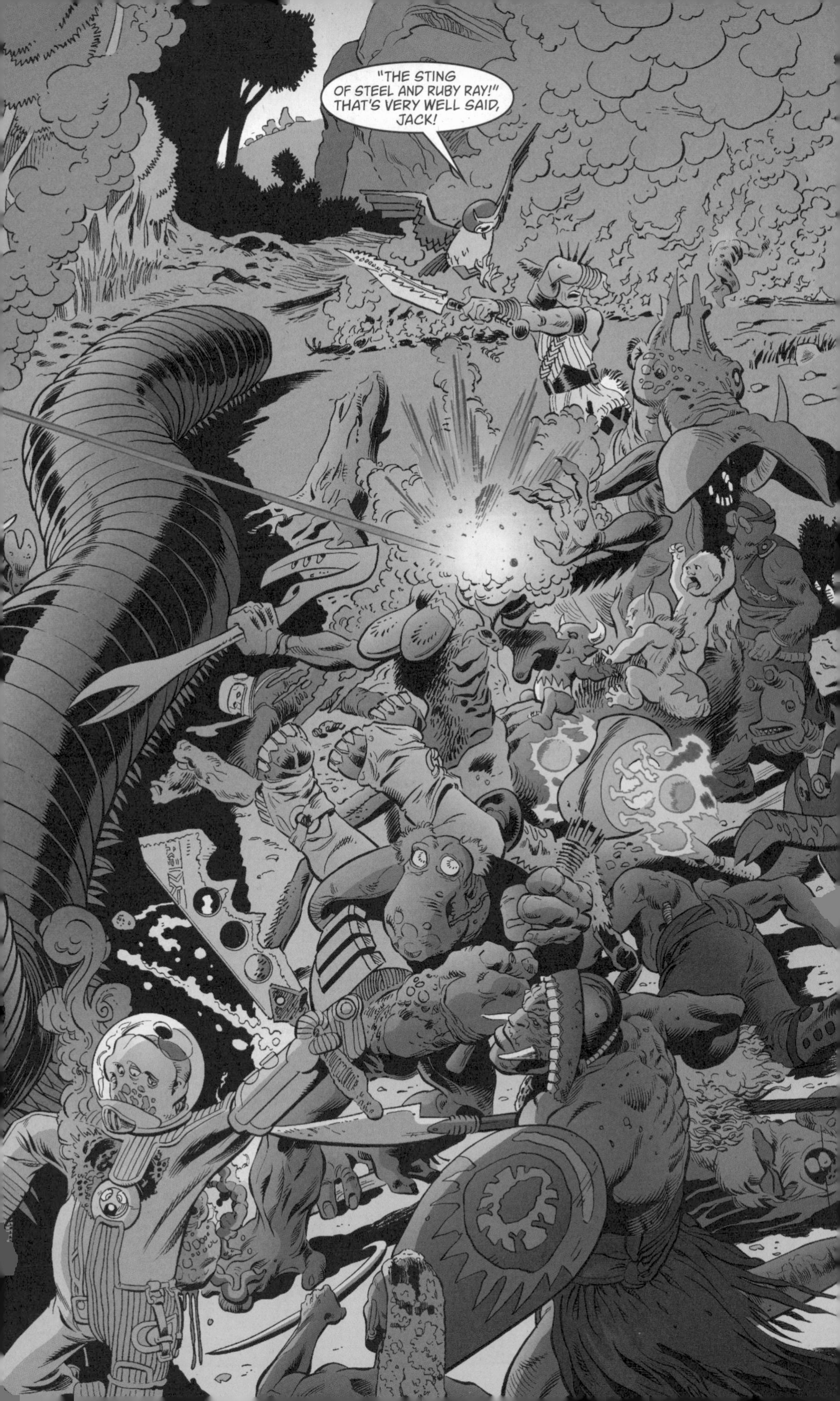
"THE STING OF STEEL AND RUBY RAY!" THAT'S VERY WELL SAID, JACK!

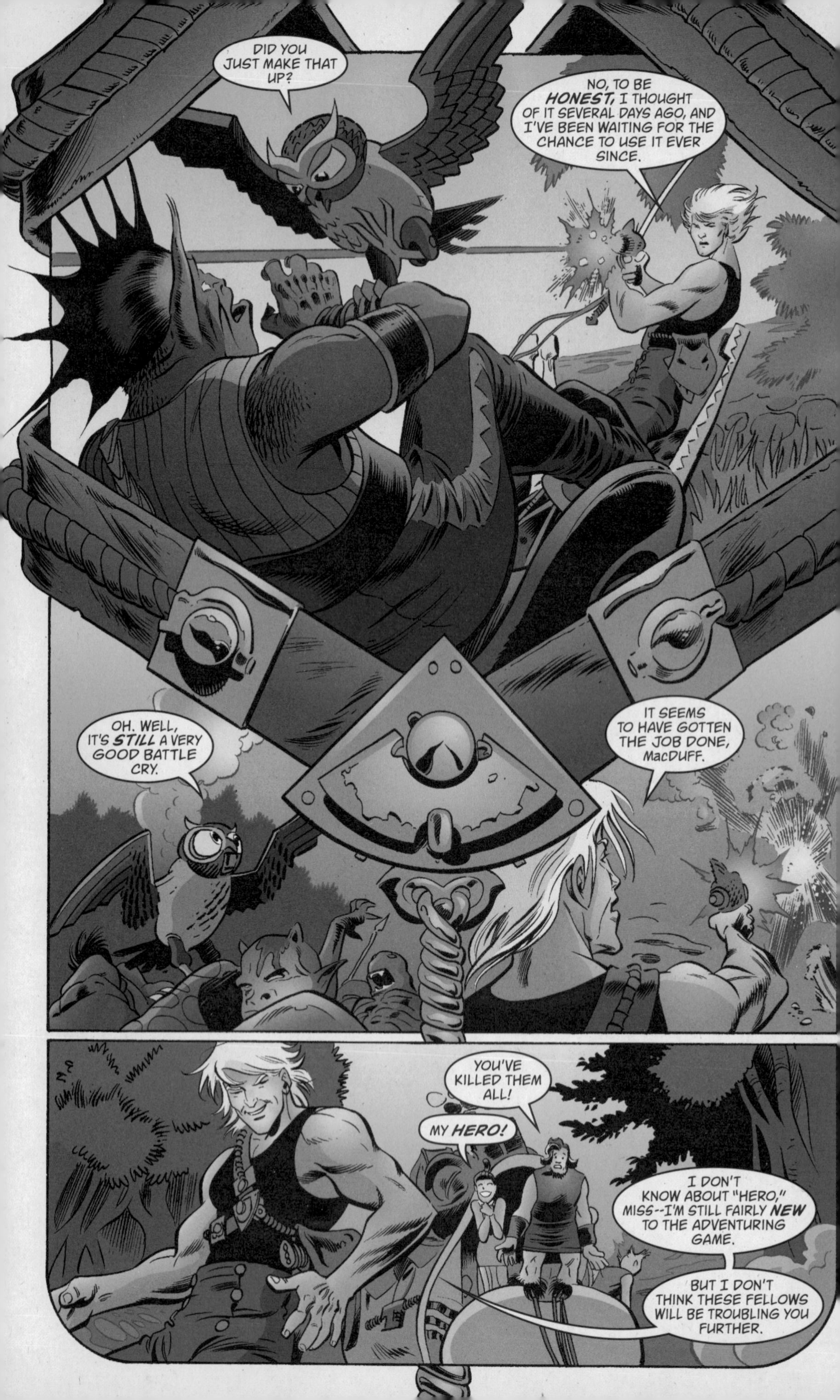
DID YOU JUST MAKE THAT UP?
NO, TO BE HONEST, I THOUGHT OF IT SEVERAL DAYS AGO, AND I'VE BEEN WAITING FOR THE CHANCE TO USE IT EVER SINCE.
OH. WELL, IT'S STILL A VERY GOOD BATTLE CRY.
IT SEEMS TO HAVE GOTTEN THE JOB DONE, MacDUFF.
YOU'VE KILLED THEM ALL!
MY HERO!
I DON'T KNOW ABOUT "HERO," MISS--I'M STILL FAIRLY NEW TO THE ADVENTURING GAME.
BUT I DON'T THINK THESE FELLOWS WILL BE TROUBLING YOU FURTHER.

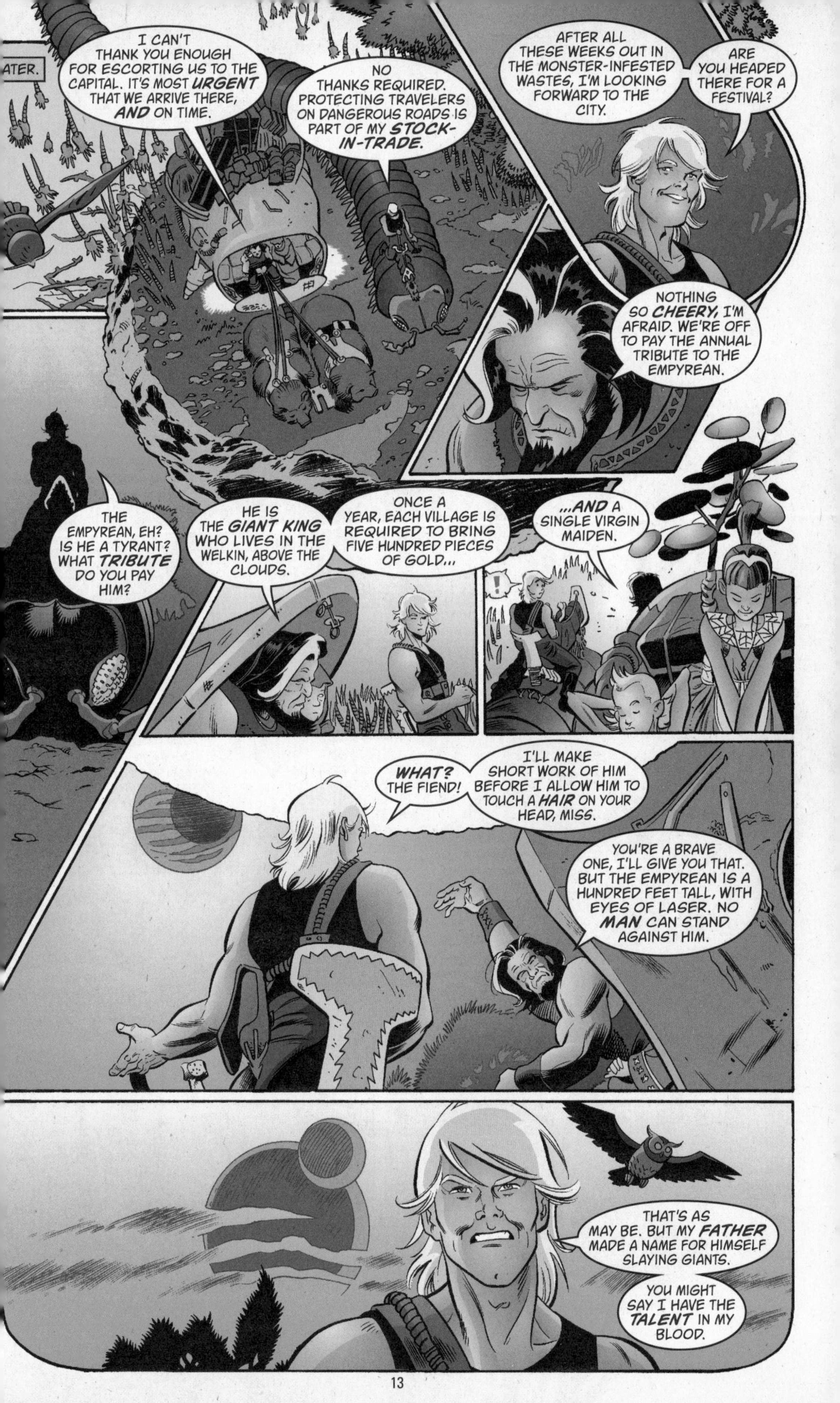
ATER.
I CAN'T THANK YOU ENOUGH FOR ESCORTING US TO THE CAPITAL. IT'S MOST URGENT THAT WE ARRIVE THERE, AND ON TIME.
NO THANKS REQUIRED. PROTECTING TRAVELERS ON DANGEROUS ROADS IS PART OF MY STOCK-IN-TRADE.
AFTER ALL THESE WEEKS OUT IN THE MONSTER-INFESTED WASTES, I'M LOOKING FORWARD TO THE CITY.
ARE YOU HEADED THERE FOR A FESTIVAL?
NOTHING SO CHEERY, I'M AFRAID. WE'RE OFF TO PAY THE ANNUAL TRIBUTE TO THE EMPYREAN.
THE EMPYREAN, EH? IS HE A TYRANT? WHAT TRIBUTE DO YOU PAY HIM?
HE IS THE GIANT KING WHO LIVES IN THE WELKIN, ABOVE THE CLOUDS.
ONCE A YEAR, EACH VILLAGE IS REQUIRED TO BRING FIVE HUNDRED PIECES OF GOLD...
...AND A SINGLE VIRGIN MAIDEN.
WHAT? THE FIEND!
I'LL MAKE SHORT WORK OF HIM BEFORE I ALLOW HIM TO TOUCH A HAIR ON YOUR HEAD, MISS.
YOU'RE A BRAVE ONE, I'LL GIVE YOU THAT. BUT THE EMPYREAN IS A HUNDRED FEET TALL, WITH EYES OF LASER. NO MAN CAN STAND AGAINST HIM.
THAT'S AS MAY BE. BUT MY FATHER MADE A NAME FOR HIMSELF SLAYING GIANTS.
YOU MIGHT SAY I HAVE THE TALENT IN MY BLOOD.

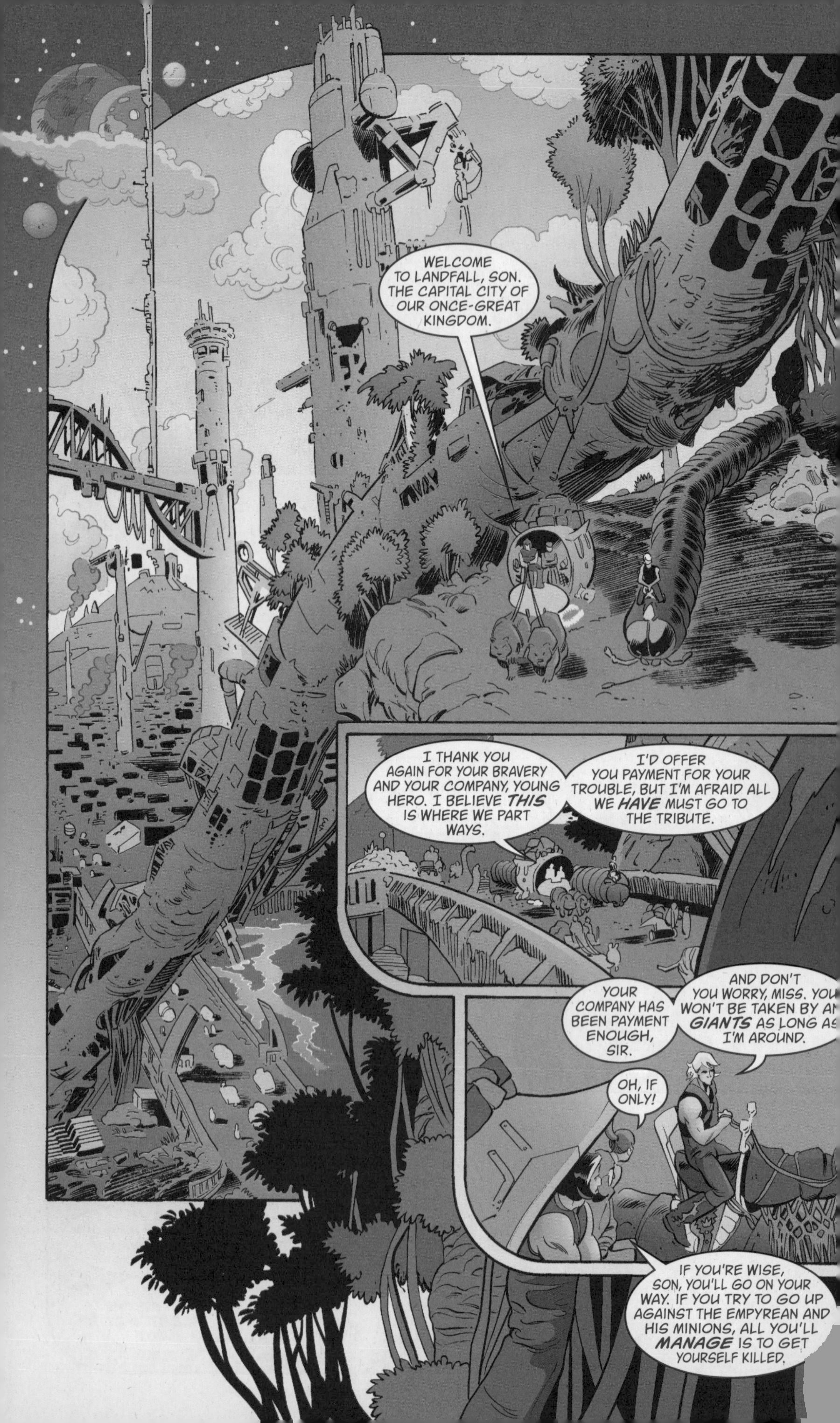
WELCOME TO LANDFALL, SON. THE CAPITAL CITY OF OUR ONCE-GREAT KINGDOM.
I THANK YOU AGAIN FOR YOUR BRAVERY AND YOUR COMPANY, YOUNG HERO. I BELIEVE *THIS* IS WHERE WE PART WAYS.
I'D OFFER YOU PAYMENT FOR YOUR TROUBLE, BUT I'M AFRAID ALL WE *HAVE* MUST GO TO THE TRIBUTE.
YOUR COMPANY HAS BEEN PAYMENT ENOUGH, SIR.
AND DON'T YOU WORRY, MISS. YOU WON'T BE TAKEN BY AN *GIANTS* AS LONG AS I'M AROUND.
OH, IF ONLY!
IF YOU'RE WISE, SON, YOU'LL GO ON YOUR WAY. IF YOU TRY TO GO UP AGAINST THE EMPYREAN AND HIS MINIONS, ALL YOU'LL *MANAGE* IS TO GET YOURSELF KILLED.

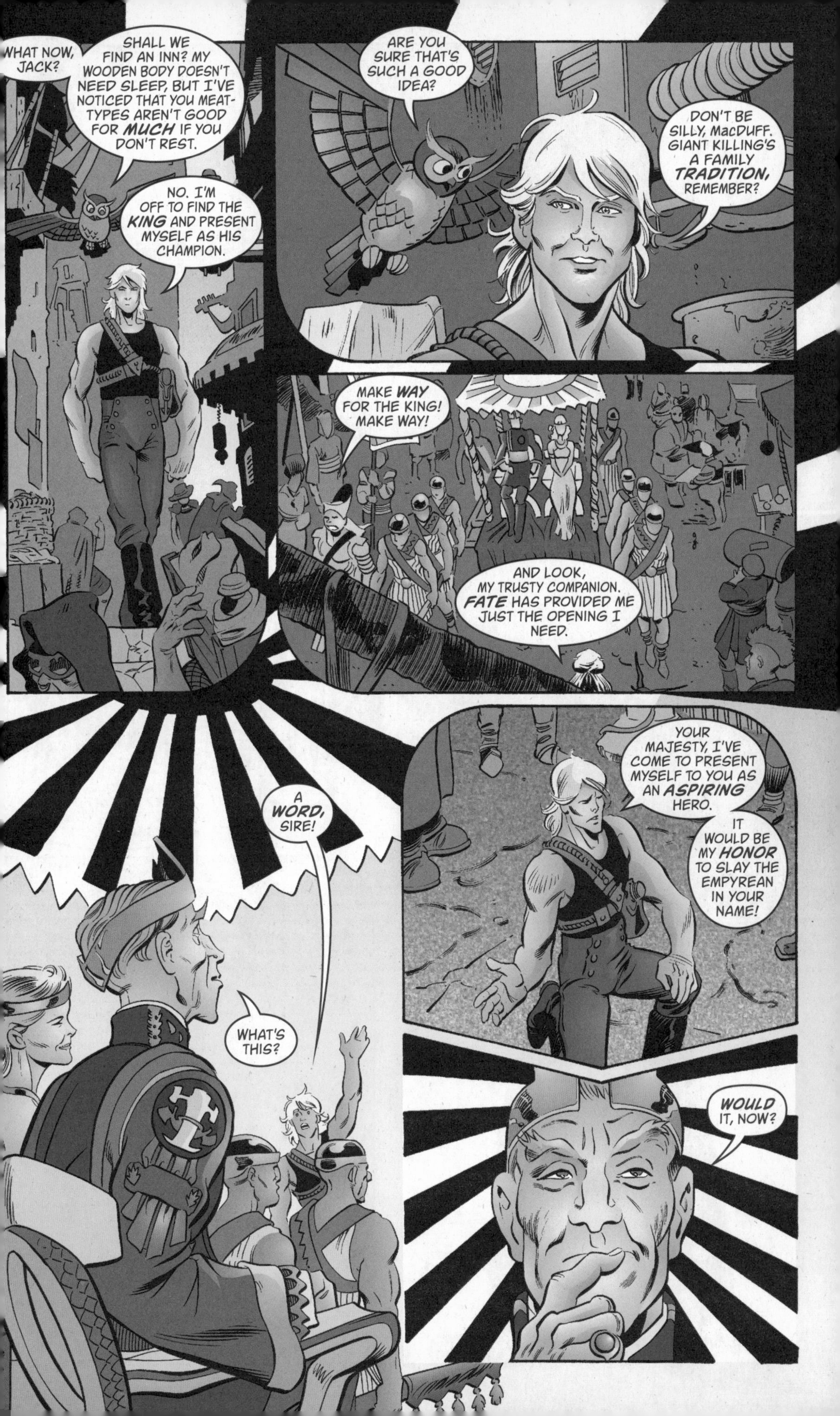

WHAT NOW, JACK?
SHALL WE FIND AN INN? MY WOODEN BODY DOESN'T NEED SLEEP, BUT I'VE NOTICED THAT YOU MEAT-TYPES AREN'T GOOD FOR MUCH IF YOU DON'T REST.
NO. I'M OFF TO FIND THE KING AND PRESENT MYSELF AS HIS CHAMPION.
ARE YOU SURE THAT'S SUCH A GOOD IDEA?
DON'T BE SILLY, MacDUFF. GIANT KILLING'S A FAMILY TRADITION, REMEMBER?
MAKE WAY FOR THE KING! MAKE WAY!
AND LOOK, MY TRUSTY COMPANION. FATE HAS PROVIDED ME JUST THE OPENING I NEED.
A WORD, SIRE!
WHAT'S THIS?
YOUR MAJESTY, I'VE COME TO PRESENT MYSELF TO YOU AS AN ASPIRING HERO.
IT WOULD BE MY HONOR TO SLAY THE EMPYREAN IN YOUR NAME!
WOULD IT, NOW?

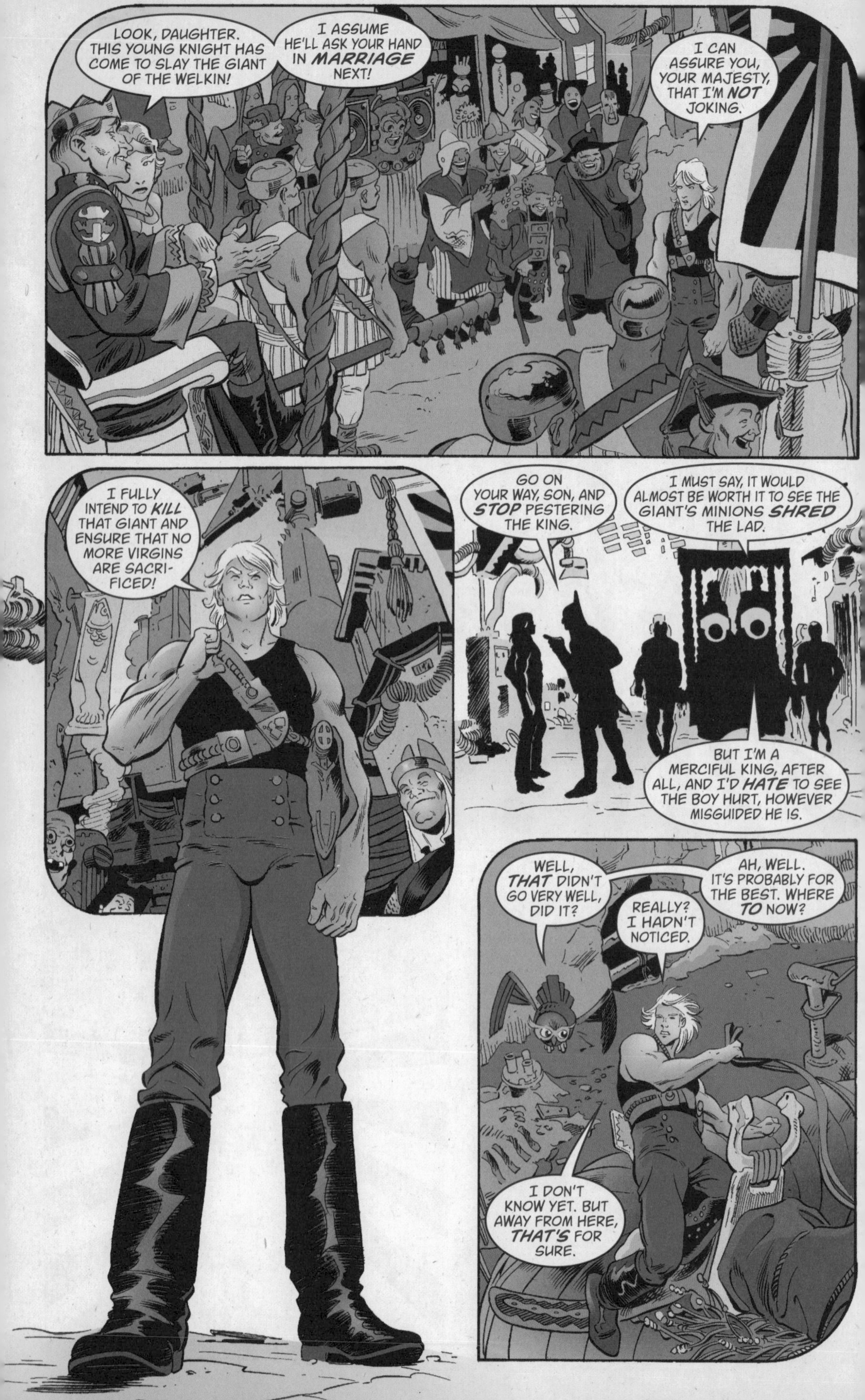
LOOK, DAUGHTER. THIS YOUNG KNIGHT HAS COME TO SLAY THE GIANT OF THE WELKIN!
I ASSUME HE'LL ASK YOUR HAND IN MARRIAGE NEXT!
I CAN ASSURE YOU, YOUR MAJESTY, THAT I'M NOT JOKING.
I FULLY INTEND TO KILL THAT GIANT AND ENSURE THAT NO MORE VIRGINS ARE SACRI- FICED!
GO ON YOUR WAY, SON, AND STOP PESTERING THE KING.
I MUST SAY, IT WOULD ALMOST BE WORTH IT TO SEE THE GIANT'S MINIONS SHRED THE LAD.
BUT I'M A MERCIFUL KING, AFTER ALL, AND I'D HATE TO SEE THE BOY HURT, HOWEVER MISGUIDED HE IS.
WELL, THAT DIDN'T GO VERY WELL, DID IT?
REALLY? I HADN'T NOTICED.
AH, WELL. IT'S PROBABLY FOR THE BEST. WHERE TO NOW?
I DON'T KNOW YET. BUT AWAY FROM HERE, THAT'S FOR SURE.

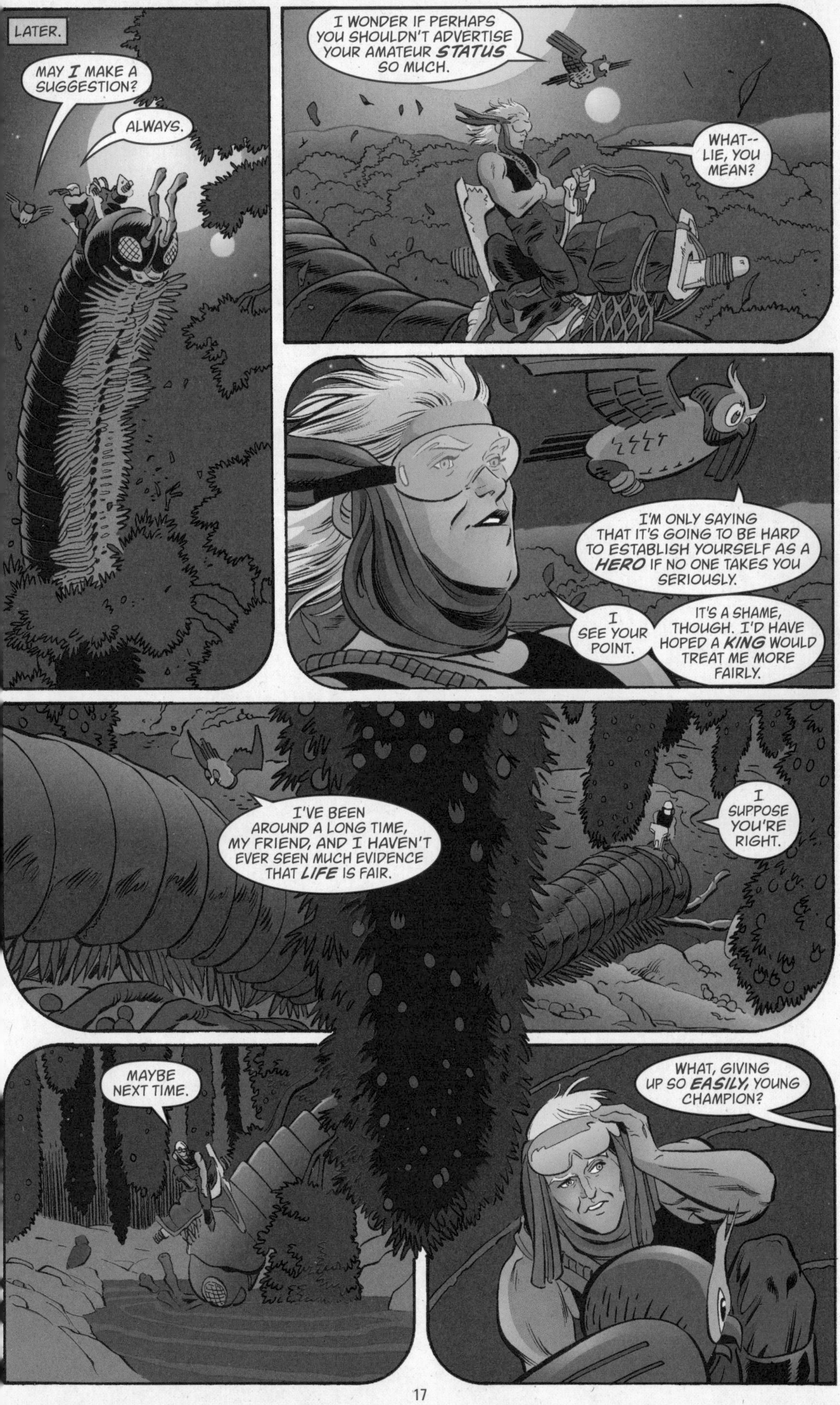
LATER.
MAY I MAKE A SUGGESTION?
ALWAYS.
I WONDER IF PERHAPS YOU SHOULDN'T ADVERTISE YOUR AMATEUR STATUS SO MUCH.
WHAT-- LIE, YOU MEAN?
I'M ONLY SAYING THAT IT'S GOING TO BE HARD TO ESTABLISH YOURSELF AS A HERO IF NO ONE TAKES YOU SERIOUSLY.
I SEE YOUR POINT.
IT'S A SHAME, THOUGH. I'D HAVE HOPED A KING WOULD TREAT ME MORE FAIRLY.
I'VE BEEN AROUND A LONG TIME, MY FRIEND, AND I HAVEN'T EVER SEEN MUCH EVIDENCE THAT LIFE IS FAIR.
I SUPPOSE YOU'RE RIGHT.
MAYBE NEXT TIME.
WHAT, GIVING UP SO EASILY, YOUNG CHAMPION?

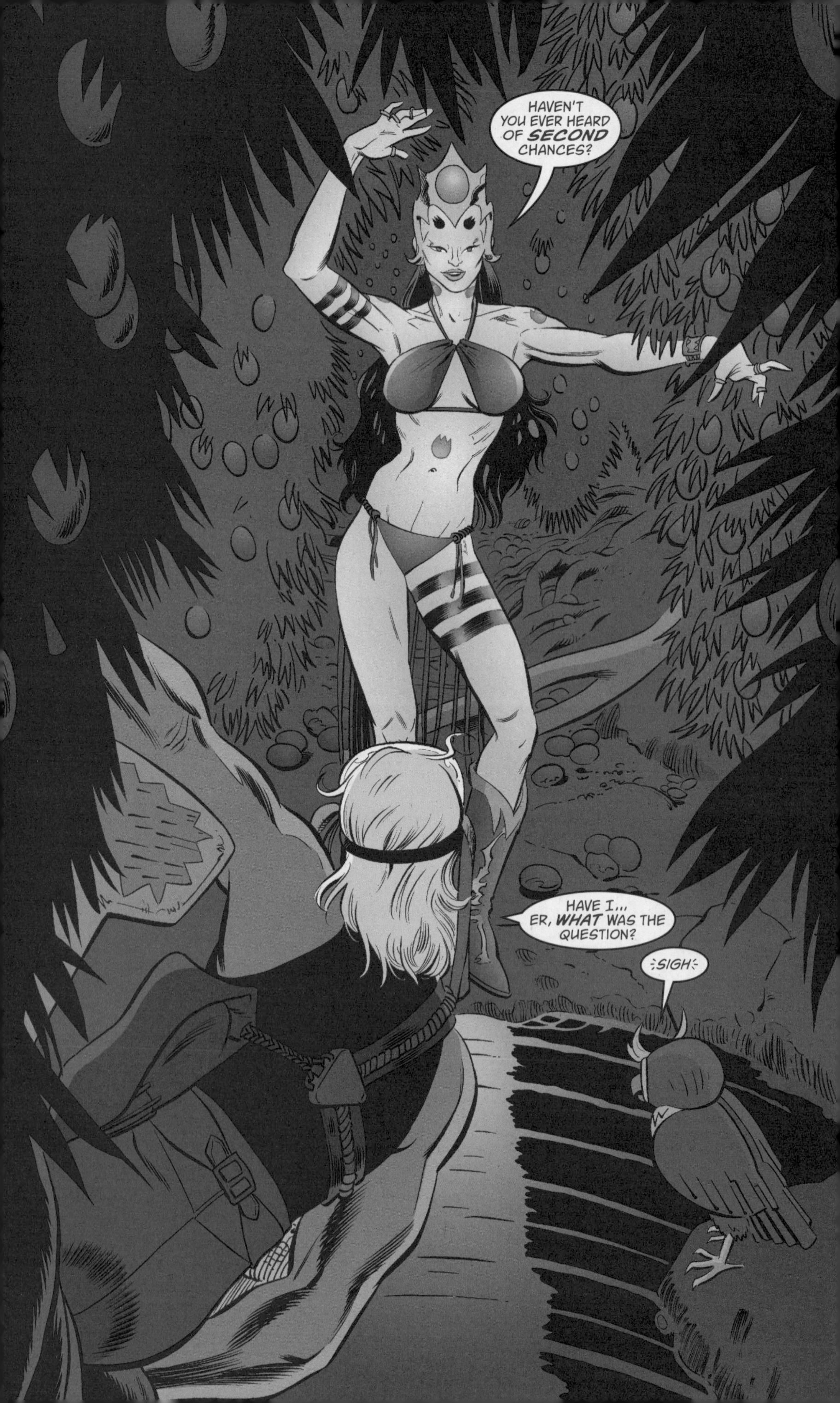
HAVEN'T YOU EVER HEARD OF SECOND CHANCES?
HAVE I... ER, WHAT WAS THE QUESTION?
SIGH

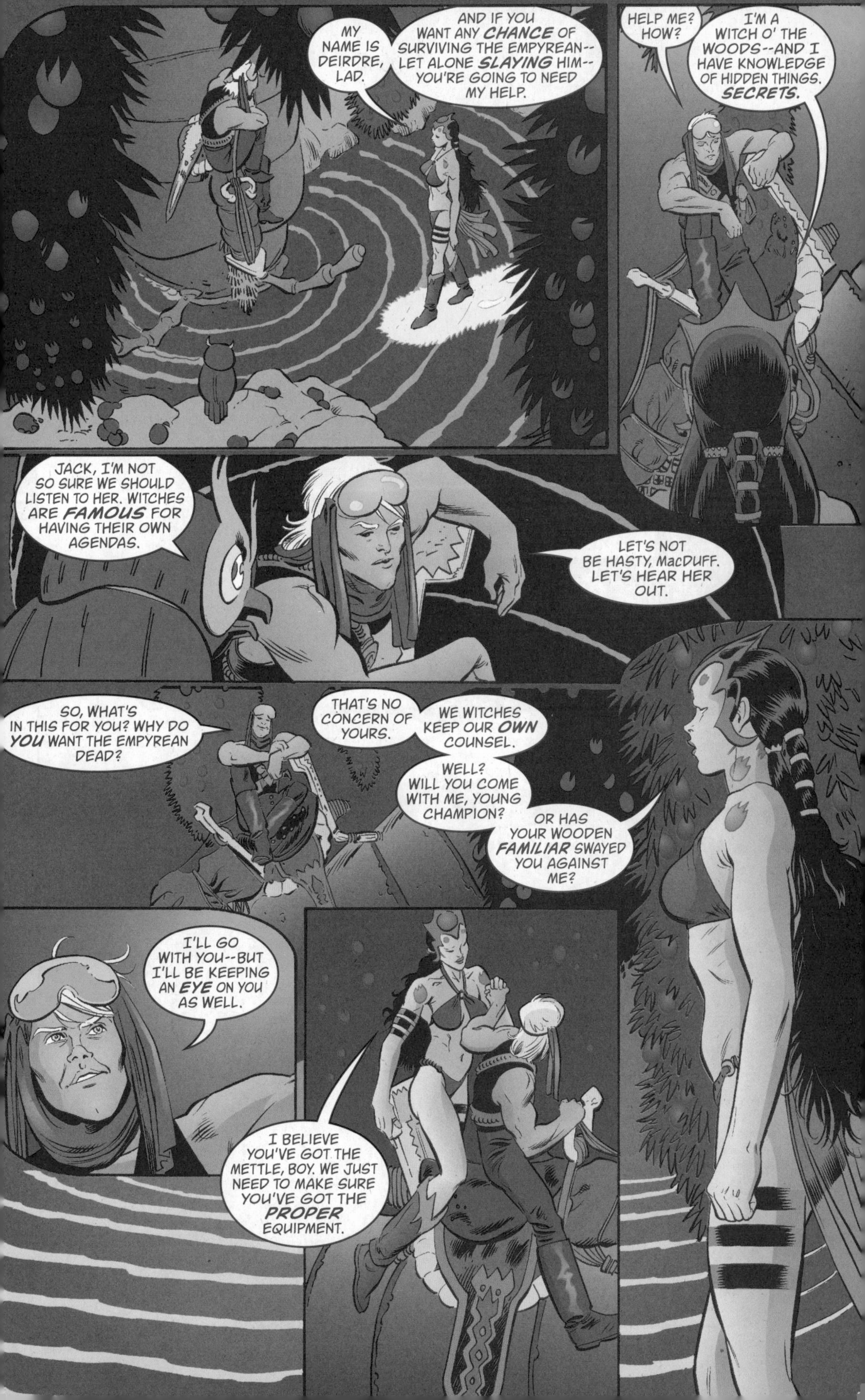

MY NAME IS DEIRDRE, LAD.
AND IF YOU WANT ANY CHANCE OF SURVIVING THE EMPYREAN-- LET ALONE SLAYING HIM-- YOU'RE GOING TO NEED MY HELP.
HELP ME? HOW?
I'M A WITCH O' THE WOODS--AND I HAVE KNOWLEDGE OF HIDDEN THINGS. SECRETS.
JACK, I'M NOT SO SURE WE SHOULD LISTEN TO HER. WITCHES ARE FAMOUS FOR HAVING THEIR OWN AGENDAS.
LET'S NOT BE HASTY, MacDUFF. LET'S HEAR HER OUT.
SO, WHAT'S IN THIS FOR YOU? WHY DO YOU WANT THE EMPYREAN DEAD?
THAT'S NO CONCERN OF YOURS.
WE WITCHES KEEP OUR OWN COUNSEL.
WELL? WILL YOU COME WITH ME, YOUNG CHAMPION?
OR HAS YOUR WOODEN FAMILIAR SWAYED YOU AGAINST ME?
I'LL GO WITH YOU--BUT I'LL BE KEEPING AN EYE ON YOU AS WELL.
I BELIEVE YOU'VE GOT THE METTLE, BOY. WE JUST NEED TO MAKE SURE YOU'VE GOT THE PROPER EQUIPMENT.

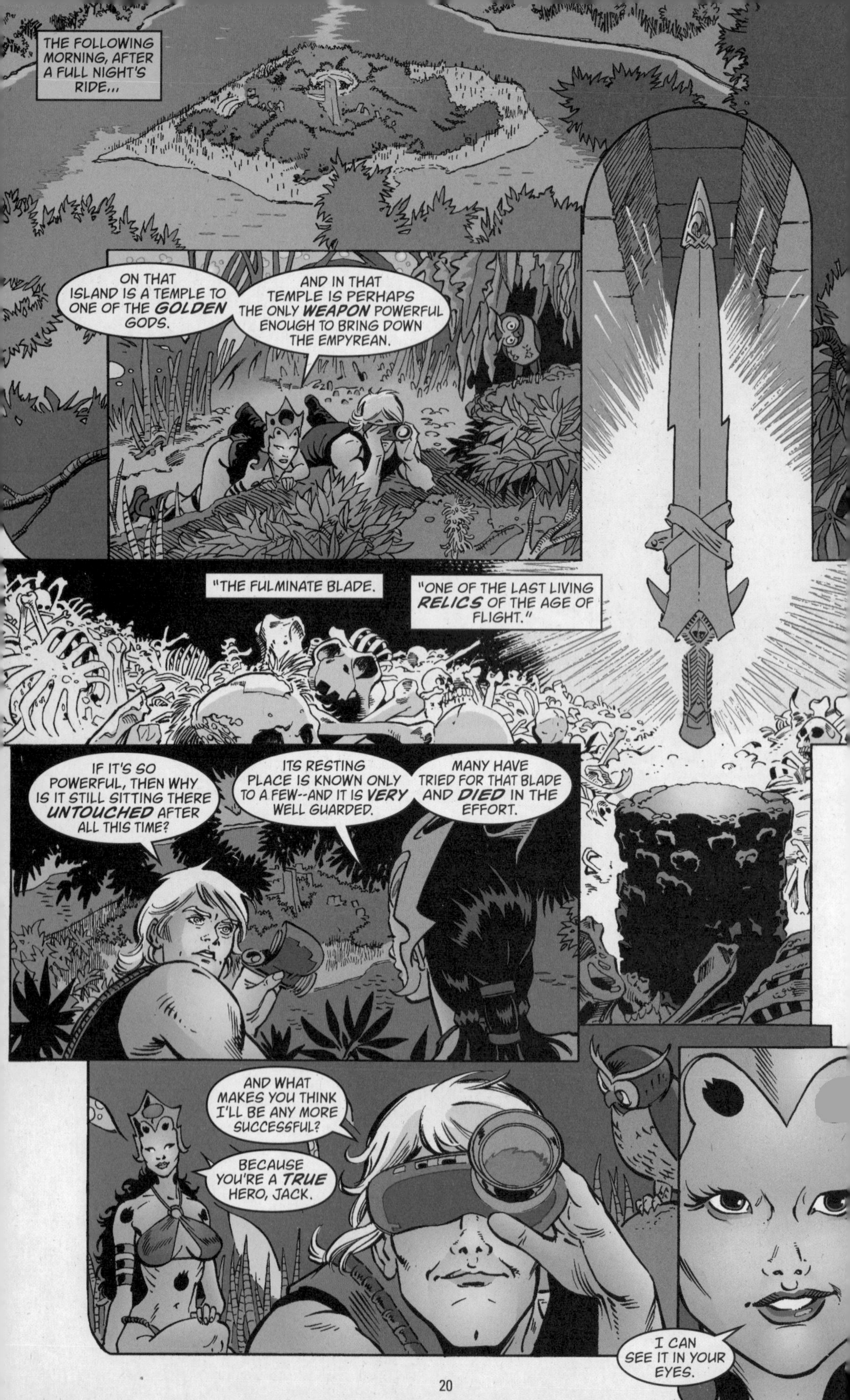
THE FOLLOWING MORNING, AFTER A FULL NIGHT'S RIDE...
ON THAT ISLAND IS A TEMPLE TO ONE OF THE GOLDEN GODS.
AND IN THAT TEMPLE IS PERHAPS THE ONLY WEAPON POWERFUL ENOUGH TO BRING DOWN THE EMPYREAN.
"THE FULMINATE BLADE.
"ONE OF THE LAST LIVING RELICS OF THE AGE OF FLIGHT."
IF IT'S SO POWERFUL, THEN WHY IS IT STILL SITTING THERE UNTOUCHED AFTER ALL THIS TIME?
ITS RESTING PLACE IS KNOWN ONLY TO A FEW--AND IT IS VERY WELL GUARDED.
MANY HAVE TRIED FOR THAT BLADE AND DIED IN THE EFFORT.
AND WHAT MAKES YOU THINK I'LL BE ANY MORE SUCCESSFUL?
BECAUSE YOU'RE A TRUE HERO, JACK.
I CAN SEE IT IN YOUR EYES.

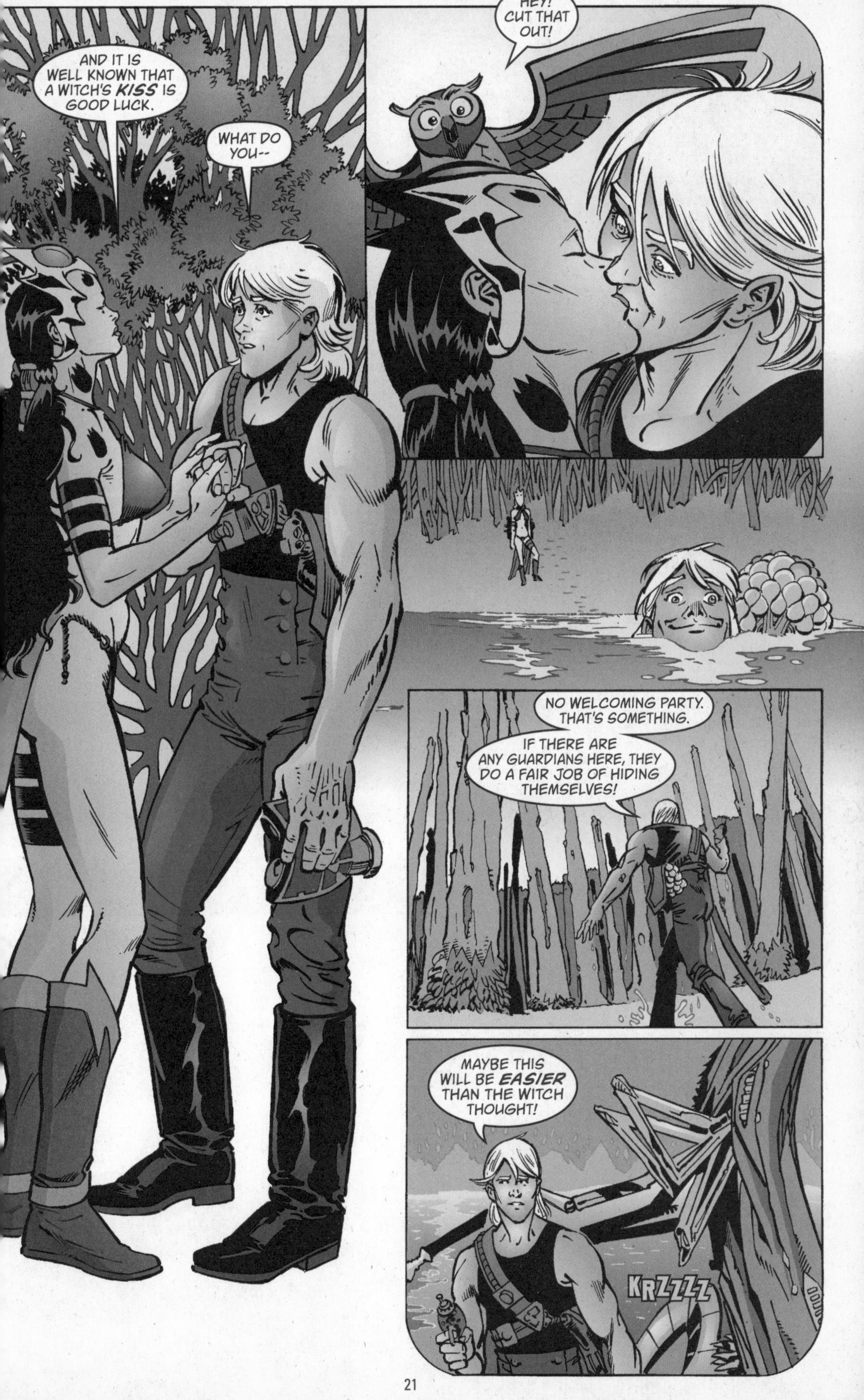
AND IT IS WELL KNOWN THAT A WITCH'S KISS IS GOOD LUCK.
WHAT DO YOU--
HEY! CUT THAT OUT!
NO WELCOMING PARTY. THAT'S SOMETHING.
IF THERE ARE ANY GUARDIANS HERE, THEY DO A FAIR JOB OF HIDING THEMSELVES!
MAYBE THIS WILL BE EASIER THAN THE WITCH THOUGHT!
KRZZZZ

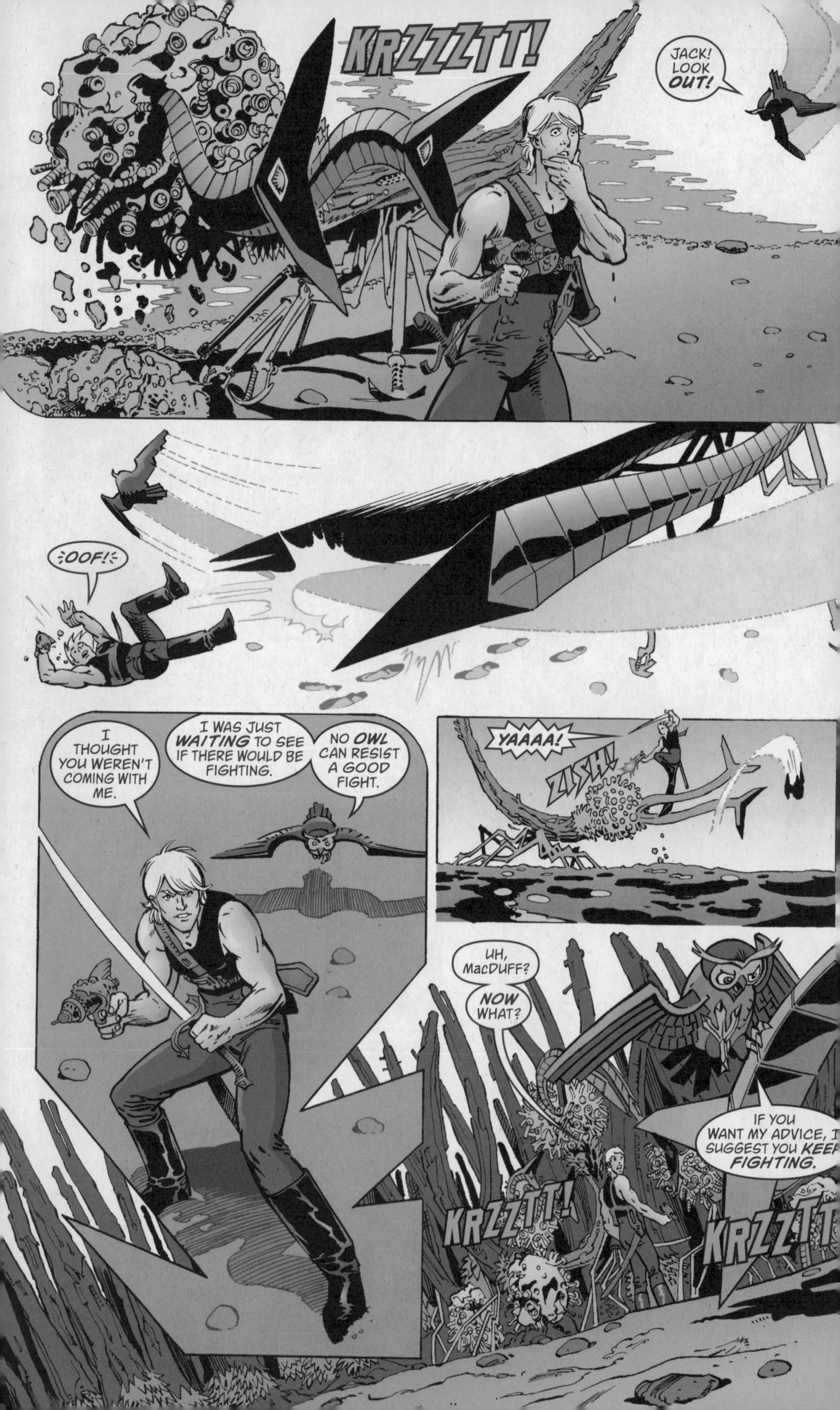
KRZZZTT!
JACK! LOOK OUT!
OOF!
I THOUGHT YOU WEREN'T COMING WITH ME.
I WAS JUST WAITING TO SEE IF THERE WOULD BE FIGHTING.
NO OWL CAN RESIST A GOOD FIGHT.
YAAAA!
ZISH!
UH, MacDUFF?
NOW WHAT?
IF YOU WANT MY ADVICE, I SUGGEST YOU KEE FIGHTING.
KRZZTT!
KRZZTT

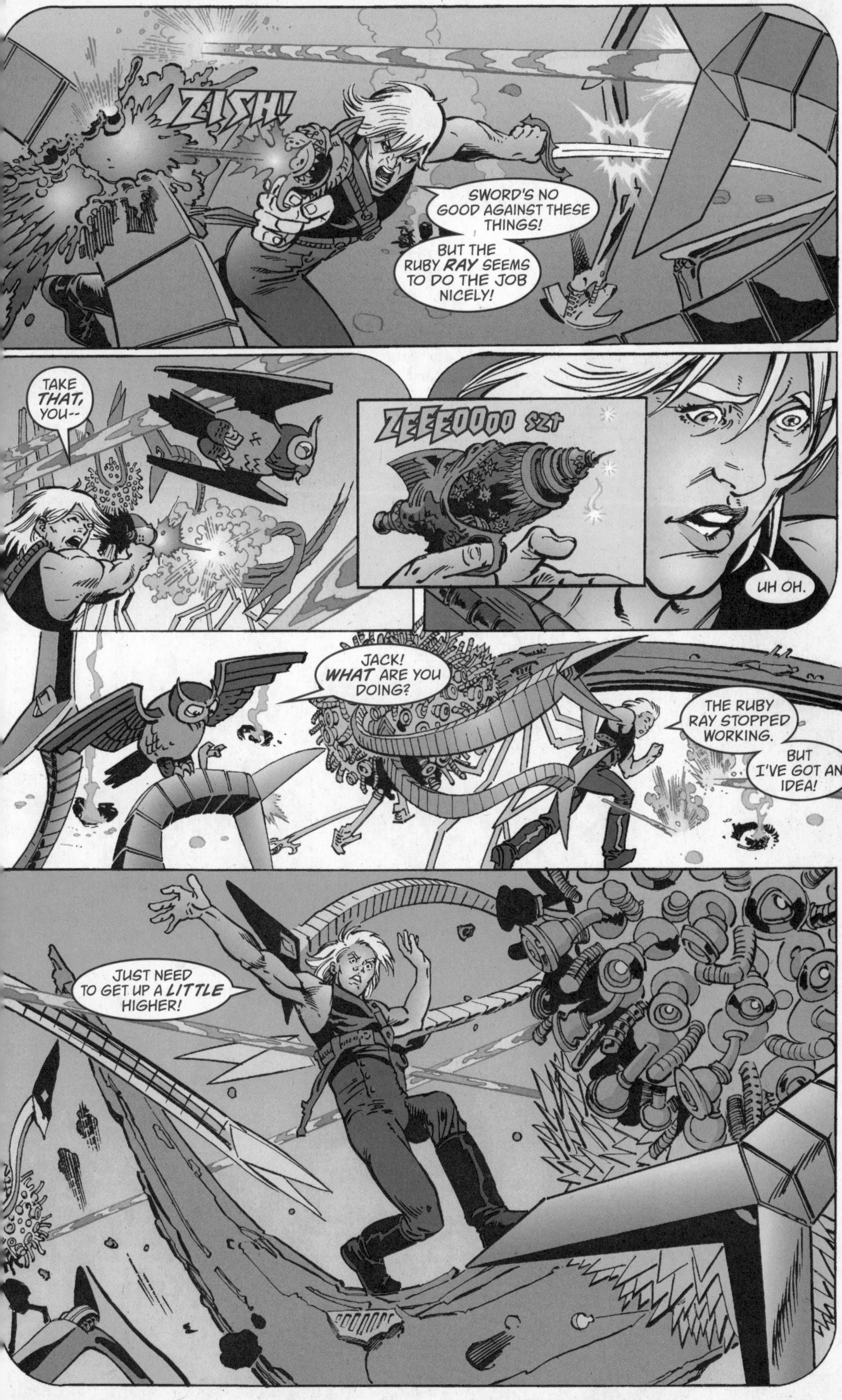
ZISH!
SWORD'S NO GOOD AGAINST THESE THINGS!
BUT THE RUBY RAY SEEMS TO DO THE JOB NICELY!
TAKE THAT, YOU--
ZEEEOOOO SZT
UH OH.
JACK! WHAT ARE YOU DOING?
THE RUBY RAY STOPPED WORKING.
BUT I'VE GOT AN IDEA!
JUST NEED TO GET UP A LITTLE HIGHER!

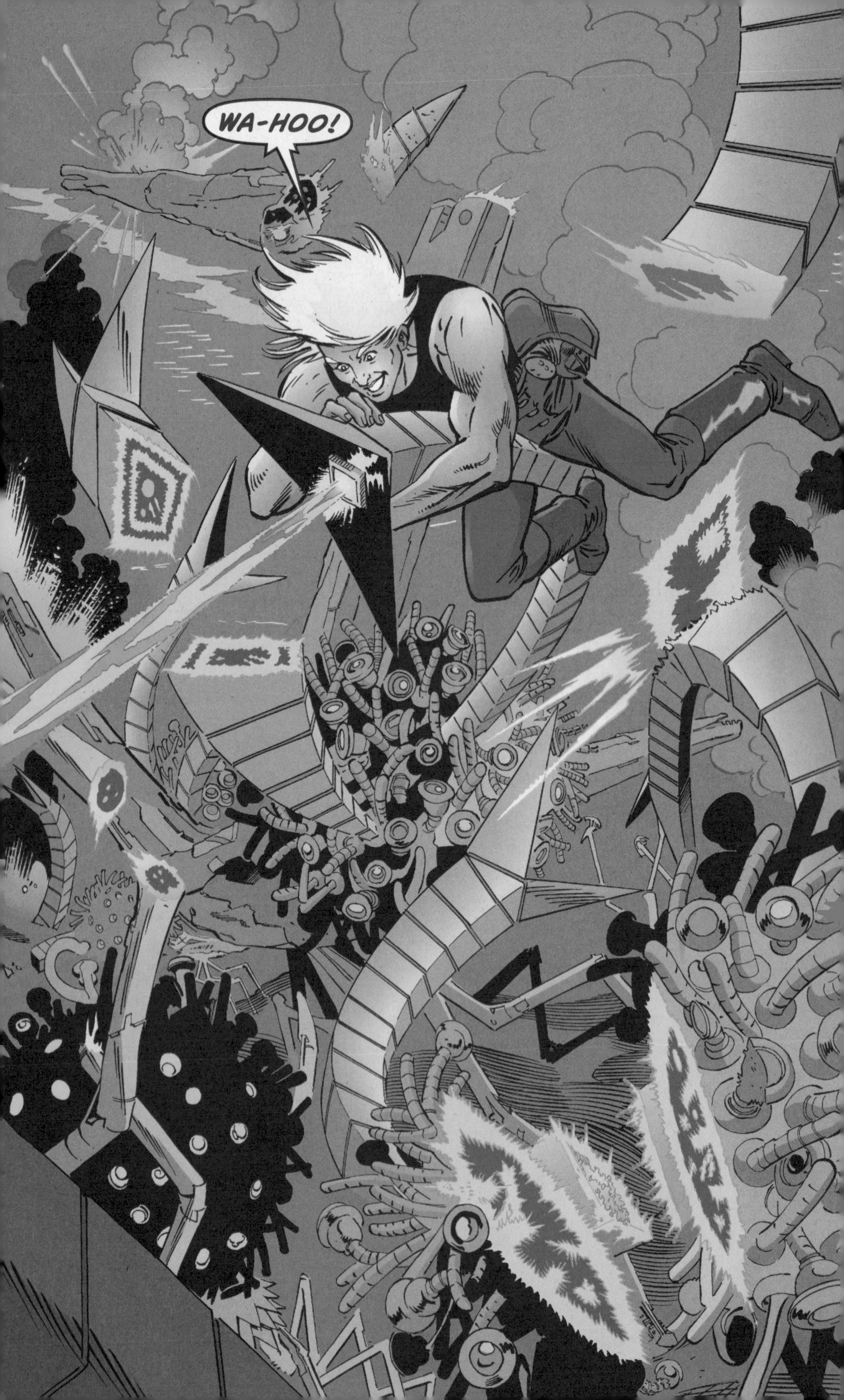
WA-HOO!

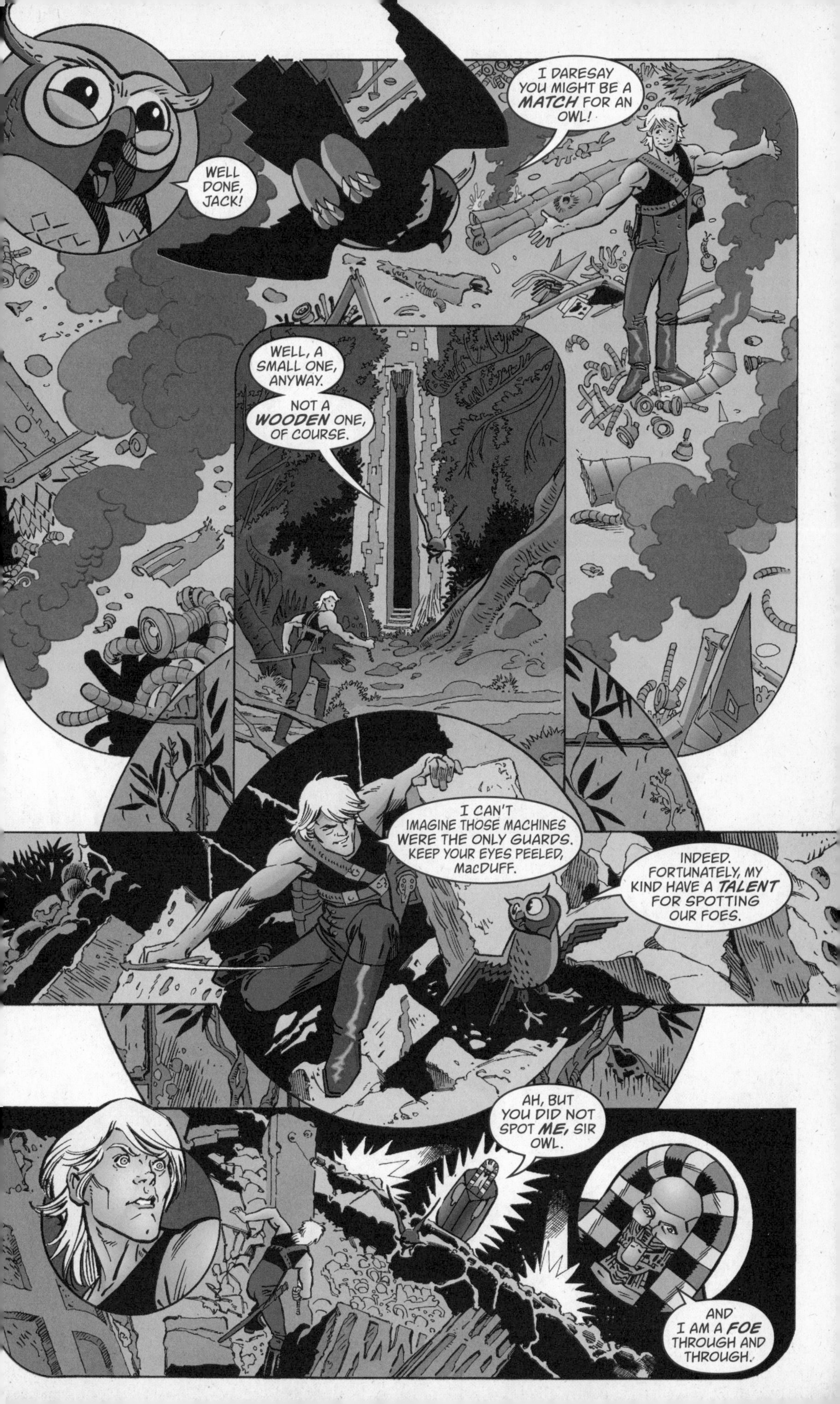
WELL DONE, JACK!
I DARESAY YOU MIGHT BE A MATCH FOR AN OWL!
WELL, A SMALL ONE, ANYWAY.
NOT A WOODEN ONE, OF COURSE.
I CAN'T IMAGINE THOSE MACHINES WERE THE ONLY GUARDS. KEEP YOUR EYES PEELED, MacDUFF.
INDEED. FORTUNATELY, MY KIND HAVE A TALENT FOR SPOTTING OUR FOES.
AH, BUT YOU DID NOT SPOT ME, SIR OWL.
AND I AM A FOE THROUGH AND THROUGH.

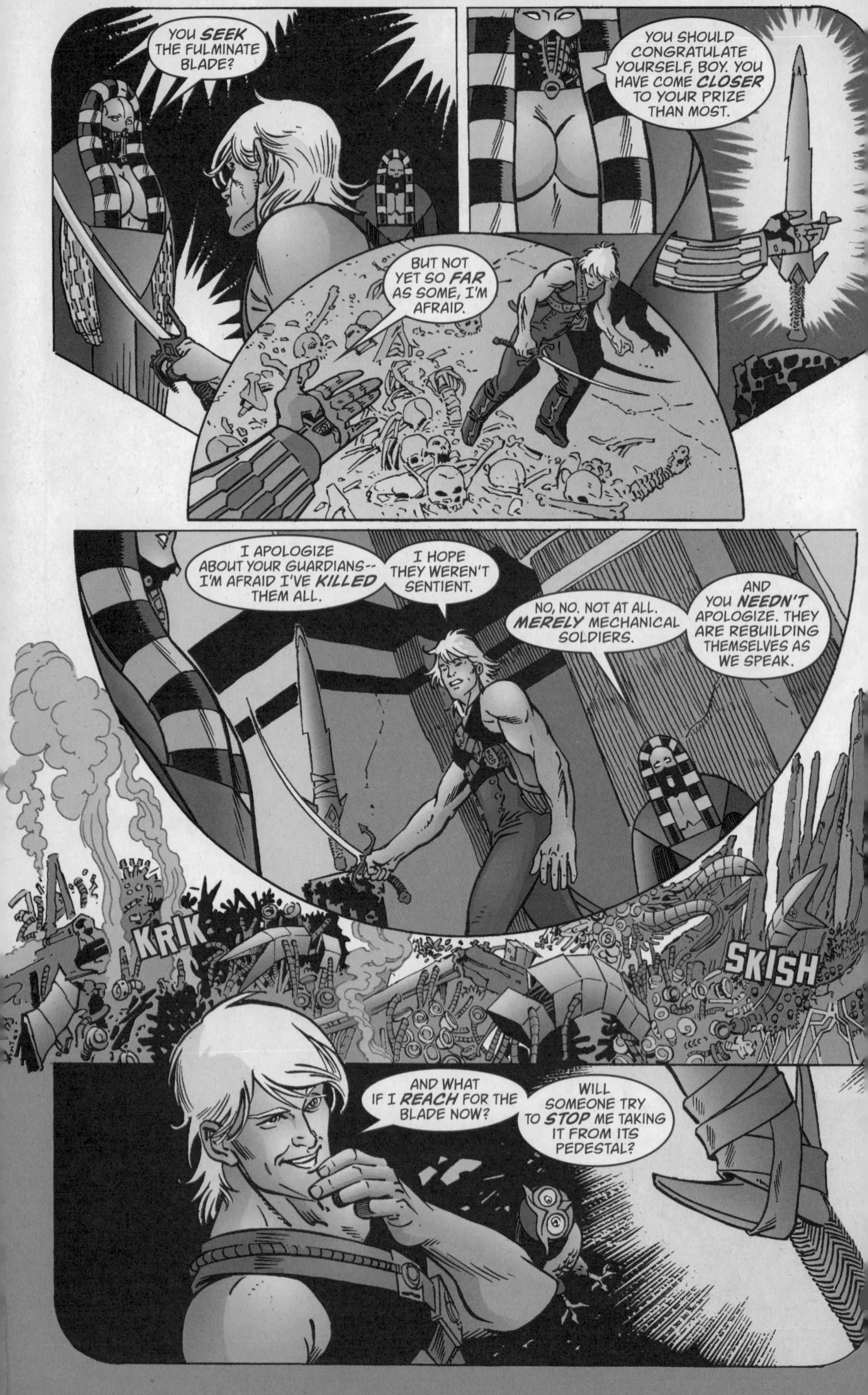

YOU SEEK THE FULMINATE BLADE?
YOU SHOULD CONGRATULATE YOURSELF, BOY. YOU HAVE COME CLOSER TO YOUR PRIZE THAN MOST.
BUT NOT YET SO FAR AS SOME, I'M AFRAID.
I APOLOGIZE ABOUT YOUR GUARDIANS-- I'M AFRAID I'VE KILLED THEM ALL.
I HOPE THEY WEREN'T SENTIENT.
NO, NO. NOT AT ALL. MERELY MECHANICAL SOLDIERS.
AND YOU NEEDN'T APOLOGIZE. THEY ARE REBUILDING THEMSELVES AS WE SPEAK.
KRIK
SKISH
AND WHAT IF I REACH FOR THE BLADE NOW?
WILL SOMEONE TRY TO STOP ME TAKING IT FROM ITS PEDESTAL?

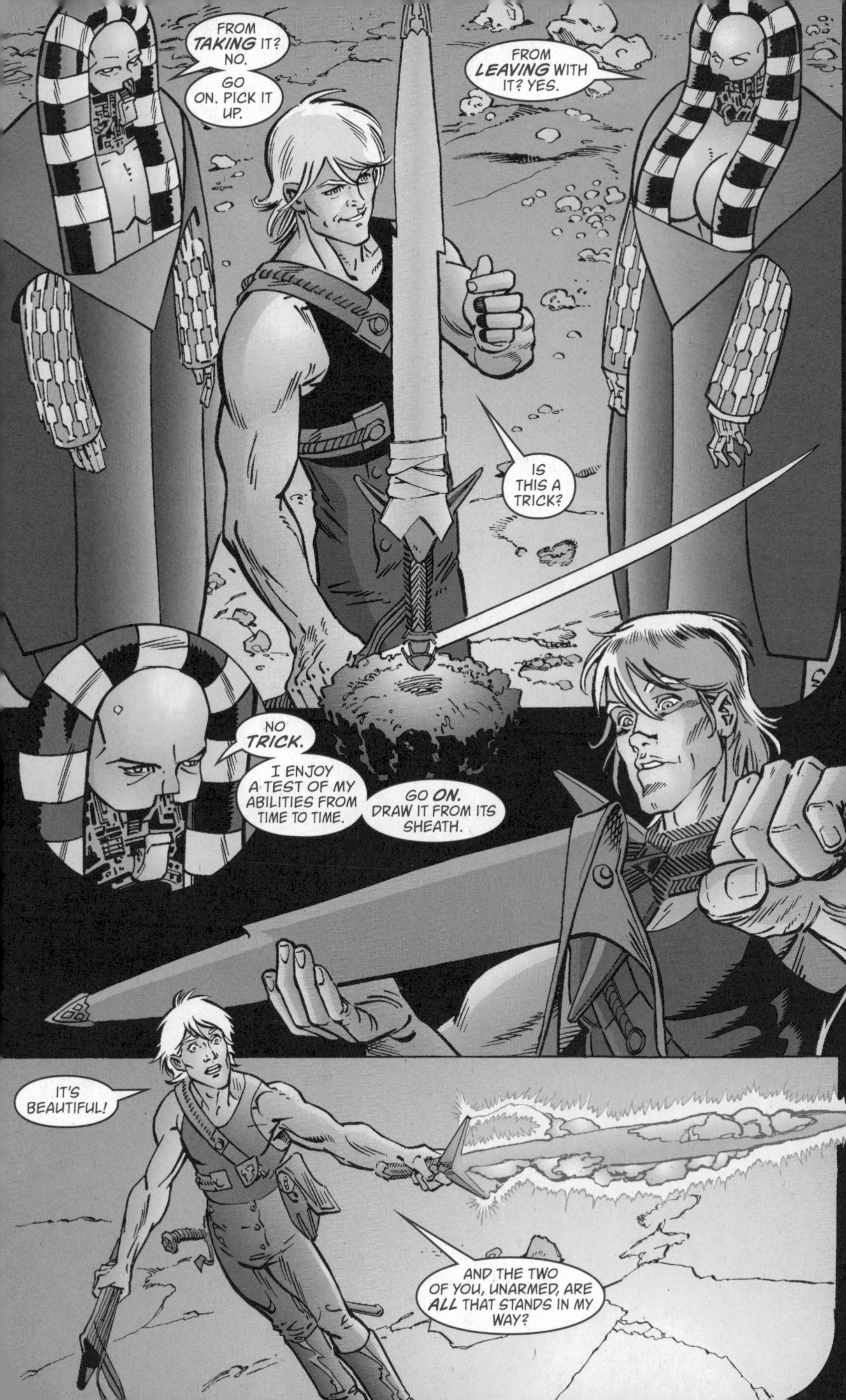
FROM TAKING IT? NO.
GO ON. PICK IT UP.
FROM LEAVING WITH IT? YES.
IS THIS A TRICK?
NO TRICK.
I ENJOY A TEST OF MY ABILITIES FROM TIME TO TIME.
GO ON. DRAW IT FROM ITS SHEATH.
IT'S BEAUTIFUL!
AND THE TWO OF YOU, UNARMED, ARE ALL THAT STANDS IN MY WAY?

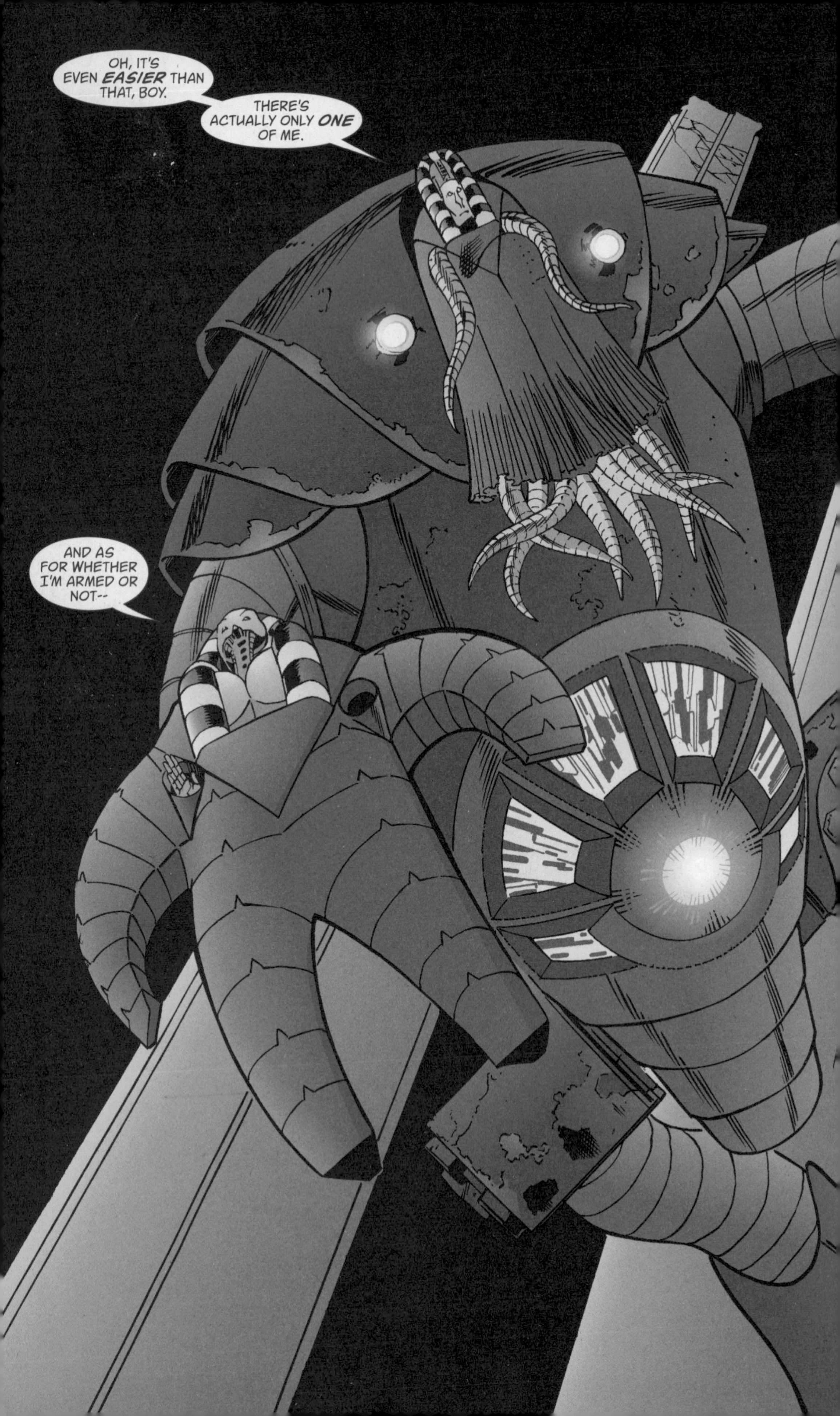
OH, IT'S EVEN EASIER THAN THAT, BOY.
THERE'S ACTUALLY ONLY ONE OF ME.
AND AS FOR WHETHER I'M ARMED OR NOT--

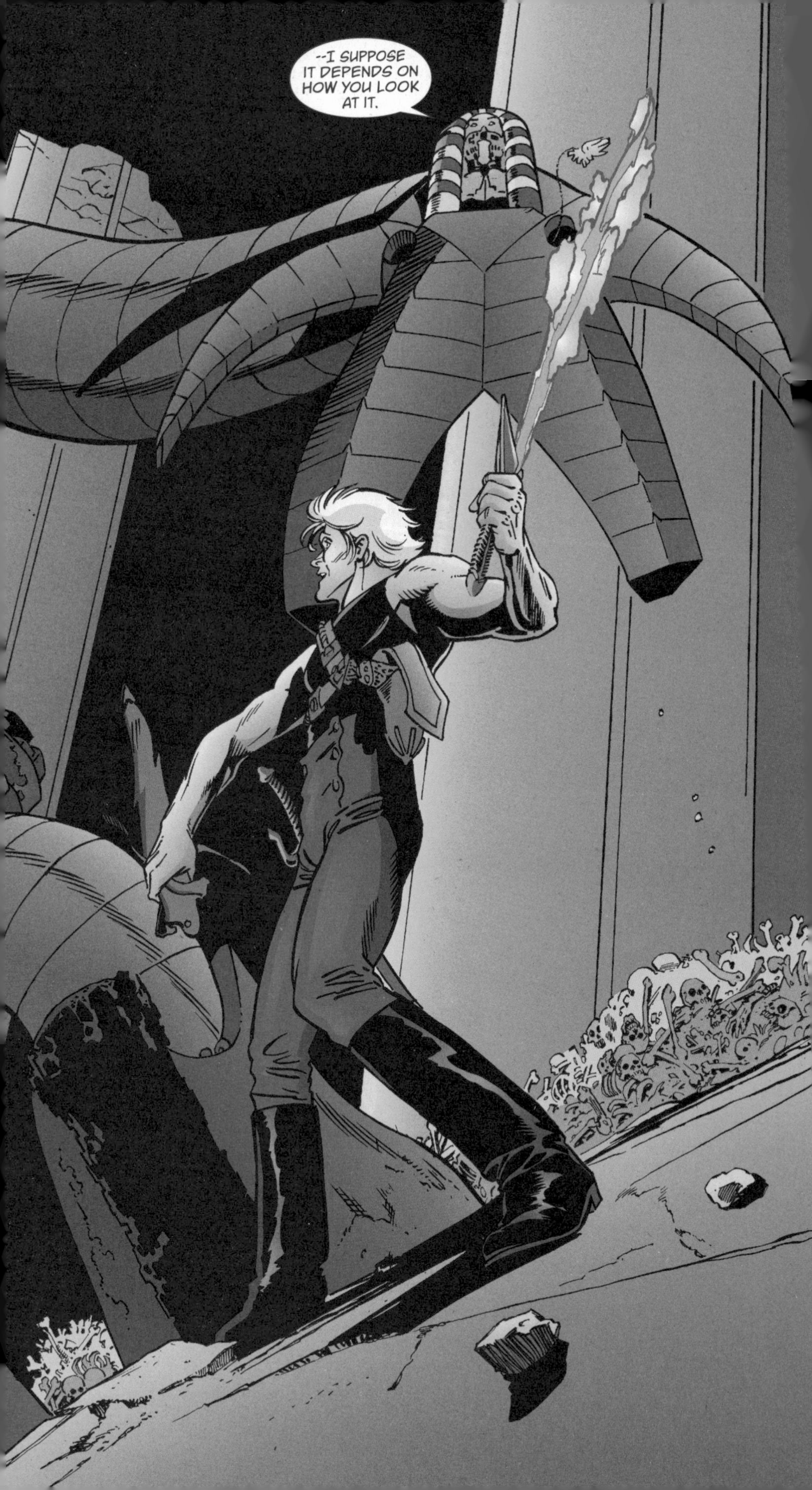
--I SUPPOSE IT DEPENDS ON HOW YOU LOOK AT IT.

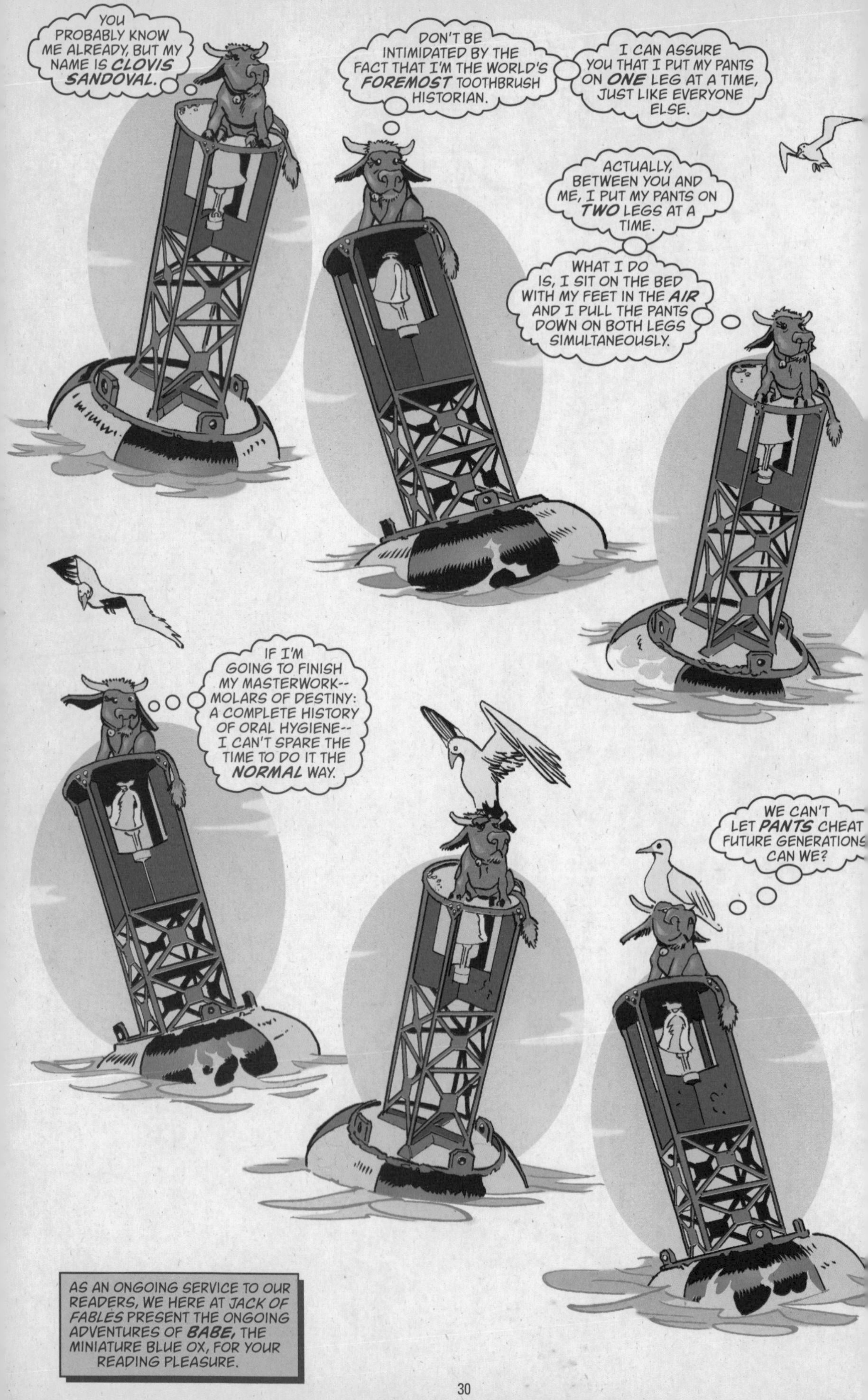

YOU PROBABLY KNOW ME ALREADY, BUT MY NAME IS CLOVIS SANDOVAL.
DON'T BE INTIMIDATED BY THE FACT THAT I'M THE WORLD'S FOREMOST TOOTHBRUSH HISTORIAN.
I CAN ASSURE YOU THAT I PUT MY PANTS ON ONE LEG AT A TIME, JUST LIKE EVERYONE ELSE.
ACTUALLY, BETWEEN YOU AND ME, I PUT MY PANTS ON TWO LEGS AT A TIME.
WHAT I DO IS, I SIT ON THE BED WITH MY FEET IN THE AIR AND I PULL THE PANTS DOWN ON BOTH LEGS SIMULTANEOUSLY.
IF I'M GOING TO FINISH MY MASTERWORK-- MOLARS OF DESTINY: A COMPLETE HISTORY OF ORAL HYGIENE-- I CAN'T SPARE THE TIME TO DO IT THE NORMAL WAY.
WE CAN'T LET PANTS CHEAT FUTURE GENERATIONS CAN WE?
AS AN ONGOING SERVICE TO OUR READERS, WE HERE AT JACK OF FABLES PRESENT THE ONGOING ADVENTURES OF BABE, THE MINIATURE BLUE OX, FOR YOUR READING PLEASURE.

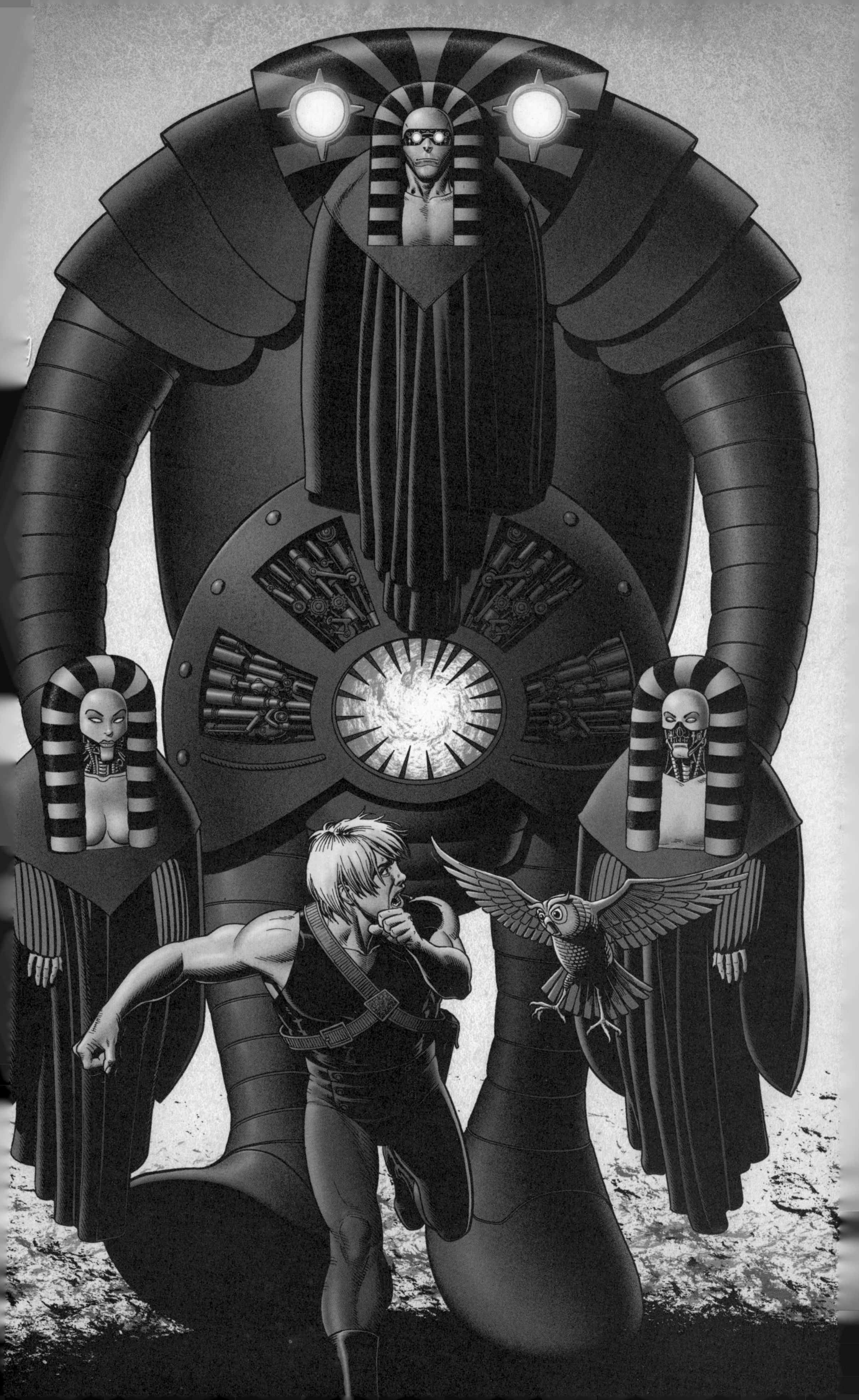

"Many a man has gotten himself killed by believing his own press."

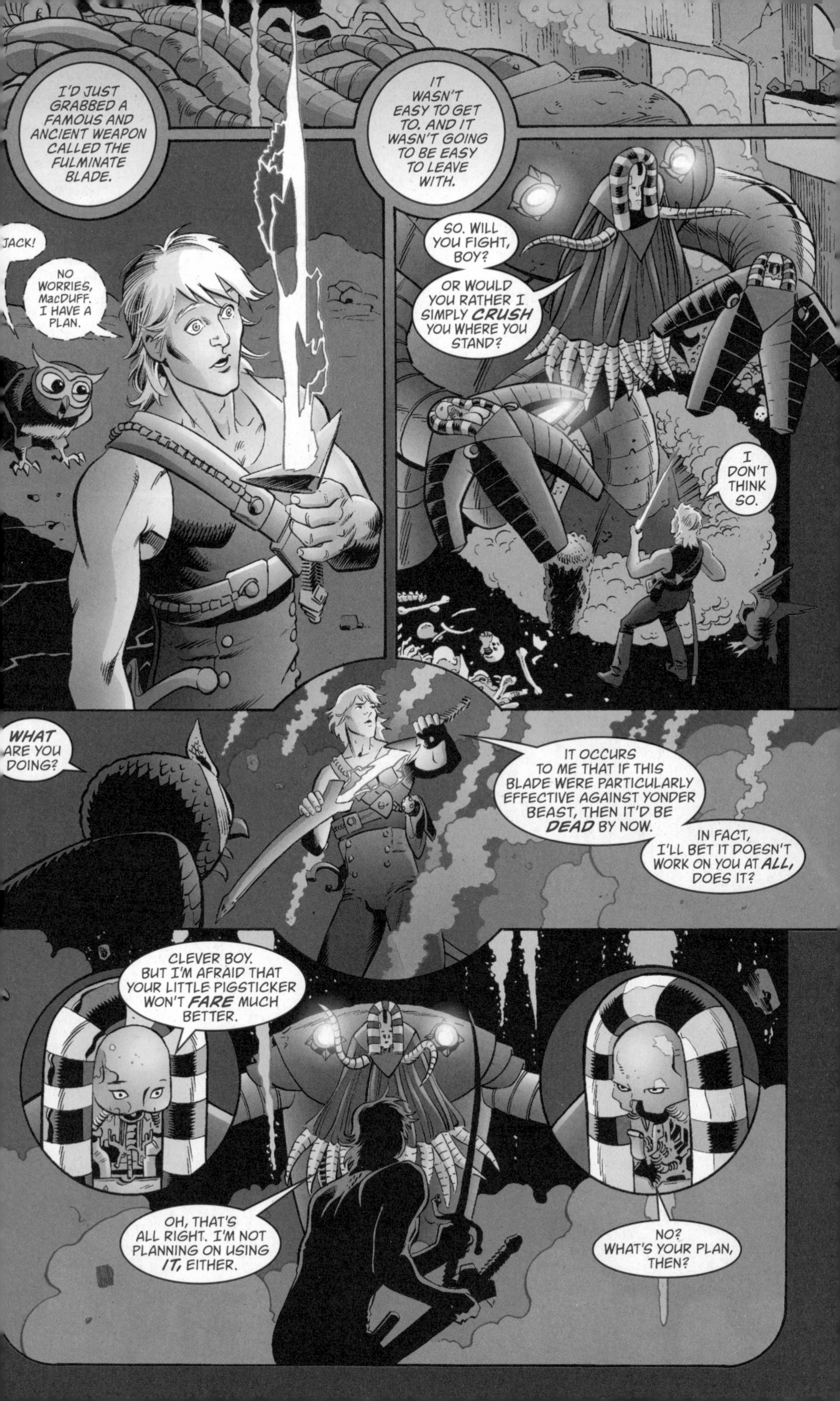

I'D JUST GRABBED A FAMOUS AND ANCIENT WEAPON CALLED THE FULMINATE BLADE.
IT WASN'T EASY TO GET TO. AND IT WASN'T GOING TO BE EASY TO LEAVE WITH.
JACK!
NO WORRIES, MacDUFF. I HAVE A PLAN.
SO. WILL YOU FIGHT, BOY?
OR WOULD YOU RATHER I SIMPLY CRUSH YOU WHERE YOU STAND?
I DON'T THINK SO.
WHAT ARE YOU DOING?
IT OCCURS TO ME THAT IF THIS BLADE WERE PARTICULARLY EFFECTIVE AGAINST YONDER BEAST, THEN IT'D BE DEAD BY NOW.
IN FACT, I'LL BET IT DOESN'T WORK ON YOU AT ALL, DOES IT?
CLEVER BOY. BUT I'M AFRAID THAT YOUR LITTLE PIGSTICKER WON'T FARE MUCH BETTER.
OH, THAT'S ALL RIGHT. I'M NOT PLANNING ON USING IT, EITHER.
NO? WHAT'S YOUR PLAN, THEN?

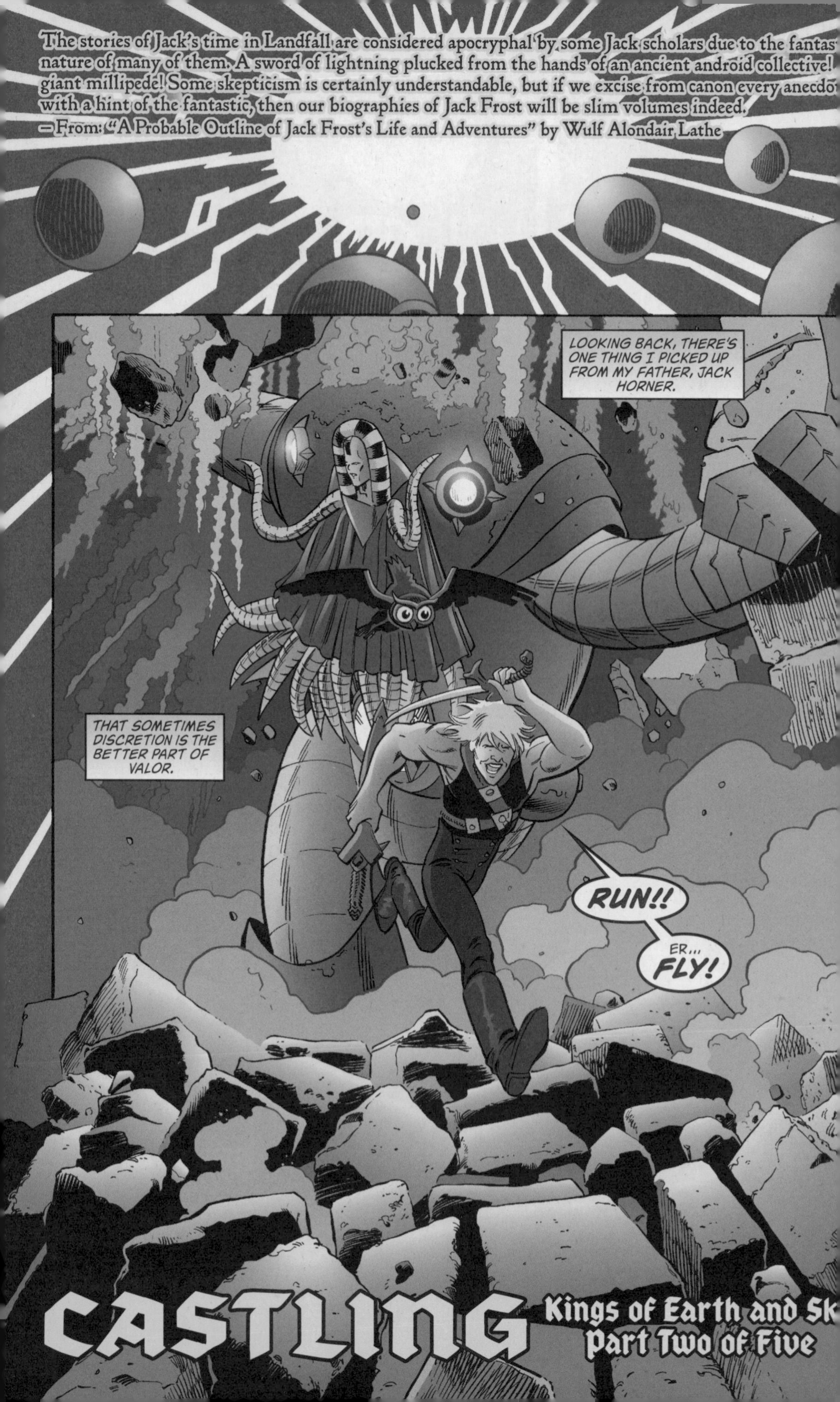
The stories of Jack's time in Landfall are considered apocryphal by some Jack scholars due to the fantas nature of many of them. A sword of lightning plucked from the hands of an ancient android collective! giant millipede! Some skepticism is certainly understandable, but if we excise from canon every anecdo with a hint of the fantastic, then our biographies of Jack Frost will be slim volumes indeed.
– From: "A Probable Outline of Jack Frost's Life and Adventures" by Wulf Alondair Lathe
LOOKING BACK, THERE'S ONE THING I PICKED UP FROM MY FATHER, JACK HORNER.
THAT SOMETIMES DISCRETION IS THE BETTER PART OF VALOR.
RUN!!
ER... FLY!
CASTLING
Kings of Earth and Sk
Part Two of Five

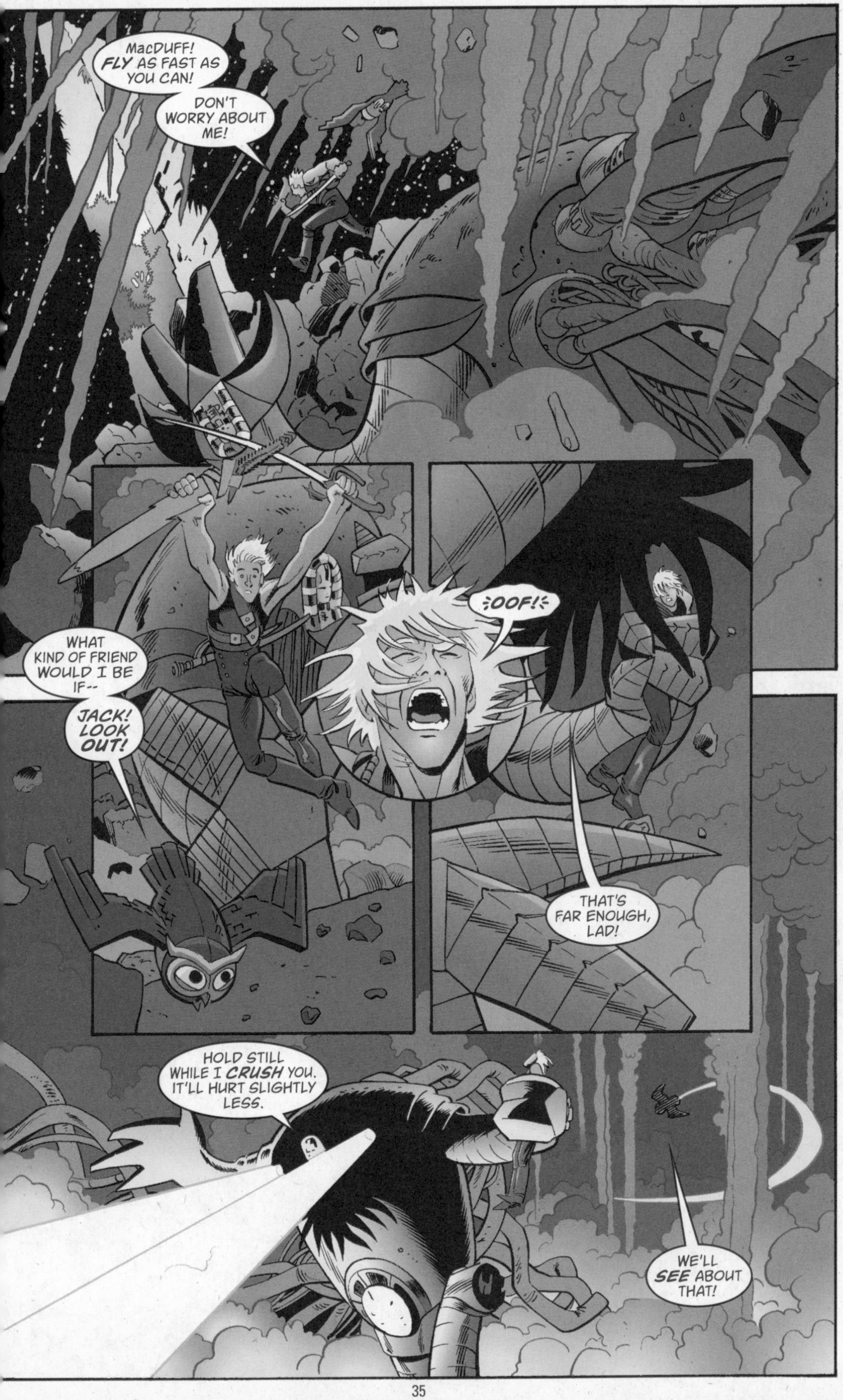
MacDUFF! FLY AS FAST AS YOU CAN!
DON'T WORRY ABOUT ME!
WHAT KIND OF FRIEND WOULD I BE IF--
JACK! LOOK OUT!
OOF!
THAT'S FAR ENOUGH, LAD!
HOLD STILL WHILE I CRUSH YOU. IT'LL HURT SLIGHTLY LESS.
WE'LL SEE ABOUT THAT!

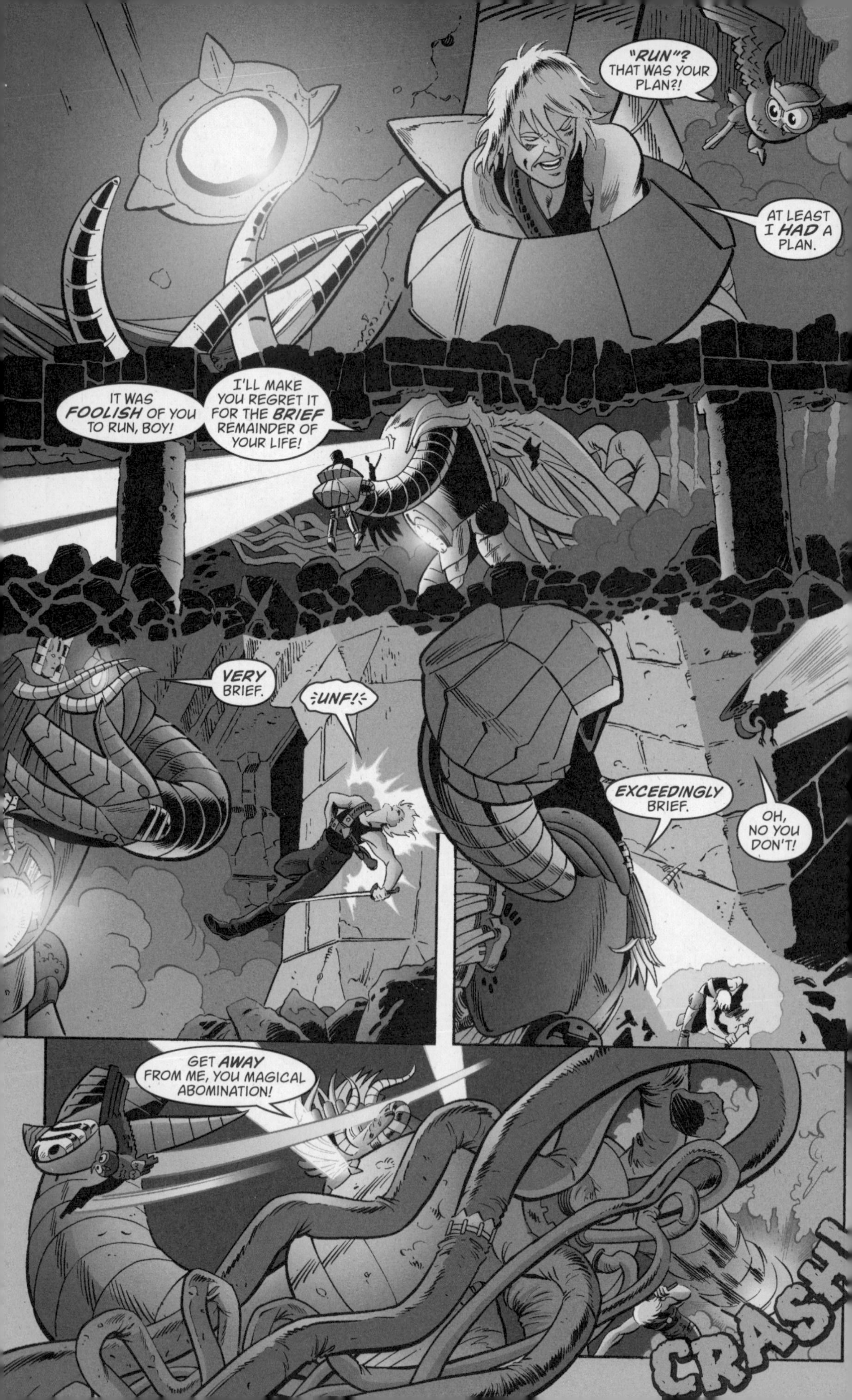
"RUN"? THAT WAS YOUR PLAN?!
AT LEAST I HAD A PLAN.
IT WAS FOOLISH OF YOU TO RUN, BOY!
I'LL MAKE YOU REGRET IT FOR THE BRIEF REMAINDER OF YOUR LIFE!
VERY BRIEF.
UNF!
EXCEEDINGLY BRIEF.
OH, NO YOU DON'T!
GET AWAY FROM ME, YOU MAGICAL ABOMINATION!
CRASH!

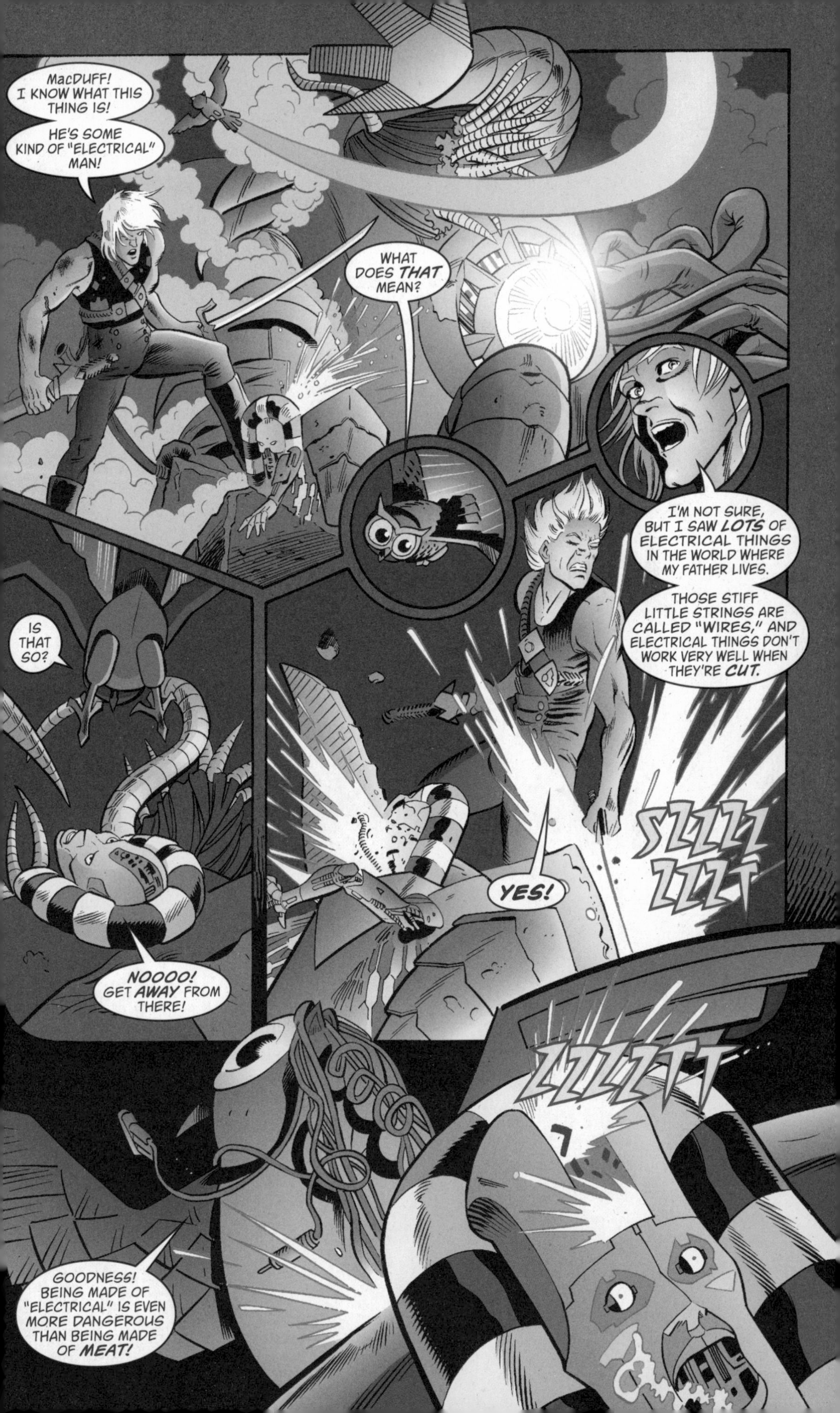
MacDUFF! I KNOW WHAT THIS THING IS!
HE'S SOME KIND OF "ELECTRICAL" MAN!
WHAT DOES THAT MEAN?
I'M NOT SURE, BUT I SAW LOTS OF ELECTRICAL THINGS IN THE WORLD WHERE MY FATHER LIVES.
THOSE STIFF LITTLE STRINGS ARE CALLED "WIRES," AND ELECTRICAL THINGS DON'T WORK VERY WELL WHEN THEY'RE CUT.
IS THAT SO?
NOOOO! GET AWAY FROM THERE!
YES!
SZZZZ ZZZT
ZZZZTT
GOODNESS! BEING MADE OF "ELECTRICAL" IS EVEN MORE DANGEROUS THAN BEING MADE OF MEAT!

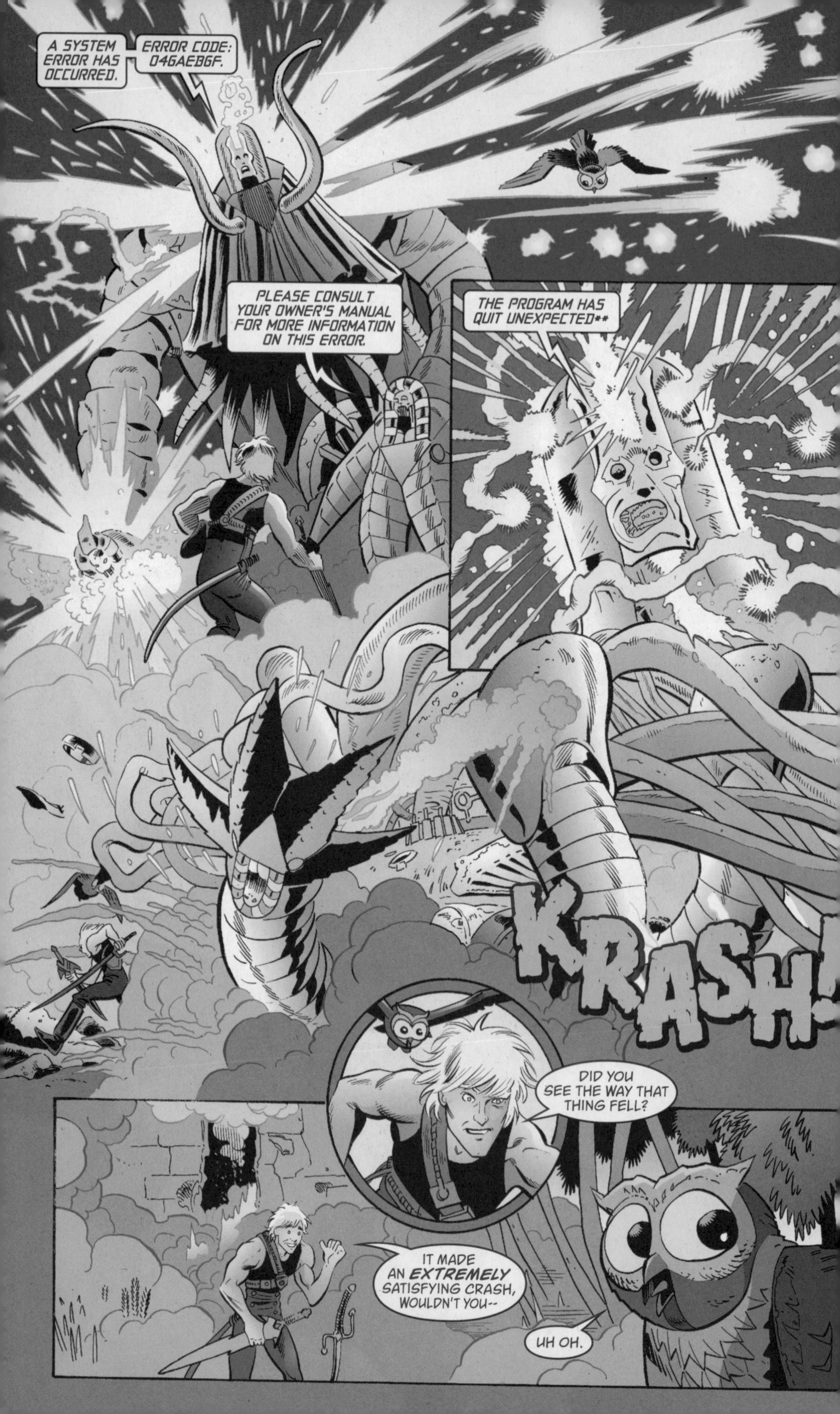
A SYSTEM ERROR HAS OCCURRED.
ERROR CODE: 046AEB6F.
PLEASE CONSULT YOUR OWNER'S MANUAL FOR MORE INFORMATION ON THIS ERROR.
THE PROGRAM HAS QUIT UNEXPECTED**
KRASH!
DID YOU SEE THE WAY THAT THING FELL?
IT MADE AN *EXTREMELY* SATISFYING CRASH, WOULDN'T YOU--
UH OH.

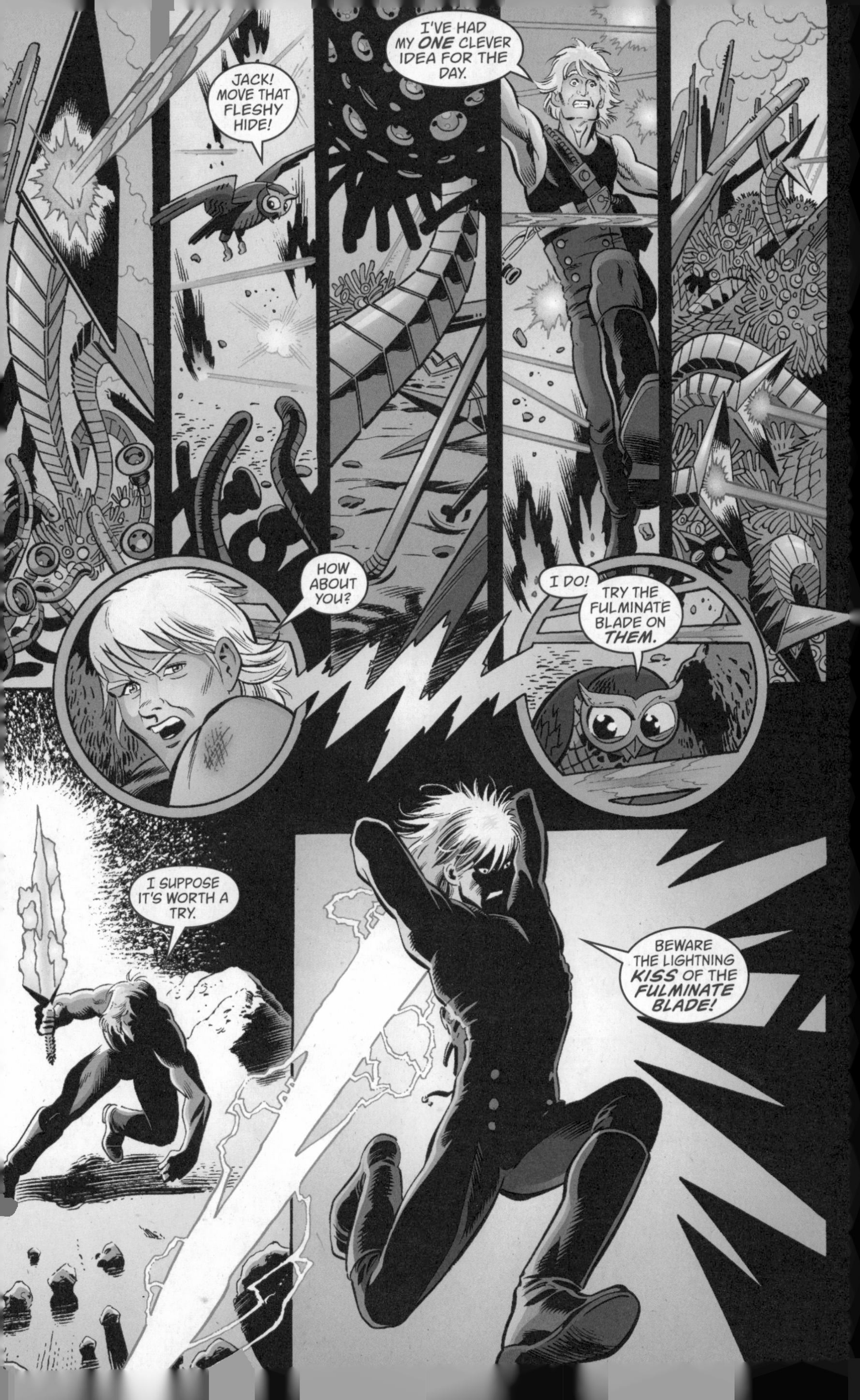
JACK! MOVE THAT FLESHY HIDE!
I'VE HAD MY ONE CLEVER IDEA FOR THE DAY.
HOW ABOUT YOU?
I DO!
TRY THE FULMINATE BLADE ON THEM.
I SUPPOSE IT'S WORTH A TRY.
BEWARE THE LIGHTNING KISS OF THE FULMINATE BLADE!

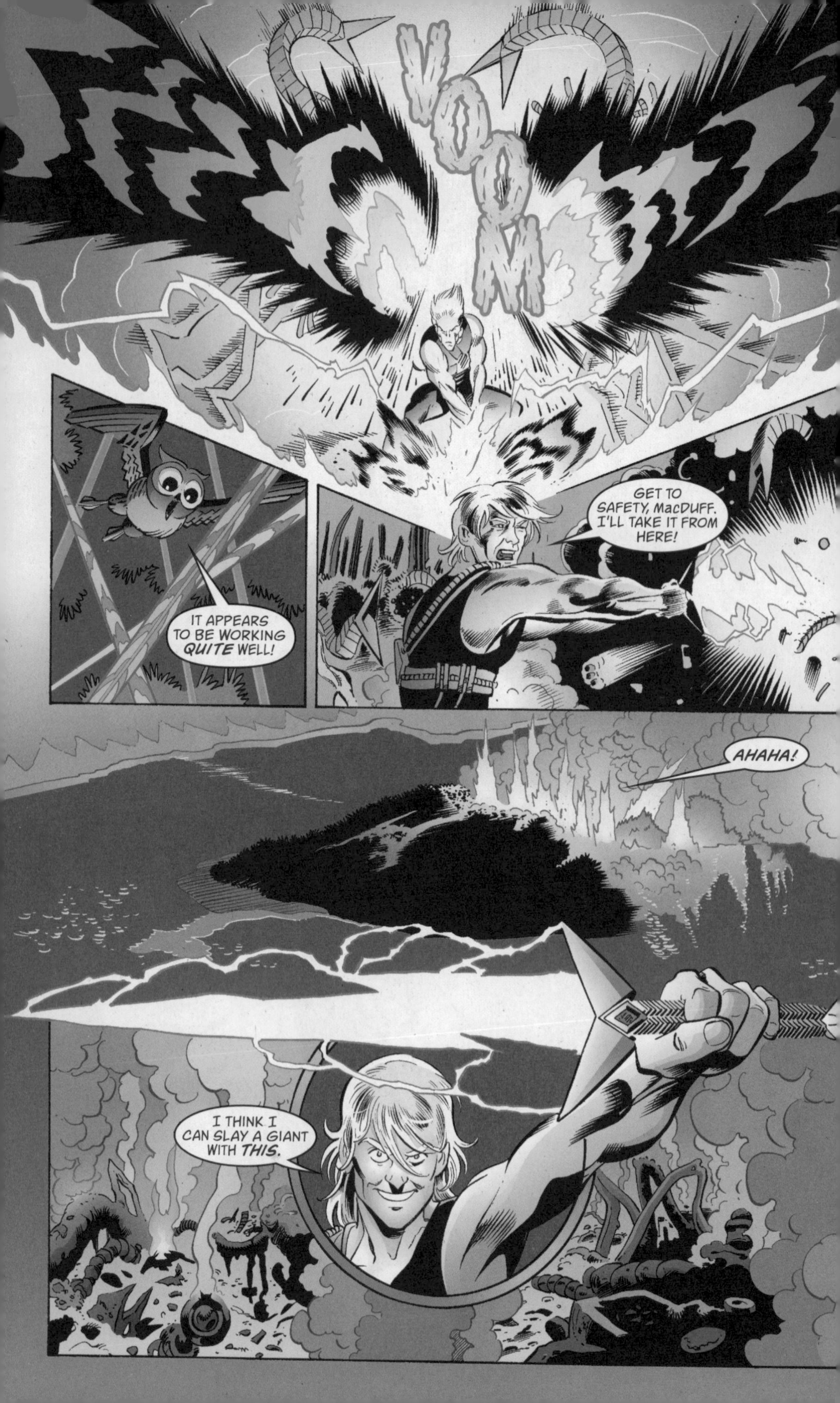
VOOOM
IT APPEARS TO BE WORKING QUITE WELL!
GET TO SAFETY, MacDUFF. I'LL TAKE IT FROM HERE!
AHAHA!
I THINK I CAN SLAY A GIANT WITH THIS.

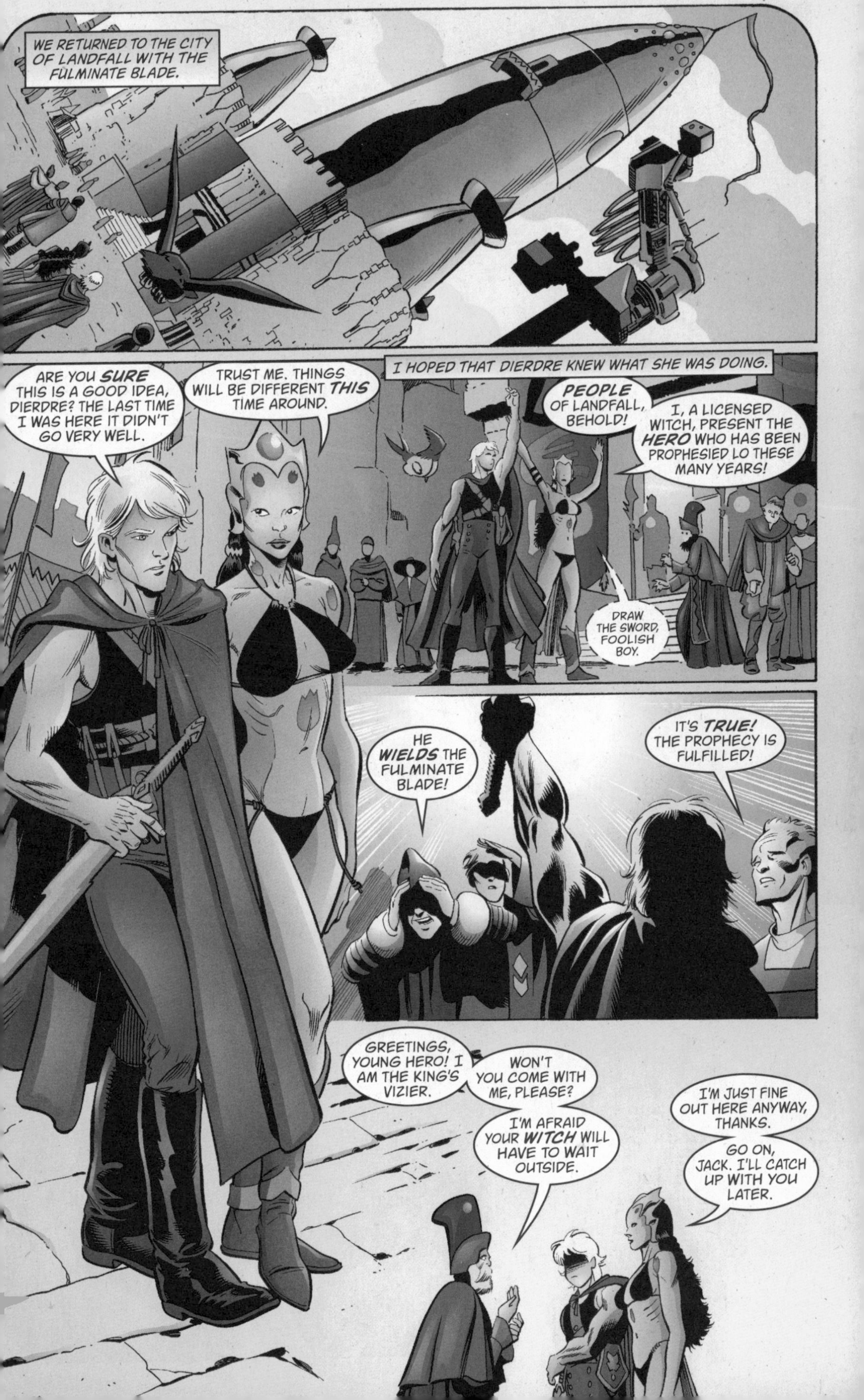

WE RETURNED TO THE CITY OF LANDFALL WITH THE FULMINATE BLADE.
ARE YOU SURE THIS IS A GOOD IDEA, DIERDRE? THE LAST TIME I WAS HERE IT DIDN'T GO VERY WELL.
TRUST ME. THINGS WILL BE DIFFERENT THIS TIME AROUND.
I HOPED THAT DIERDRE KNEW WHAT SHE WAS DOING.
PEOPLE OF LANDFALL, BEHOLD!
I, A LICENSED WITCH, PRESENT THE HERO WHO HAS BEEN PROPHESIED LO THESE MANY YEARS!
DRAW THE SWORD, FOOLISH BOY.
HE WIELDS THE FULMINATE BLADE!
IT'S TRUE! THE PROPHECY IS FULFILLED!
GREETINGS, YOUNG HERO! I AM THE KING'S VIZIER.
WON'T YOU COME WITH ME, PLEASE?
I'M AFRAID YOUR WITCH WILL HAVE TO WAIT OUTSIDE.
I'M JUST FINE OUT HERE ANYWAY, THANKS.
GO ON, JACK. I'LL CATCH UP WITH YOU LATER.

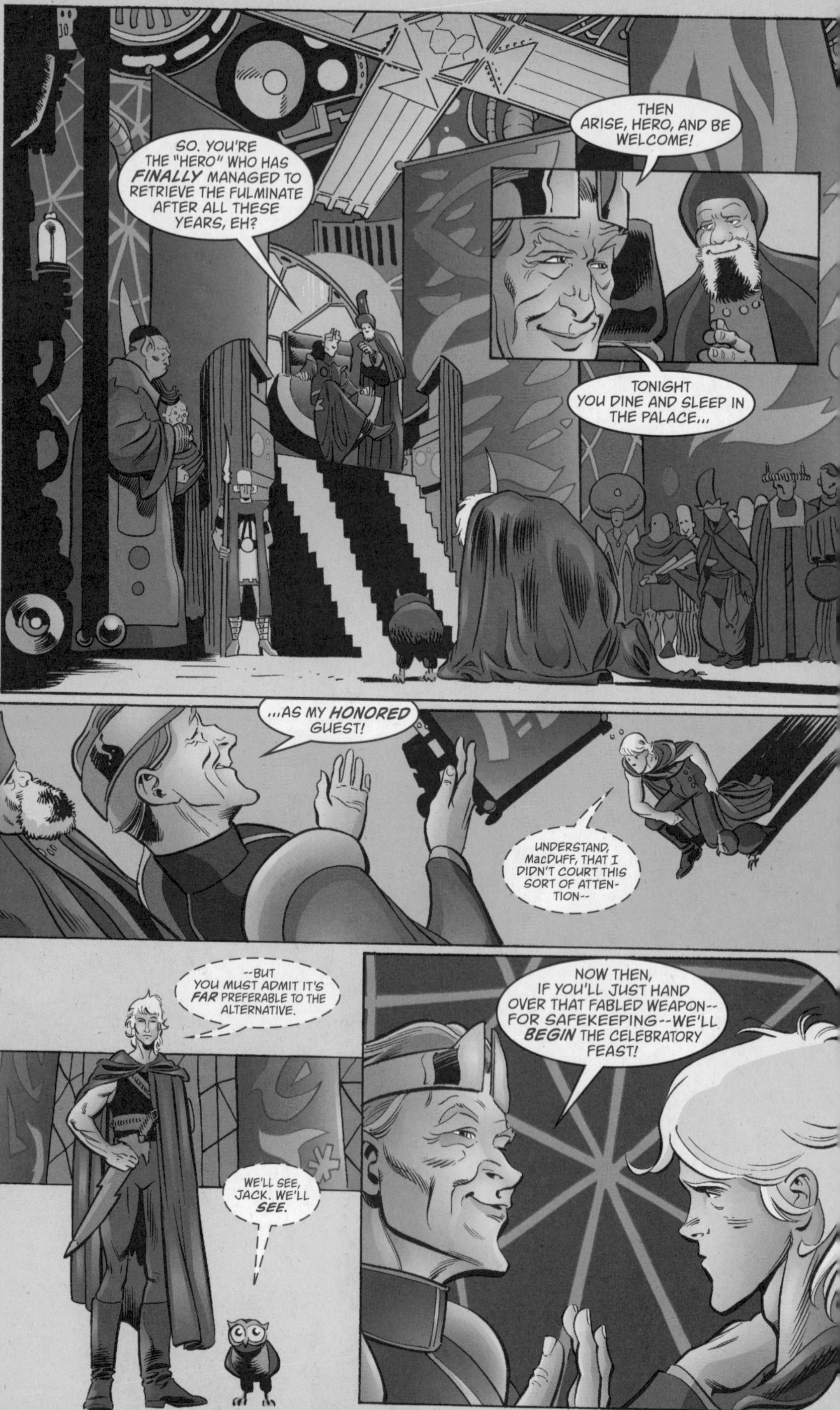
SO. YOU'RE THE "HERO" WHO HAS FINALLY MANAGED TO RETRIEVE THE FULMINATE AFTER ALL THESE YEARS, EH?
THEN ARISE, HERO, AND BE WELCOME!
TONIGHT YOU DINE AND SLEEP IN THE PALACE...
...AS MY HONORED GUEST!
UNDERSTAND, MacDUFF, THAT I DIDN'T COURT THIS SORT OF ATTEN-TION--
--BUT YOU MUST ADMIT IT'S FAR PREFERABLE TO THE ALTERNATIVE.
WE'LL SEE, JACK. WE'LL SEE.
NOW THEN, IF YOU'LL JUST HAND OVER THAT FABLED WEAPON--FOR SAFEKEEPING--WE'LL BEGIN THE CELEBRATORY FEAST!

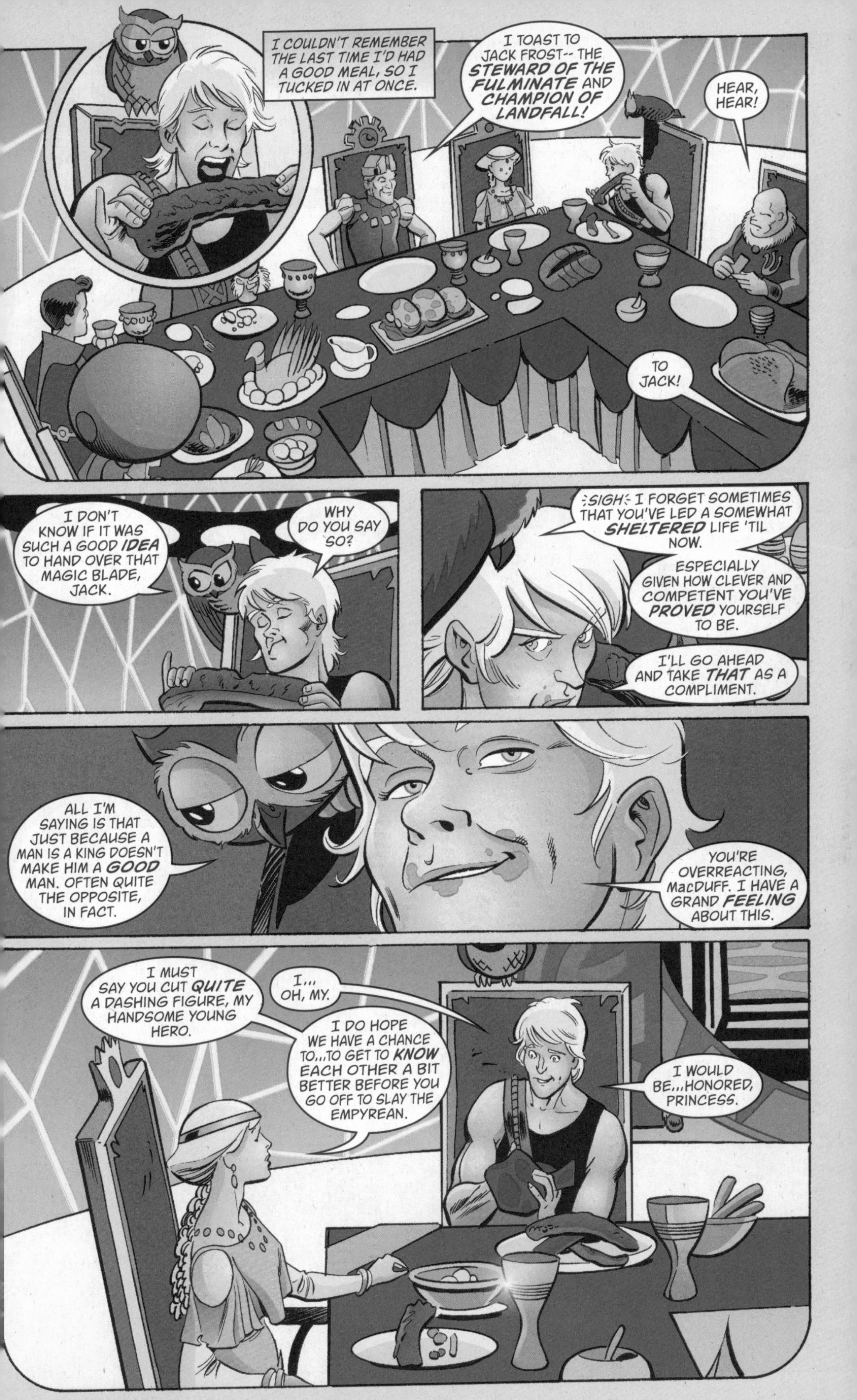

I COULDN'T REMEMBER THE LAST TIME I'D HAD A GOOD MEAL, SO I TUCKED IN AT ONCE.
I TOAST TO JACK FROST-- THE STEWARD OF THE FULMINATE AND CHAMPION OF LANDFALL!
HEAR, HEAR!
TO JACK!
I DON'T KNOW IF IT WAS SUCH A GOOD IDEA TO HAND OVER THAT MAGIC BLADE, JACK.
WHY DO YOU SAY SO?
SIGH I FORGET SOMETIMES THAT YOU'VE LED A SOMEWHAT SHELTERED LIFE 'TIL NOW.
ESPECIALLY GIVEN HOW CLEVER AND COMPETENT YOU'VE PROVED YOURSELF TO BE.
I'LL GO AHEAD AND TAKE THAT AS A COMPLIMENT.
ALL I'M SAYING IS THAT JUST BECAUSE A MAN IS A KING DOESN'T MAKE HIM A GOOD MAN. OFTEN QUITE THE OPPOSITE, IN FACT.
YOU'RE OVERREACTING, MacDUFF. I HAVE A GRAND FEELING ABOUT THIS.
I MUST SAY YOU CUT QUITE A DASHING FIGURE, MY HANDSOME YOUNG HERO.
I... OH, MY.
I DO HOPE WE HAVE A CHANCE TO...TO GET TO KNOW EACH OTHER A BIT BETTER BEFORE YOU GO OFF TO SLAY THE EMPYREAN.
I WOULD BE...HONORED, PRINCESS.

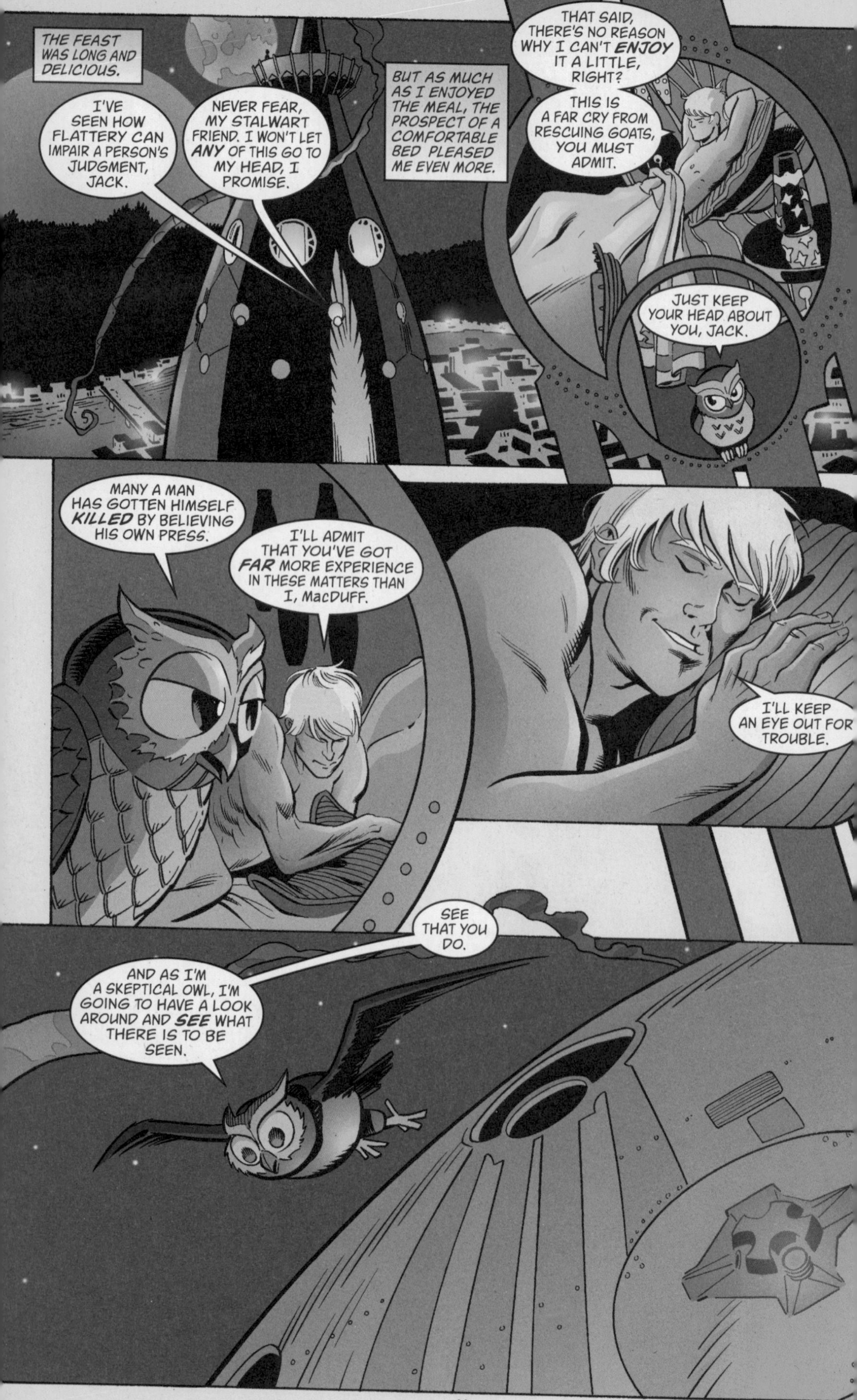
THE FEAST WAS LONG AND DELICIOUS.
I'VE SEEN HOW FLATTERY CAN IMPAIR A PERSON'S JUDGMENT, JACK.
NEVER FEAR, MY STALWART FRIEND. I WON'T LET ANY OF THIS GO TO MY HEAD, I PROMISE.
BUT AS MUCH AS I ENJOYED THE MEAL, THE PROSPECT OF A COMFORTABLE BED PLEASED ME EVEN MORE.
THAT SAID, THERE'S NO REASON WHY I CAN'T ENJOY IT A LITTLE, RIGHT?
THIS IS A FAR CRY FROM RESCUING GOATS, YOU MUST ADMIT.
JUST KEEP YOUR HEAD ABOUT YOU, JACK.
MANY A MAN HAS GOTTEN HIMSELF KILLED BY BELIEVING HIS OWN PRESS.
I'LL ADMIT THAT YOU'VE GOT FAR MORE EXPERIENCE IN THESE MATTERS THAN I, MacDUFF.
I'LL KEEP AN EYE OUT FOR TROUBLE.
SEE THAT YOU DO.
AND AS I'M A SKEPTICAL OWL, I'M GOING TO HAVE A LOOK AROUND AND SEE WHAT THERE IS TO BE SEEN.

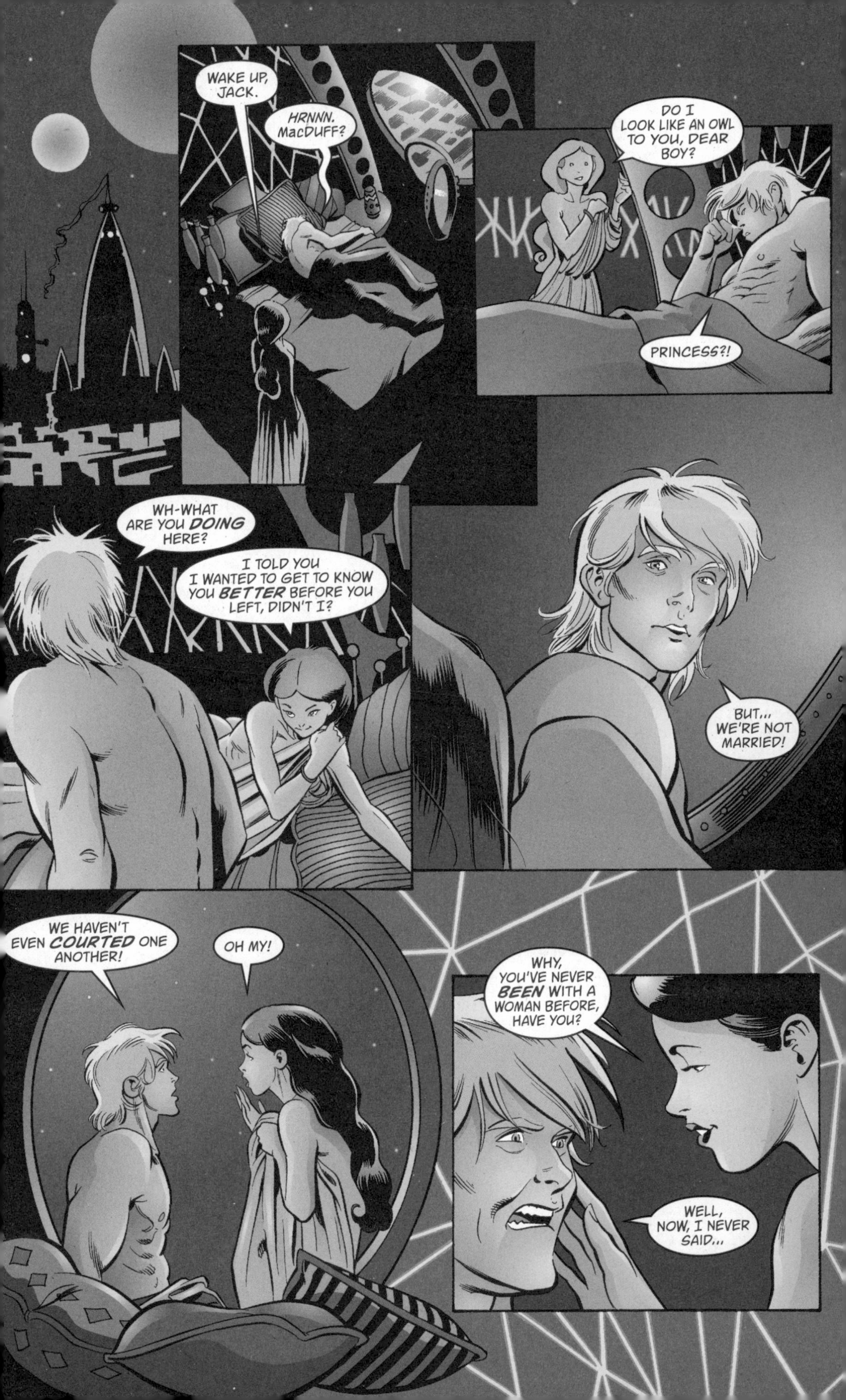
WAKE UP, JACK.
HRNNN. MacDUFF?
DO I LOOK LIKE AN OWL TO YOU, DEAR BOY?
PRINCESS?!
WH-WHAT ARE YOU DOING HERE?
I TOLD YOU I WANTED TO GET TO KNOW YOU BETTER BEFORE YOU LEFT, DIDN'T I?
BUT... WE'RE NOT MARRIED!
WE HAVEN'T EVEN COURTED ONE ANOTHER!
OH MY!
WHY, YOU'VE NEVER BEEN WITH A WOMAN BEFORE, HAVE YOU?
WELL, NOW, I NEVER SAID...

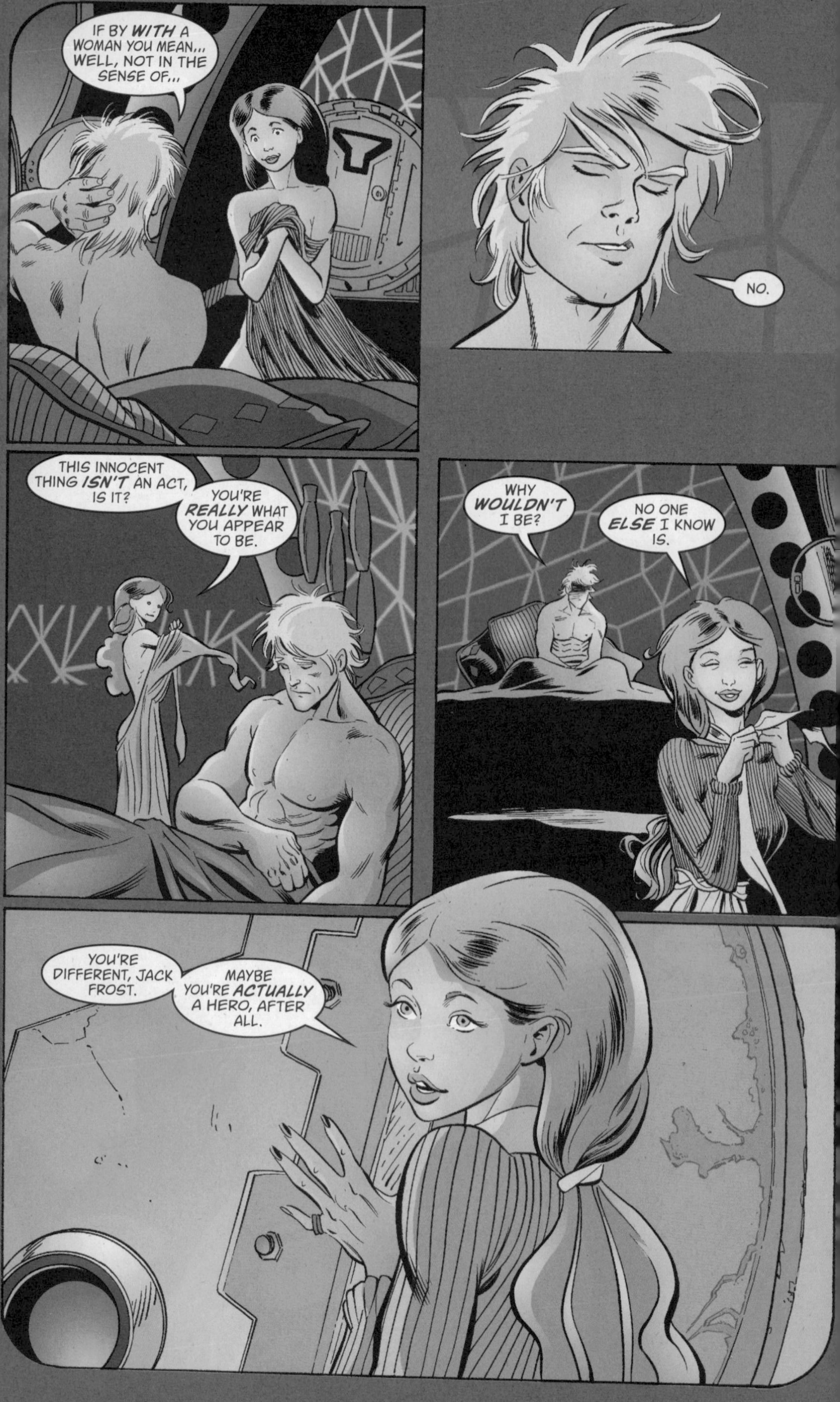
IF BY WITH A WOMAN YOU MEAN... WELL, NOT IN THE SENSE OF...
NO.
THIS INNOCENT THING ISN'T AN ACT, IS IT?
YOU'RE REALLY WHAT YOU APPEAR TO BE.
WHY WOULDN'T I BE?
NO ONE ELSE I KNOW IS.
YOU'RE DIFFERENT, JACK FROST.
MAYBE YOU'RE ACTUALLY A HERO, AFTER ALL.

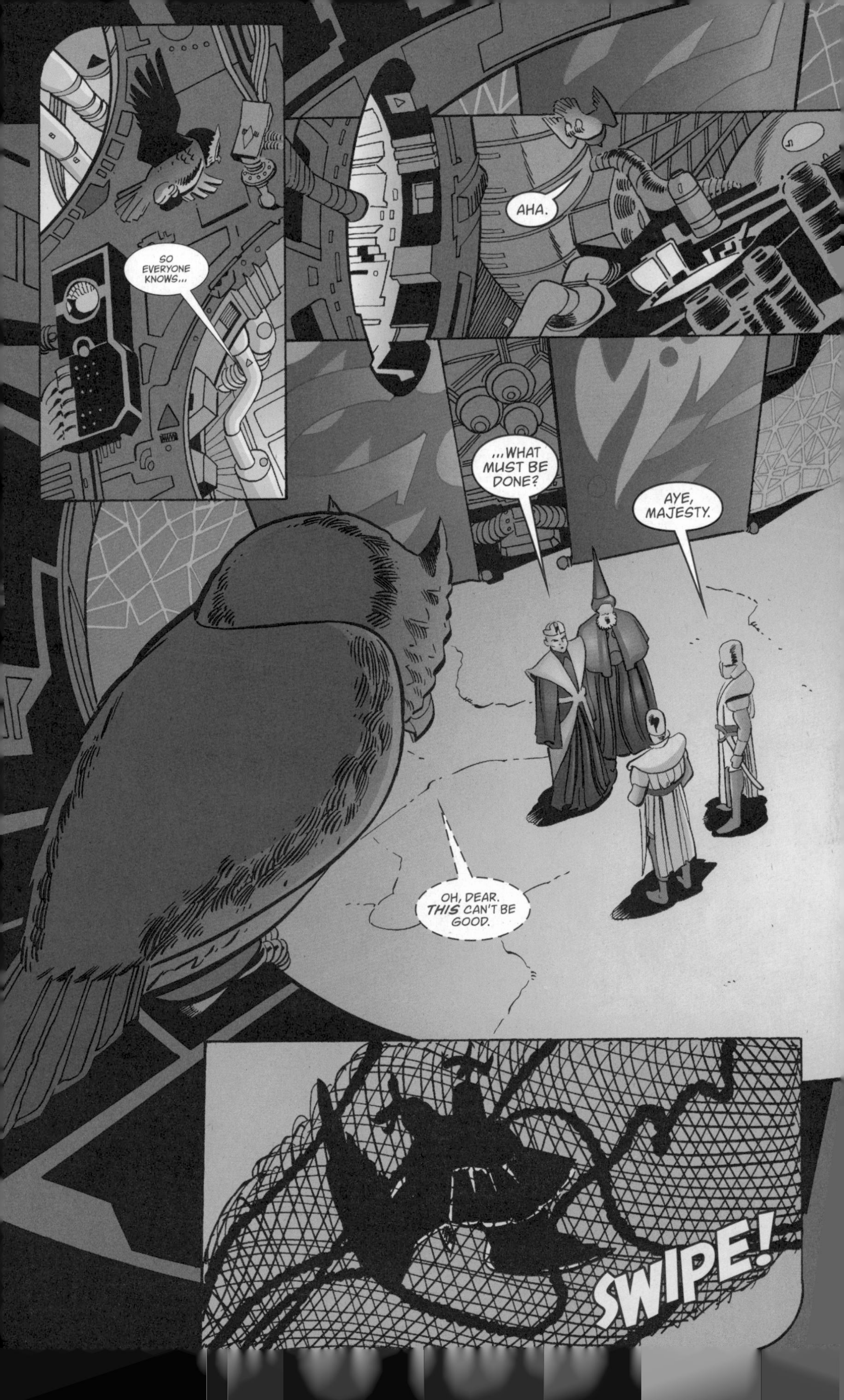

SO EVERYONE KNOWS...
AHA.
...WHAT MUST BE DONE?
AYE, MAJESTY.
OH, DEAR. THIS CAN'T BE GOOD.
SWIPE!

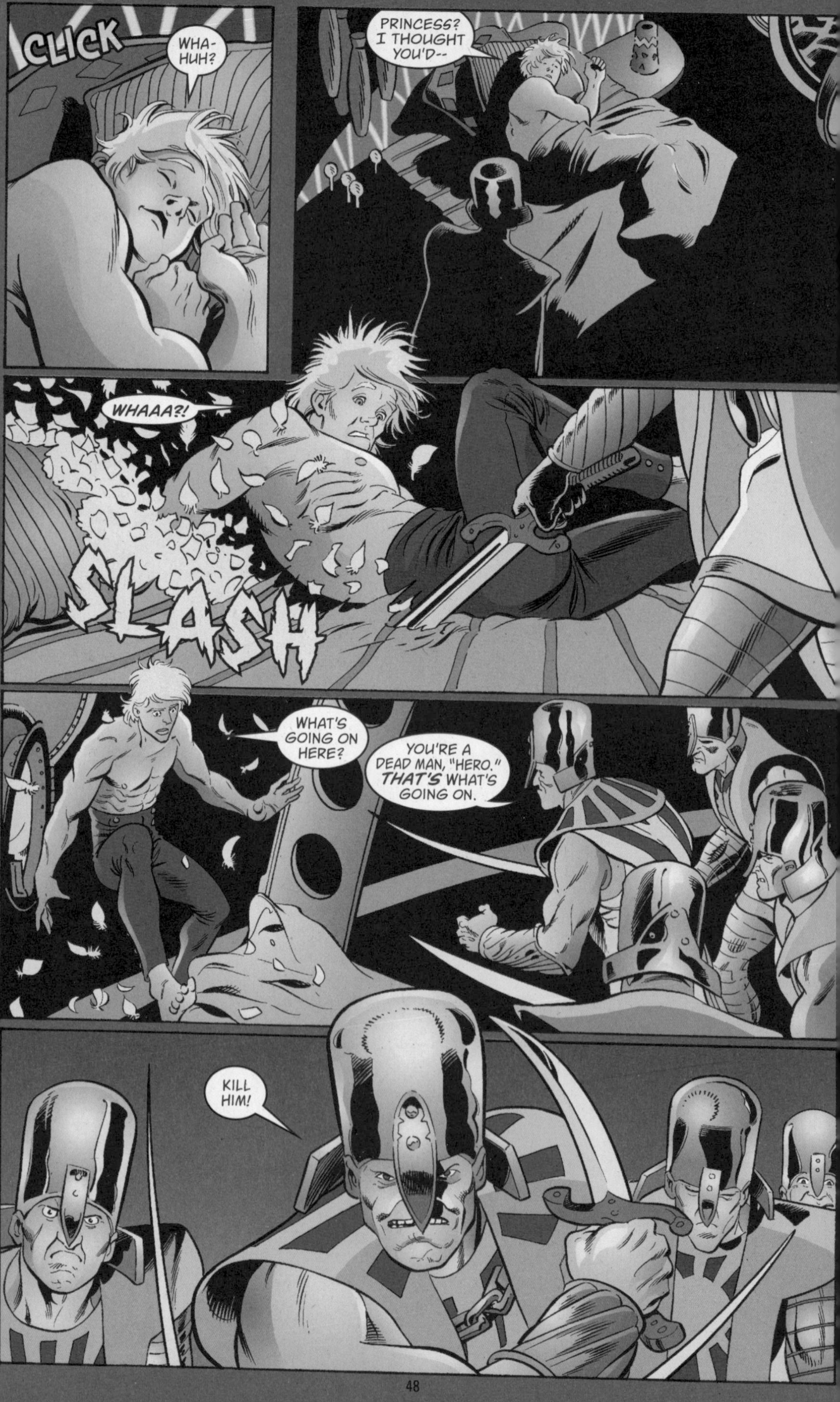
CLICK
WHA-HUH?
PRINCESS? I THOUGHT YOU'D--
WHAAA?!
SLASH
WHAT'S GOING ON HERE?
YOU'RE A DEAD MAN, "HERO." THAT'S WHAT'S GOING ON.
KILL HIM!

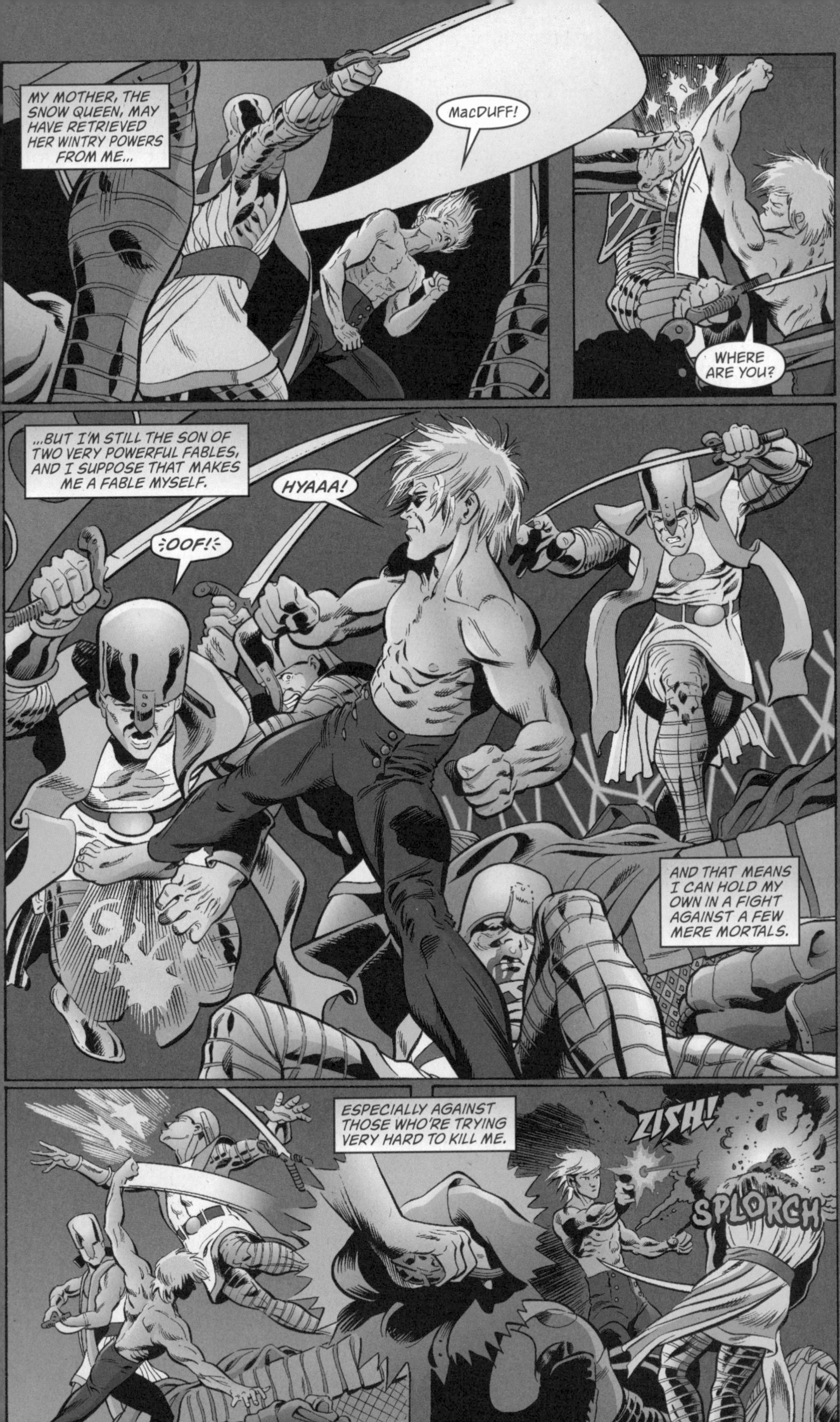
MY MOTHER, THE SNOW QUEEN, MAY HAVE RETRIEVED HER WINTRY POWERS FROM ME...
MacDUFF!
WHERE ARE YOU?
...BUT I'M STILL THE SON OF TWO VERY POWERFUL FABLES, AND I SUPPOSE THAT MAKES ME A FABLE MYSELF.
HYAAA!
OOF!
AND THAT MEANS I CAN HOLD MY OWN IN A FIGHT AGAINST A FEW MERE MORTALS.
ESPECIALLY AGAINST THOSE WHO'RE TRYING VERY HARD TO KILL ME.
ZISH!
SPLORCH

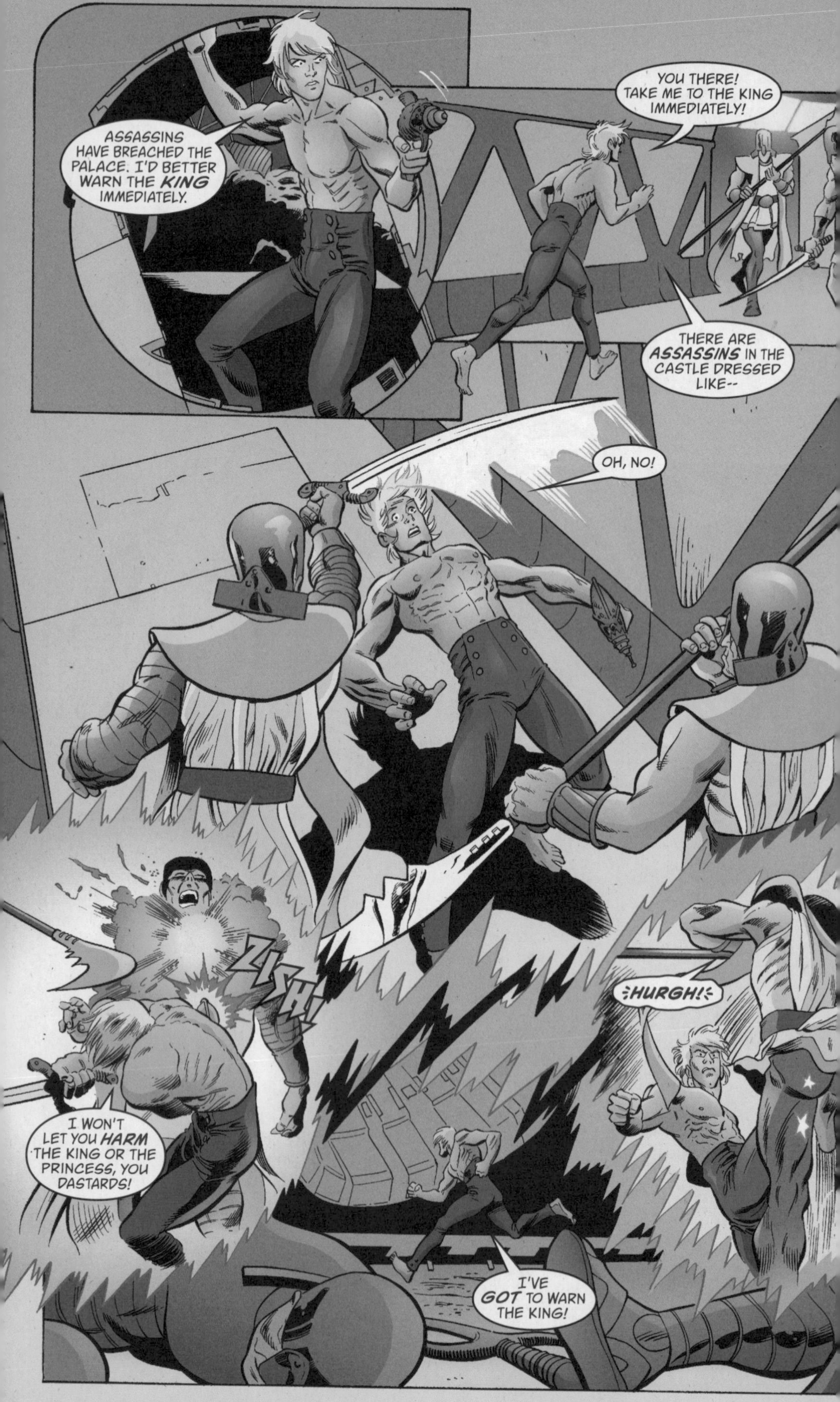
ASSASSINS HAVE BREACHED THE PALACE. I'D BETTER WARN THE KING IMMEDIATELY.
YOU THERE! TAKE ME TO THE KING IMMEDIATELY!
THERE ARE ASSASSINS IN THE CASTLE DRESSED LIKE--
OH, NO!
ZISH!
HURGH!
I WON'T LET YOU HARM THE KING OR THE PRINCESS, YOU DASTARDS!
I'VE GOT TO WARN THE KING!

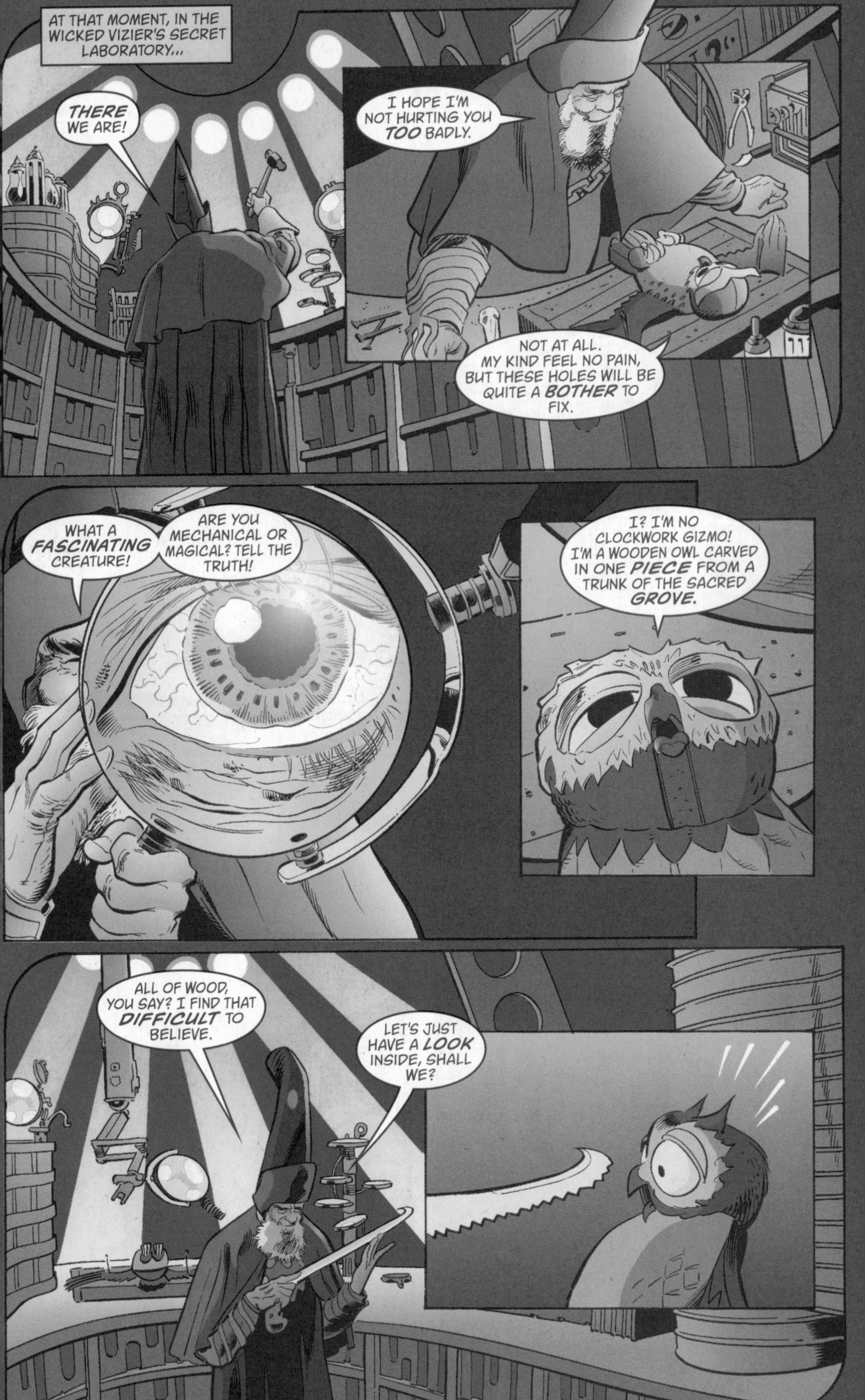
AT THAT MOMENT, IN THE WICKED VIZIER'S SECRET LABORATORY...
THERE WE ARE!
I HOPE I'M NOT HURTING YOU TOO BADLY.
NOT AT ALL. MY KIND FEEL NO PAIN, BUT THESE HOLES WILL BE QUITE A BOTHER TO FIX.
WHAT A FASCINATING CREATURE!
ARE YOU MECHANICAL OR MAGICAL? TELL THE TRUTH!
I? I'M NO CLOCKWORK GIZMO! I'M A WOODEN OWL CARVED IN ONE PIECE FROM A TRUNK OF THE SACRED GROVE.
ALL OF WOOD, YOU SAY? I FIND THAT DIFFICULT TO BELIEVE.
LET'S JUST HAVE A LOOK INSIDE, SHALL WE?

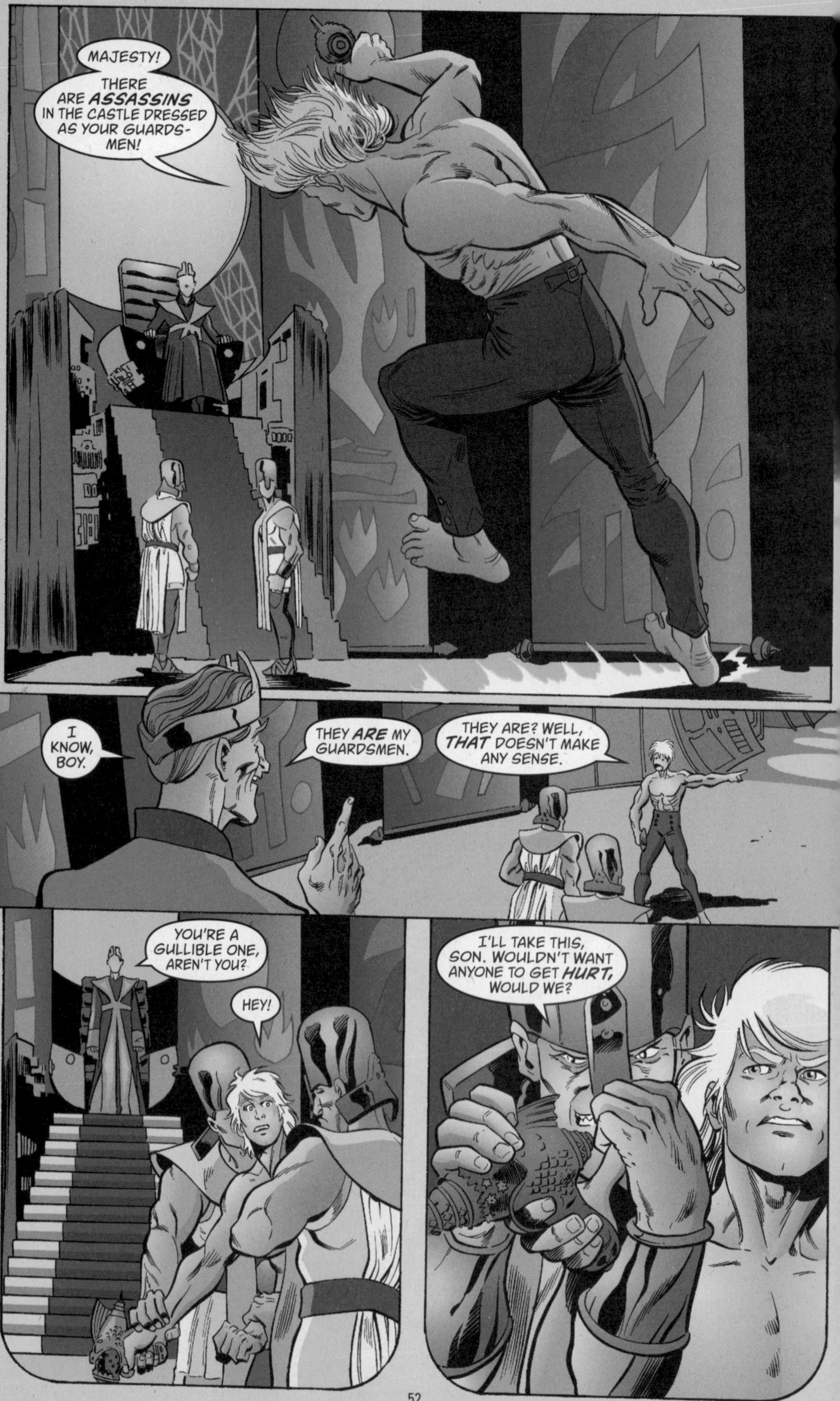
MAJESTY! THERE ARE ASSASSINS IN THE CASTLE DRESSED AS YOUR GUARDS-MEN!
I KNOW, BOY.
THEY ARE MY GUARDSMEN.
THEY ARE? WELL, THAT DOESN'T MAKE ANY SENSE.
YOU'RE A GULLIBLE ONE, AREN'T YOU?
HEY!
I'LL TAKE THIS, SON. WOULDN'T WANT ANYONE TO GET HURT, WOULD WE?

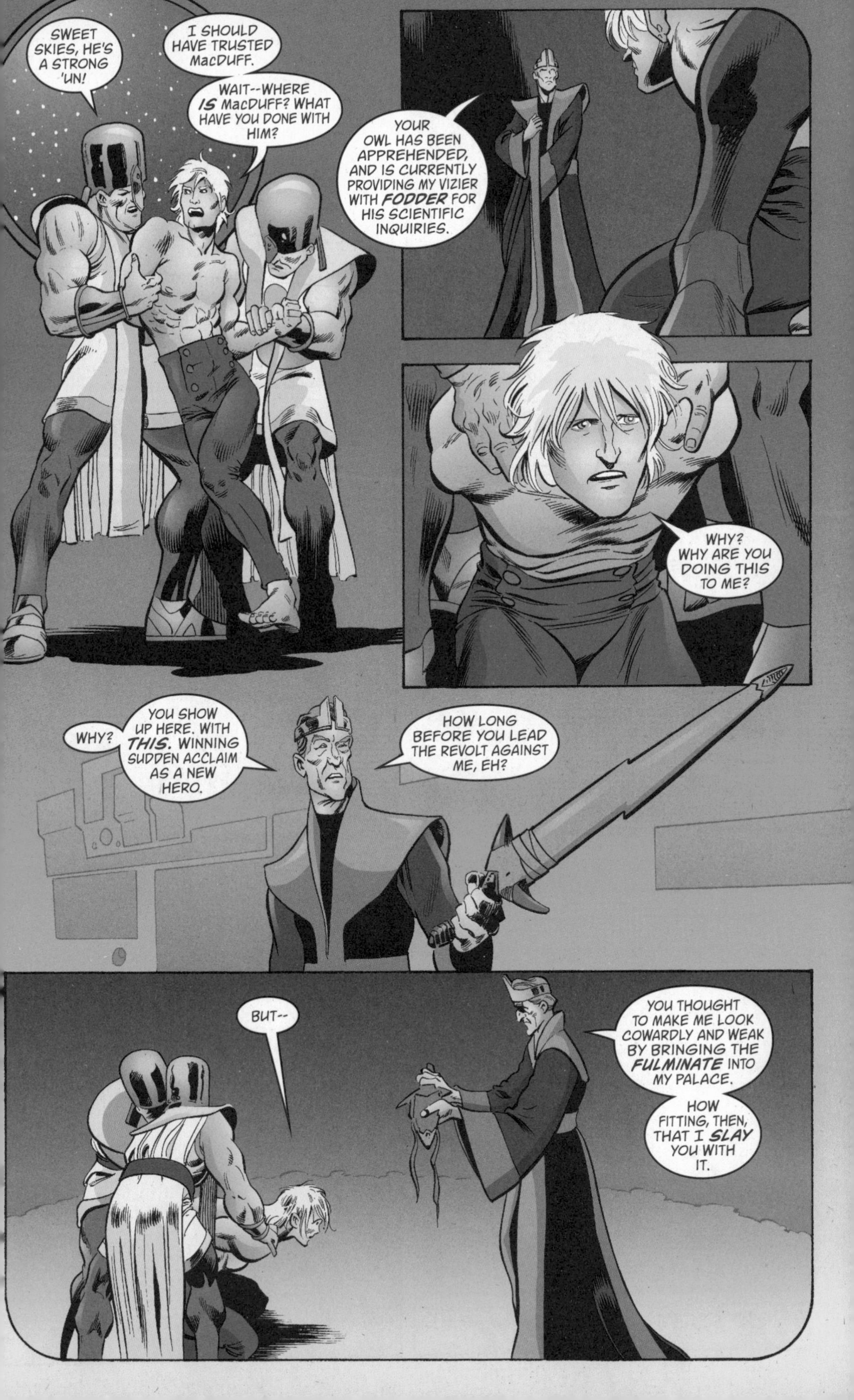
SWEET SKIES, HE'S A STRONG 'UN!
I SHOULD HAVE TRUSTED MacDUFF.
WAIT--WHERE IS MacDUFF? WHAT HAVE YOU DONE WITH HIM?
YOUR OWL HAS BEEN APPREHENDED, AND IS CURRENTLY PROVIDING MY VIZIER WITH FODDER FOR HIS SCIENTIFIC INQUIRIES.
WHY? WHY ARE YOU DOING THIS TO ME?
WHY?
YOU SHOW UP HERE. WITH THIS. WINNING SUDDEN ACCLAIM AS A NEW HERO.
HOW LONG BEFORE YOU LEAD THE REVOLT AGAINST ME, EH?
BUT--
YOU THOUGHT TO MAKE ME LOOK COWARDLY AND WEAK BY BRINGING THE FULMINATE INTO MY PALACE.
HOW FITTING, THEN, THAT I SLAY YOU WITH IT.

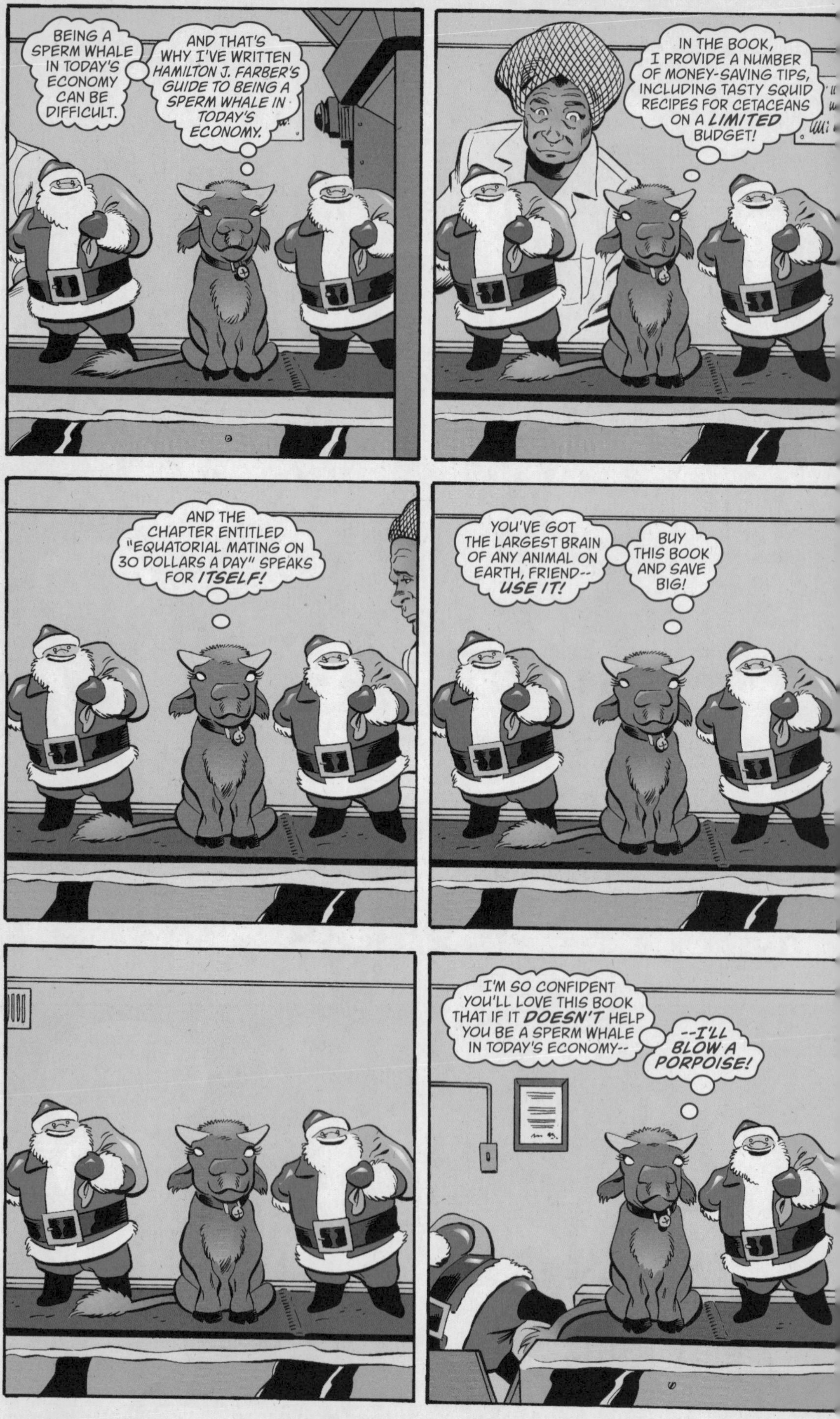
BEING A SPERM WHALE IN TODAY'S ECONOMY CAN BE DIFFICULT.
AND THAT'S WHY I'VE WRITTEN HAMILTON J. FARBER'S GUIDE TO BEING A SPERM WHALE IN TODAY'S ECONOMY.
IN THE BOOK, I PROVIDE A NUMBER OF MONEY-SAVING TIPS, INCLUDING TASTY SQUID RECIPES FOR CETACEANS ON A LIMITED BUDGET!
AND THE CHAPTER ENTITLED "EQUATORIAL MATING ON 30 DOLLARS A DAY" SPEAKS FOR ITSELF!
YOU'VE GOT THE LARGEST BRAIN OF ANY ANIMAL ON EARTH, FRIEND-- USE IT!
BUY THIS BOOK AND SAVE BIG!
I'M SO CONFIDENT YOU'LL LOVE THIS BOOK THAT IF IT DOESN'T HELP YOU BE A SPERM WHALE IN TODAY'S ECONOMY--
--I'LL BLOW A PORPOISE!

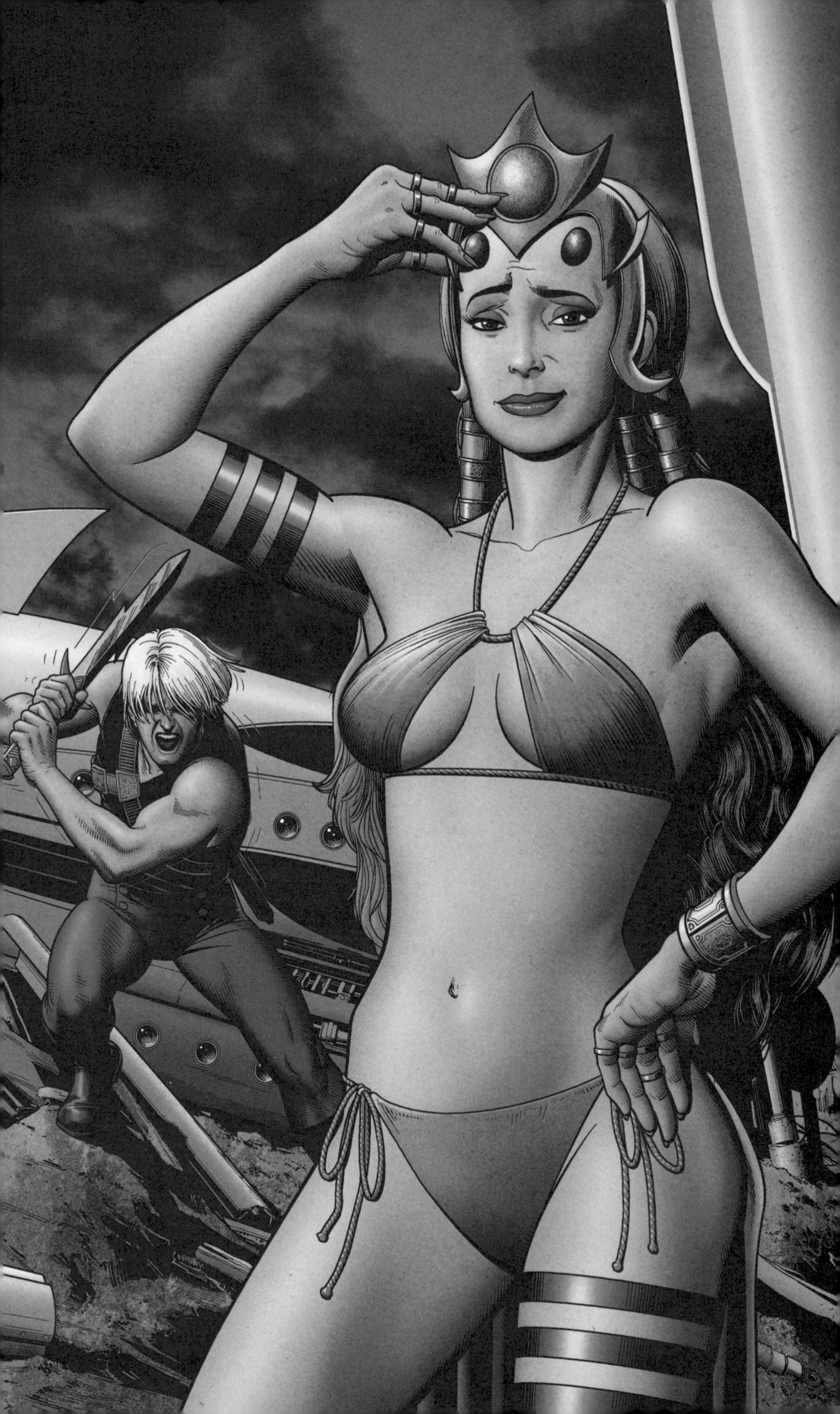

"You think I'm going to let you waltz in and take all the glory for this?"

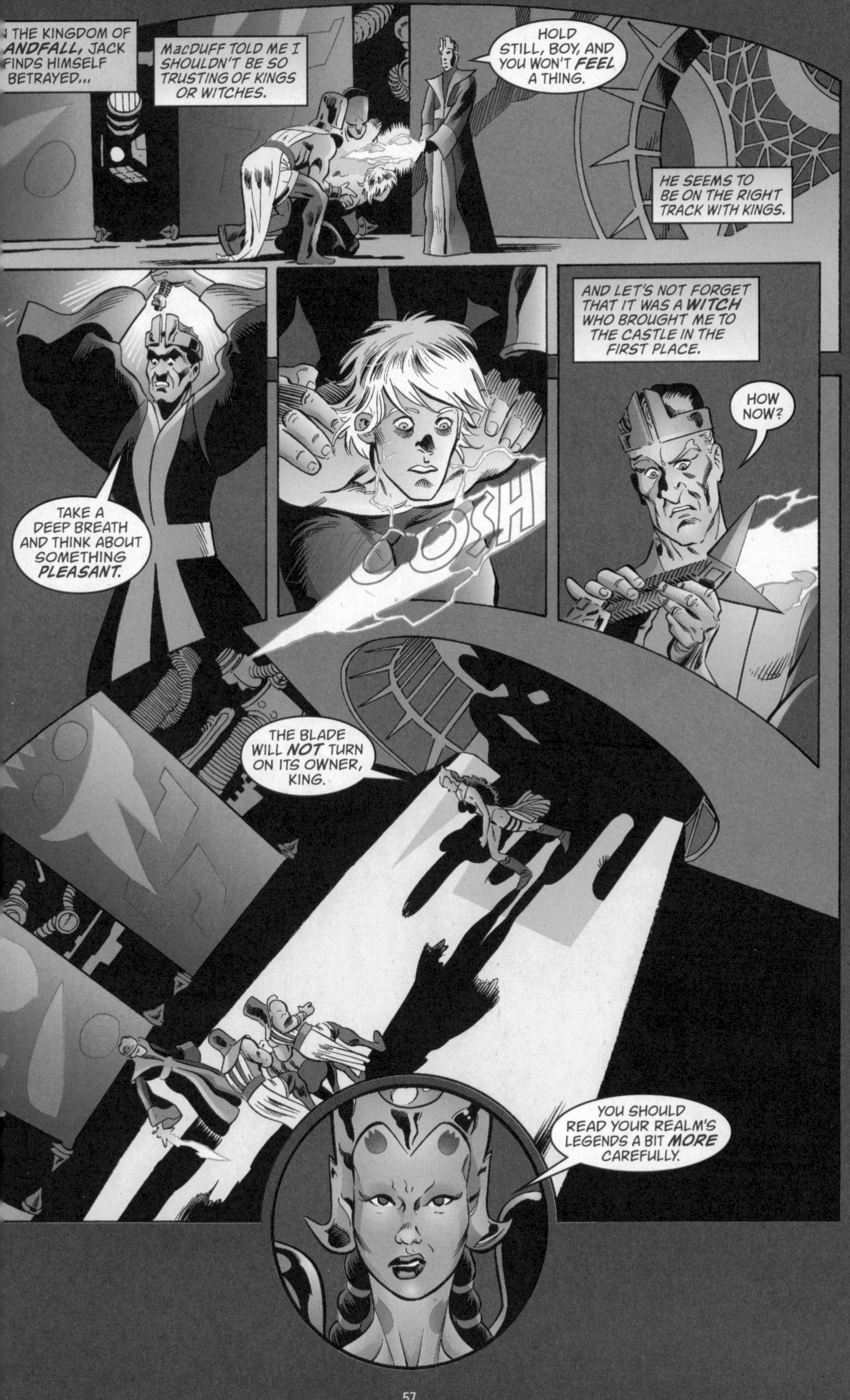

N THE KINGDOM OF ANDFALL, JACK FINDS HIMSELF BETRAYED...
MacDUFF TOLD ME I SHOULDN'T BE SO TRUSTING OF KINGS OR WITCHES.
HOLD STILL, BOY, AND YOU WON'T FEEL A THING.
HE SEEMS TO BE ON THE RIGHT TRACK WITH KINGS.
TAKE A DEEP BREATH AND THINK ABOUT SOMETHING PLEASANT.
AND LET'S NOT FORGET THAT IT WAS A WITCH WHO BROUGHT ME TO THE CASTLE IN THE FIRST PLACE.
HOW NOW?
THE BLADE WILL NOT TURN ON ITS OWNER, KING.
YOU SHOULD READ YOUR REALM'S LEGENDS A BIT MORE CAREFULLY.

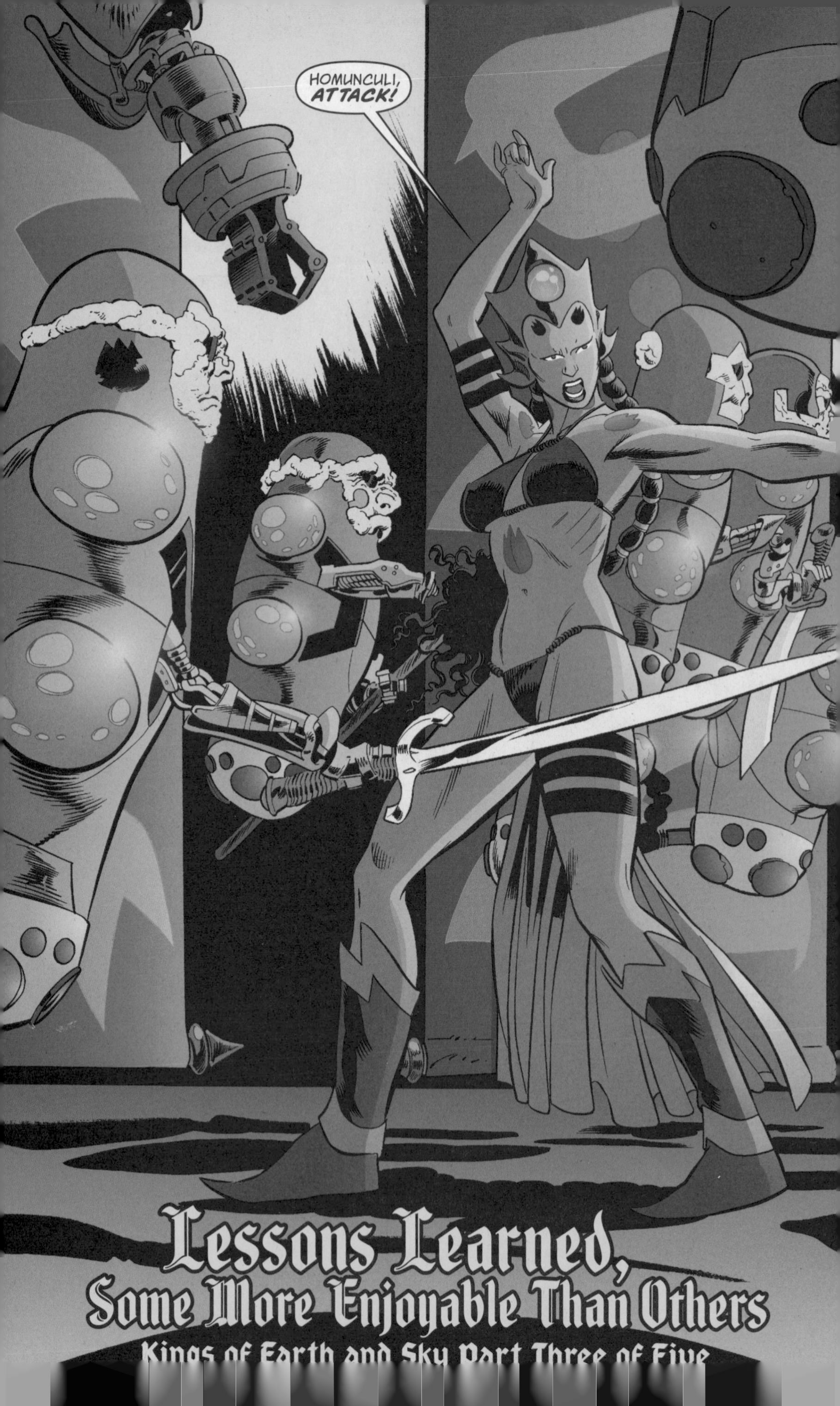
HOMUNCULI, ATTACK!
Lessons Learned,
Some More Enjoyable Than Others
Kings of Earth and Sky Part Three of Five

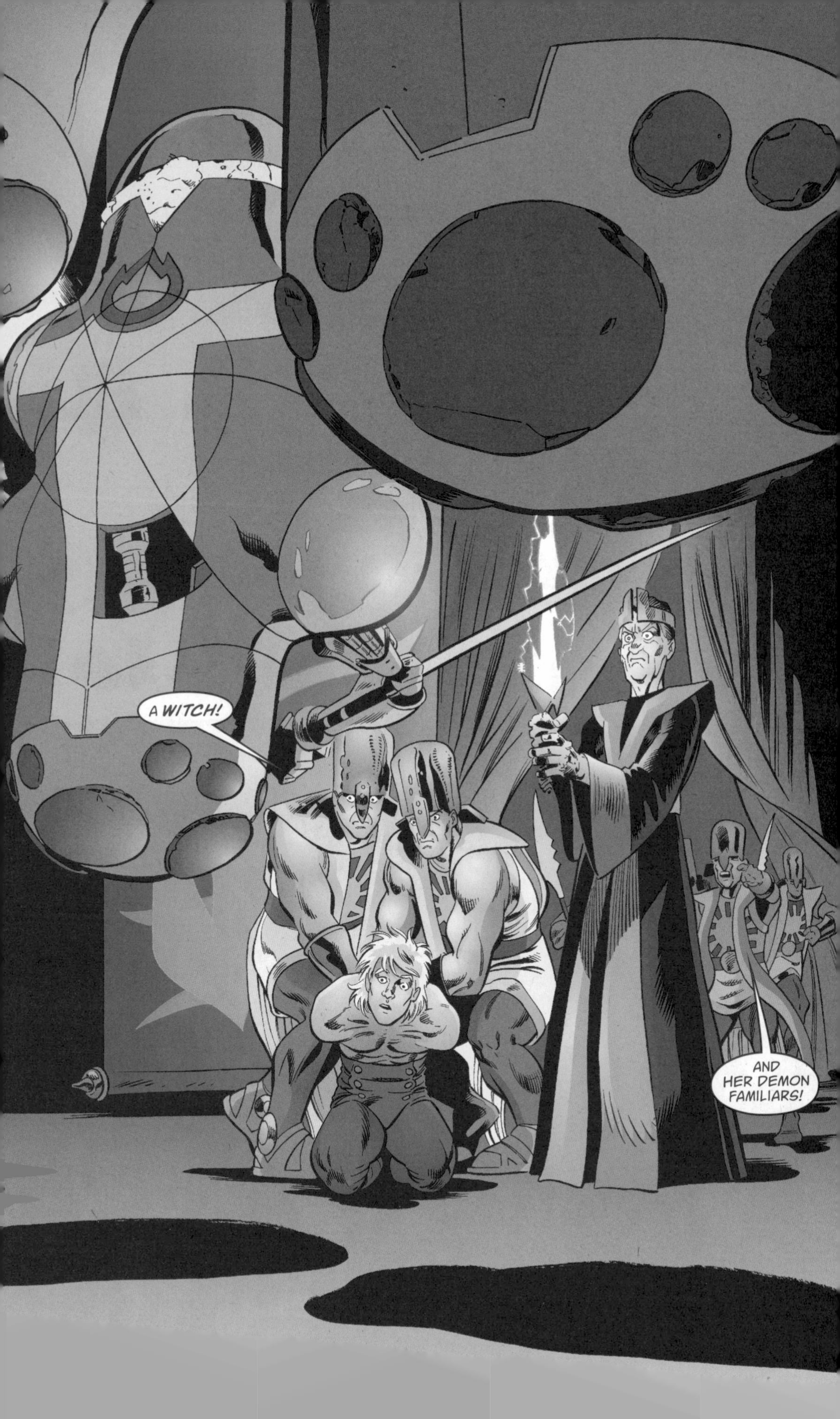
A WITCH!
AND HER DEMON FAMILIARS!

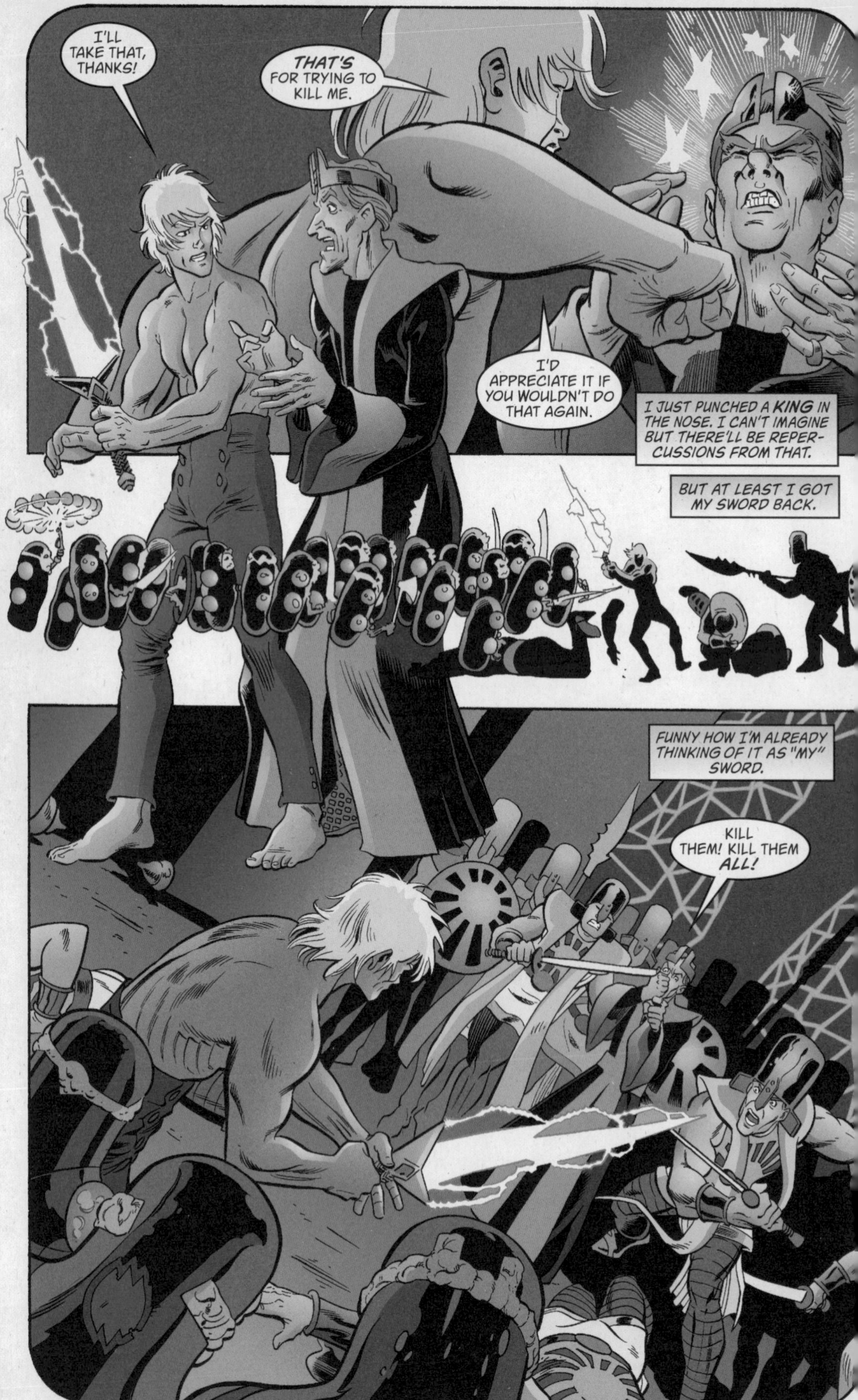

I'LL TAKE THAT, THANKS!
THAT'S FOR TRYING TO KILL ME.
I'D APPRECIATE IT IF YOU WOULDN'T DO THAT AGAIN.
I JUST PUNCHED A KING IN THE NOSE. I CAN'T IMAGINE BUT THERE'LL BE REPERCUSSIONS FROM THAT.
BUT AT LEAST I GOT MY SWORD BACK.
FUNNY HOW I'M ALREADY THINKING OF IT AS "MY" SWORD.
KILL THEM! KILL THEM ALL!

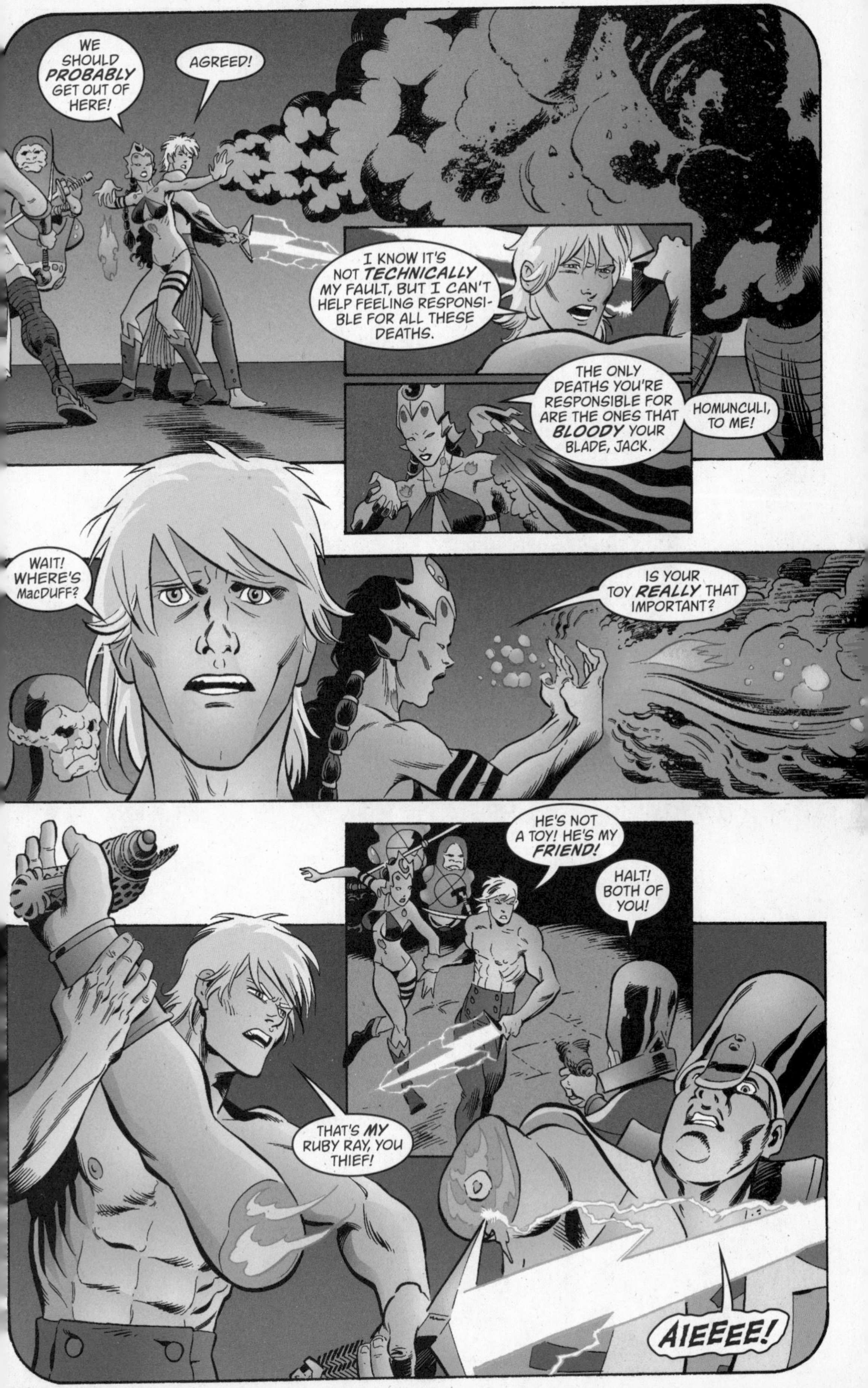

WE SHOULD PROBABLY GET OUT OF HERE!
AGREED!
I KNOW IT'S NOT TECHNICALLY MY FAULT, BUT I CAN'T HELP FEELING RESPONSIBLE FOR ALL THESE DEATHS.
THE ONLY DEATHS YOU'RE RESPONSIBLE FOR ARE THE ONES THAT BLOODY YOUR BLADE, JACK.
HOMUNCULI, TO ME!
WAIT! WHERE'S MacDUFF?
IS YOUR TOY REALLY THAT IMPORTANT?
HE'S NOT A TOY! HE'S MY FRIEND!
HALT! BOTH OF YOU!
THAT'S MY RUBY RAY, YOU THIEF!
AIEEEE!

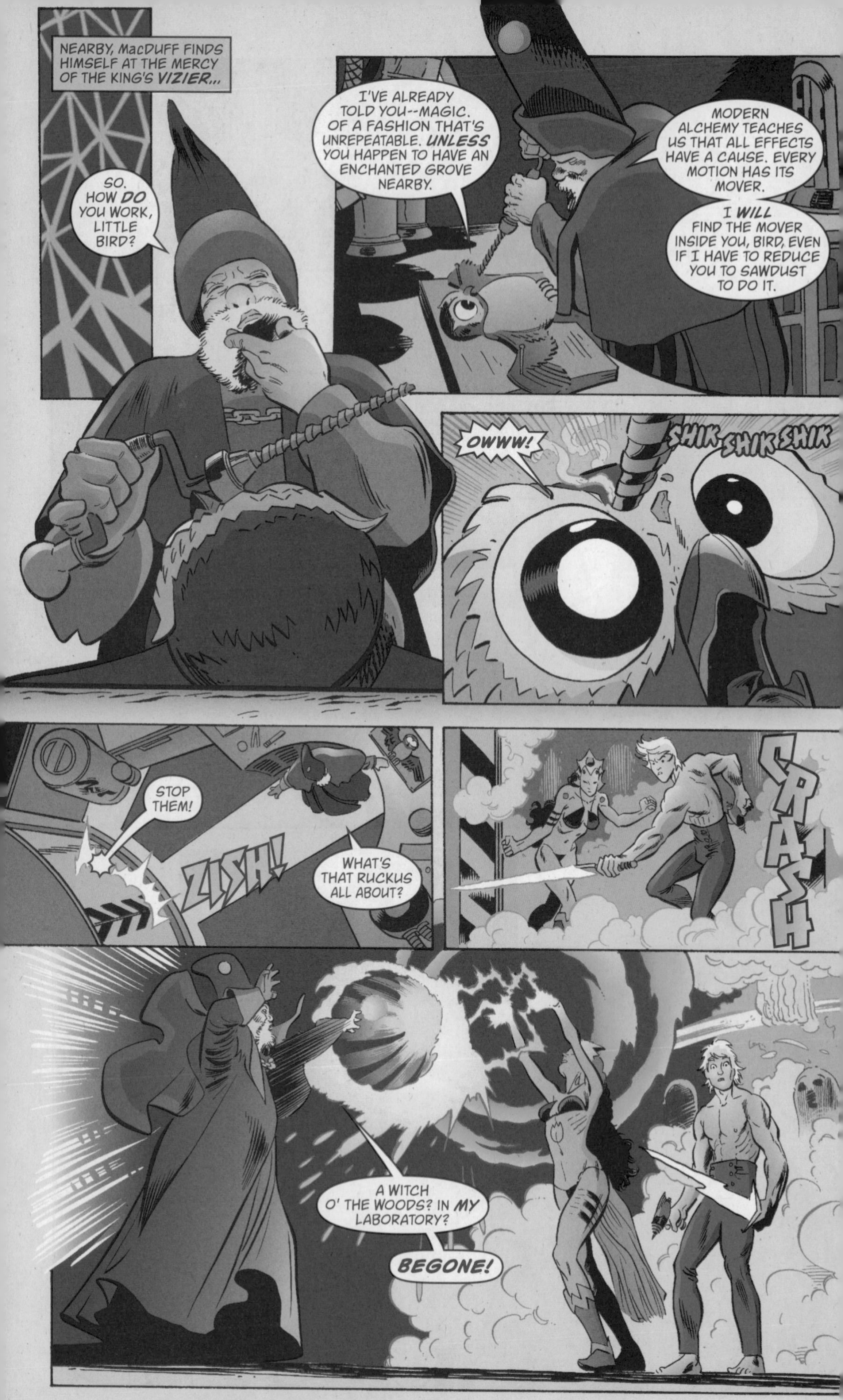
NEARBY, MacDUFF FINDS HIMSELF AT THE MERCY OF THE KING'S VIZIER...
SO. HOW DO YOU WORK, LITTLE BIRD?
I'VE ALREADY TOLD YOU--MAGIC. OF A FASHION THAT'S UNREPEATABLE. UNLESS YOU HAPPEN TO HAVE AN ENCHANTED GROVE NEARBY.
MODERN ALCHEMY TEACHES US THAT ALL EFFECTS HAVE A CAUSE. EVERY MOTION HAS ITS MOVER.
I WILL FIND THE MOVER INSIDE YOU, BIRD, EVEN IF I HAVE TO REDUCE YOU TO SAWDUST TO DO IT.
OWWW!
SHIK SHIK SHIK
STOP THEM!
ZISH!
WHAT'S THAT RUCKUS ALL ABOUT?
CRASH
A WITCH O' THE WOODS? IN MY LABORATORY?
BEGONE!

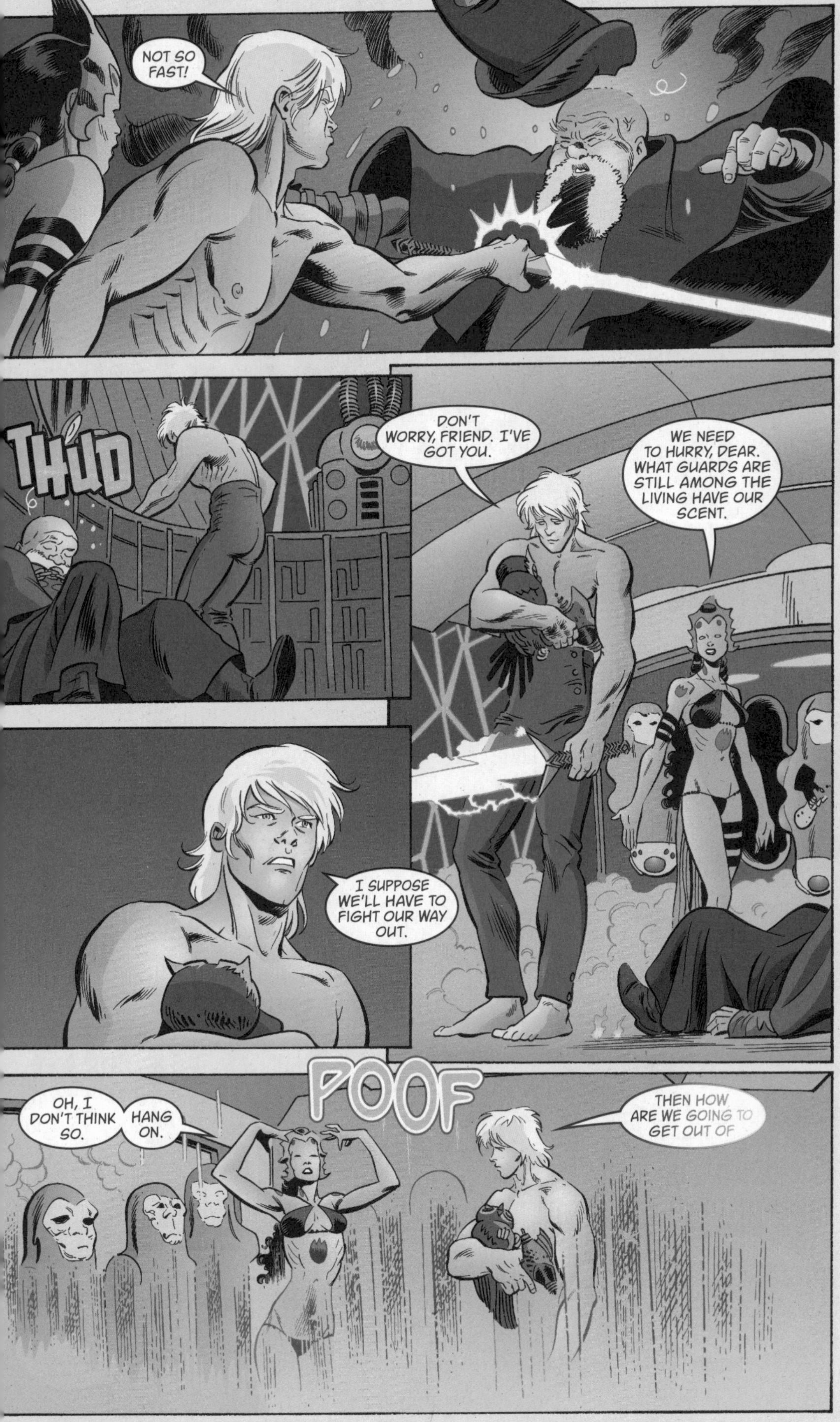
NOT SO FAST!
THUD
DON'T WORRY, FRIEND. I'VE GOT YOU.
WE NEED TO HURRY, DEAR. WHAT GUARDS ARE STILL AMONG THE LIVING HAVE OUR SCENT.
I SUPPOSE WE'LL HAVE TO FIGHT OUR WAY OUT.
OH, I DON'T THINK SO.
HANG ON.
POOF
THEN HOW ARE WE GOING TO GET OUT OF

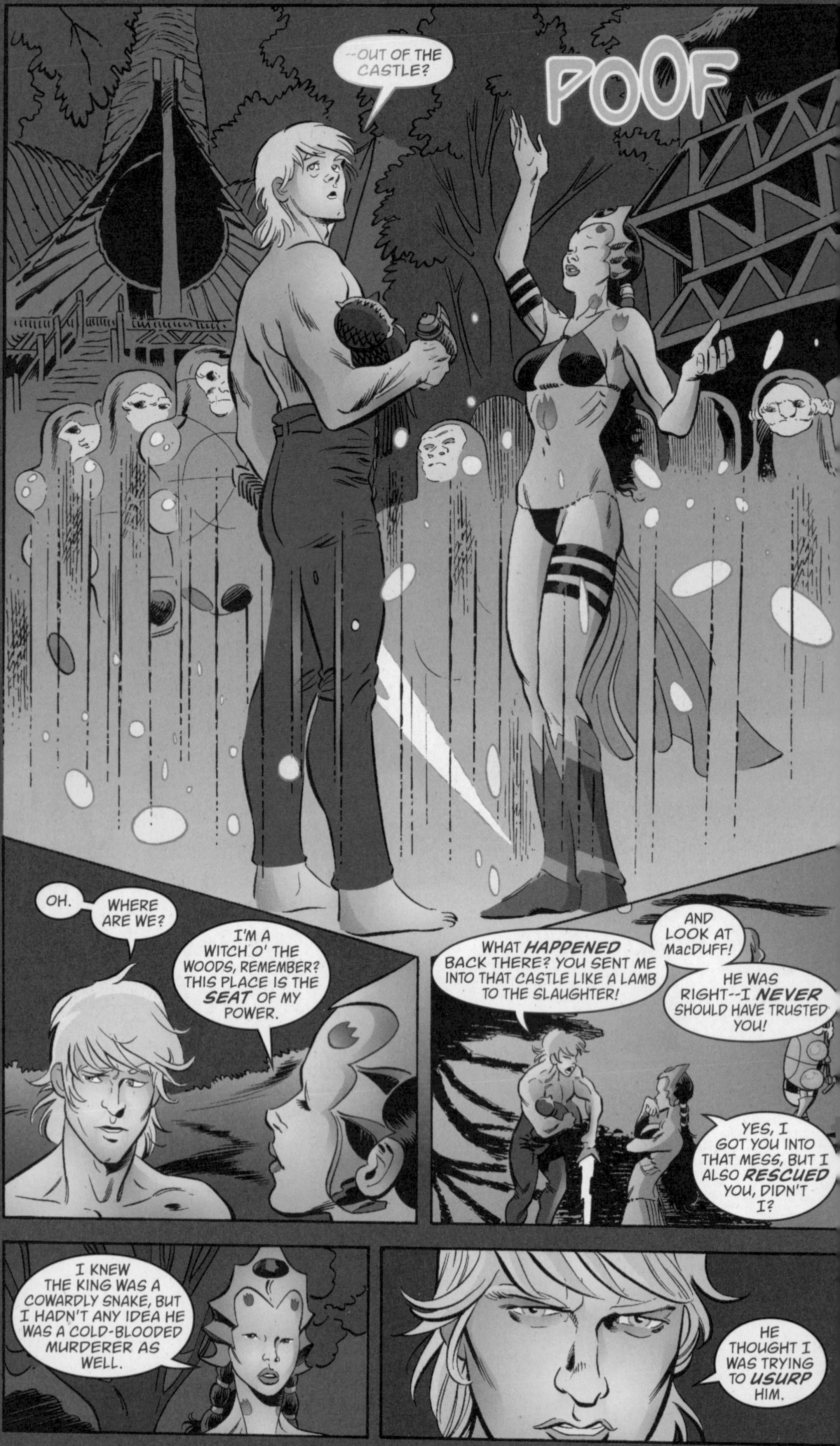

--OUT OF THE CASTLE?
POOF
OH.
WHERE ARE WE?
I'M A WITCH O' THE WOODS, REMEMBER? THIS PLACE IS THE SEAT OF MY POWER.
WHAT HAPPENED BACK THERE? YOU SENT ME INTO THAT CASTLE LIKE A LAMB TO THE SLAUGHTER!
AND LOOK AT MacDUFF!
HE WAS RIGHT--I NEVER SHOULD HAVE TRUSTED YOU!
YES, I GOT YOU INTO THAT MESS, BUT I ALSO RESCUED YOU, DIDN'T I?
I KNEW THE KING WAS A COWARDLY SNAKE, BUT I HADN'T ANY IDEA HE WAS A COLD-BLOODED MURDERER AS WELL.
HE THOUGHT I WAS TRYING TO USURP HIM.

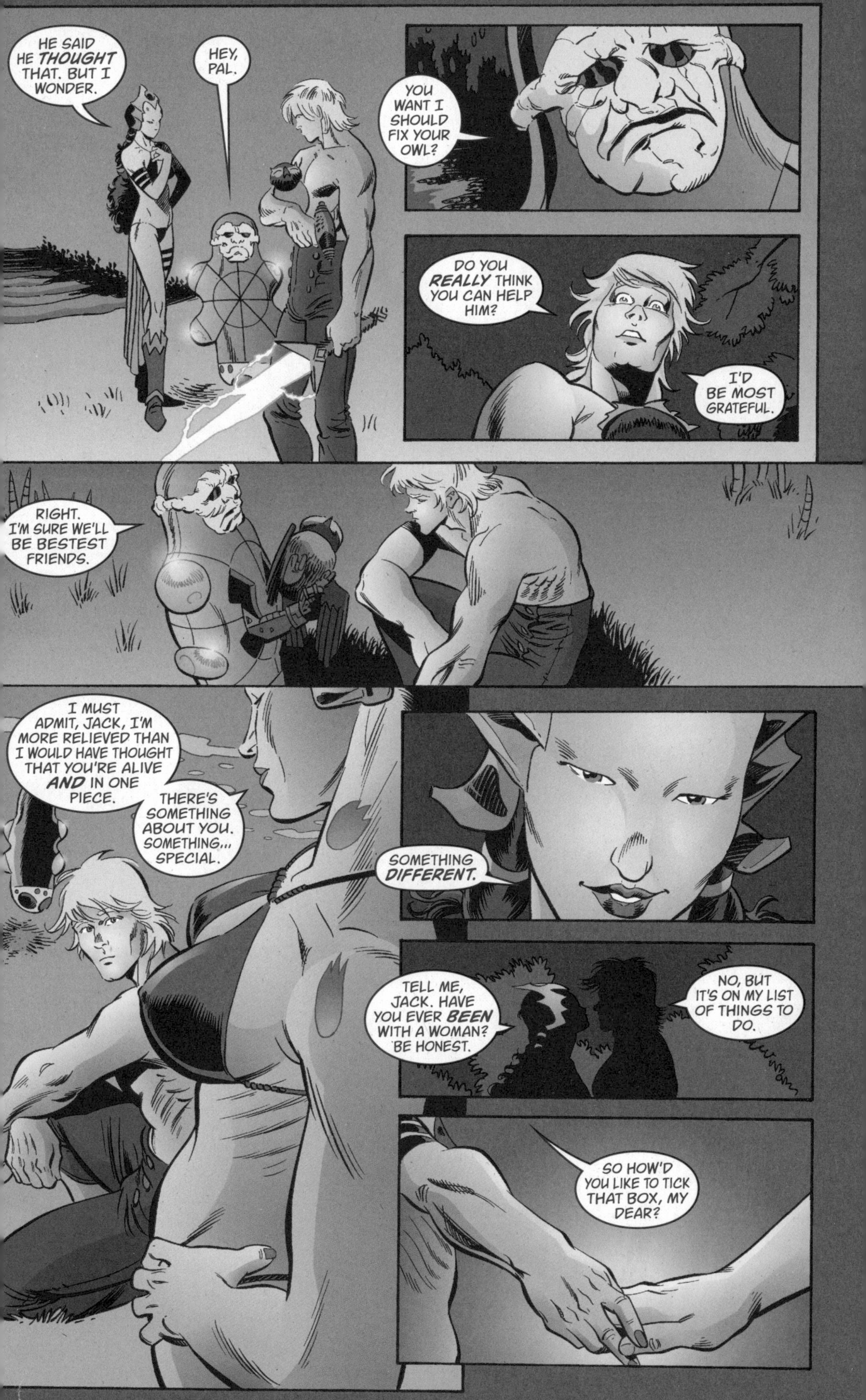
HE SAID HE THOUGHT THAT. BUT I WONDER.
HEY, PAL.
YOU WANT I SHOULD FIX YOUR OWL?
DO YOU REALLY THINK YOU CAN HELP HIM?
I'D BE MOST GRATEFUL.
RIGHT. I'M SURE WE'LL BE BESTEST FRIENDS.
I MUST ADMIT, JACK, I'M MORE RELIEVED THAN I WOULD HAVE THOUGHT THAT YOU'RE ALIVE AND IN ONE PIECE.
THERE'S SOMETHING ABOUT YOU. SOMETHING... SPECIAL.
SOMETHING DIFFERENT.
TELL ME, JACK. HAVE YOU EVER BEEN WITH A WOMAN? BE HONEST.
NO, BUT IT'S ON MY LIST OF THINGS TO DO.
SO HOW'D YOU LIKE TO TICK THAT BOX, MY DEAR?

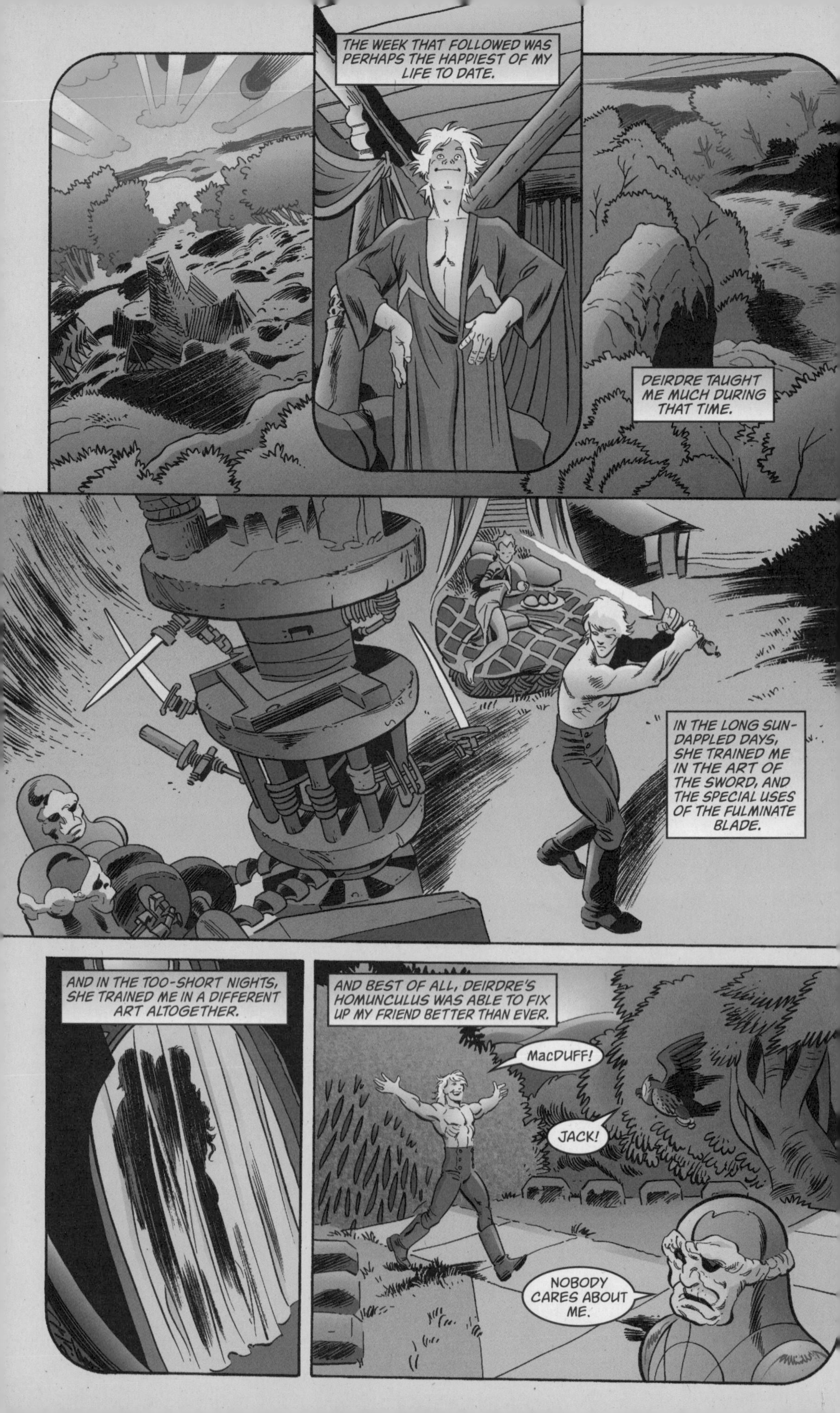
THE WEEK THAT FOLLOWED WAS PERHAPS THE HAPPIEST OF MY LIFE TO DATE.
DEIRDRE TAUGHT ME MUCH DURING THAT TIME.
IN THE LONG SUN-DAPPLED DAYS, SHE TRAINED ME IN THE ART OF THE SWORD, AND THE SPECIAL USES OF THE FULMINATE BLADE.
AND IN THE TOO-SHORT NIGHTS, SHE TRAINED ME IN A DIFFERENT ART ALTOGETHER.
AND BEST OF ALL, DEIRDRE'S HOMUNCULUS WAS ABLE TO FIX UP MY FRIEND BETTER THAN EVER.
MacDUFF!
JACK!
NOBODY CARES ABOUT ME.

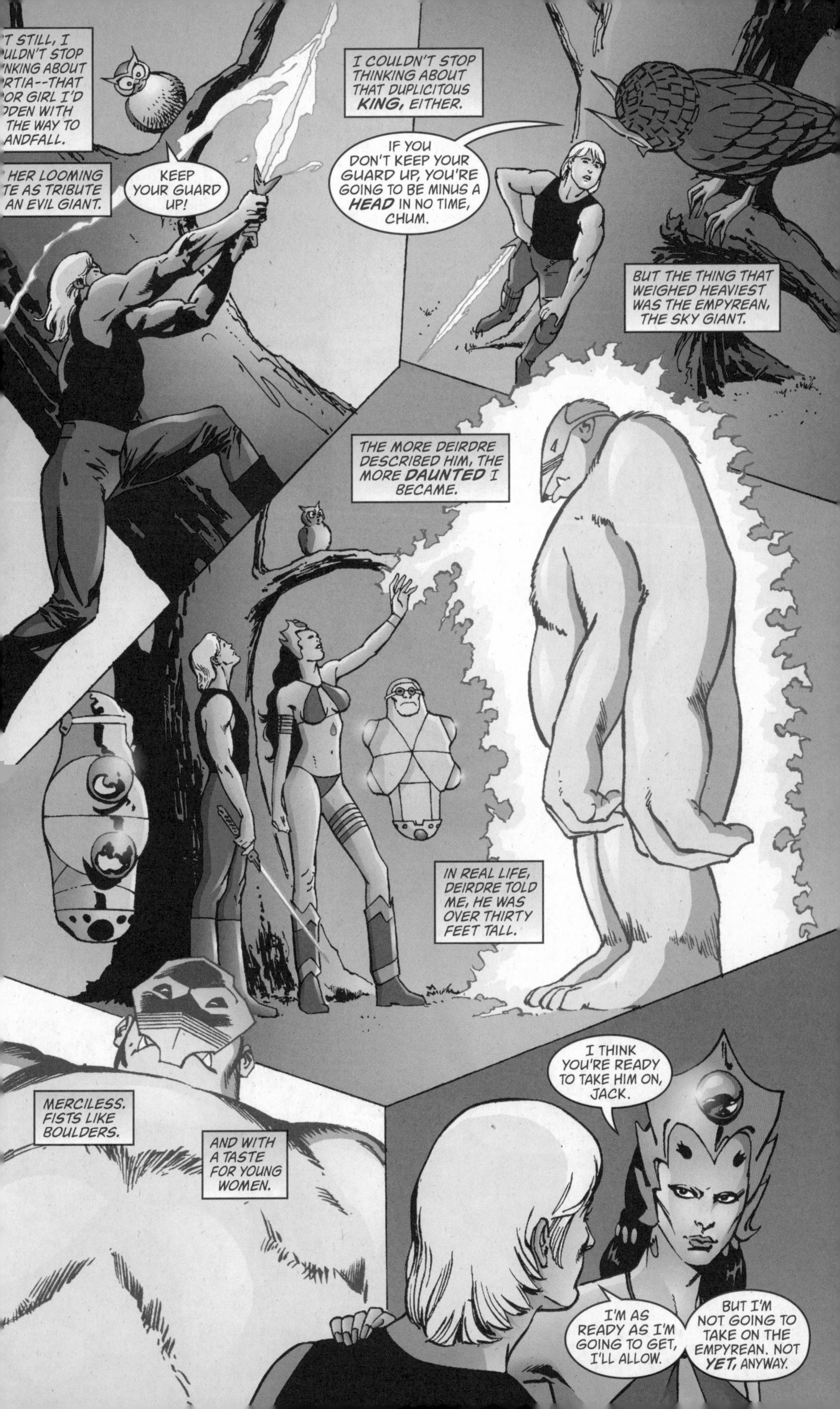
T STILL, I
ULDN'T STOP
NKING ABOUT
RTIA--THAT
OR GIRL I'D
DDEN WITH
THE WAY TO
ANDFALL.
HER LOOMING
TE AS TRIBUTE
AN EVIL GIANT.
KEEP YOUR GUARD UP!
I COULDN'T STOP THINKING ABOUT THAT DUPLICITOUS KING, EITHER.
IF YOU DON'T KEEP YOUR GUARD UP, YOU'RE GOING TO BE MINUS A HEAD IN NO TIME, CHUM.
BUT THE THING THAT WEIGHED HEAVIEST WAS THE EMPYREAN, THE SKY GIANT.
THE MORE DEIRDRE DESCRIBED HIM, THE MORE DAUNTED I BECAME.
IN REAL LIFE, DEIRDRE TOLD ME, HE WAS OVER THIRTY FEET TALL.
MERCILESS. FISTS LIKE BOULDERS.
AND WITH A TASTE FOR YOUNG WOMEN.
I THINK YOU'RE READY TO TAKE HIM ON, JACK.
I'M AS READY AS I'M GOING TO GET, I'LL ALLOW.
BUT I'M NOT GOING TO TAKE ON THE EMPYREAN. NOT YET, ANYWAY.

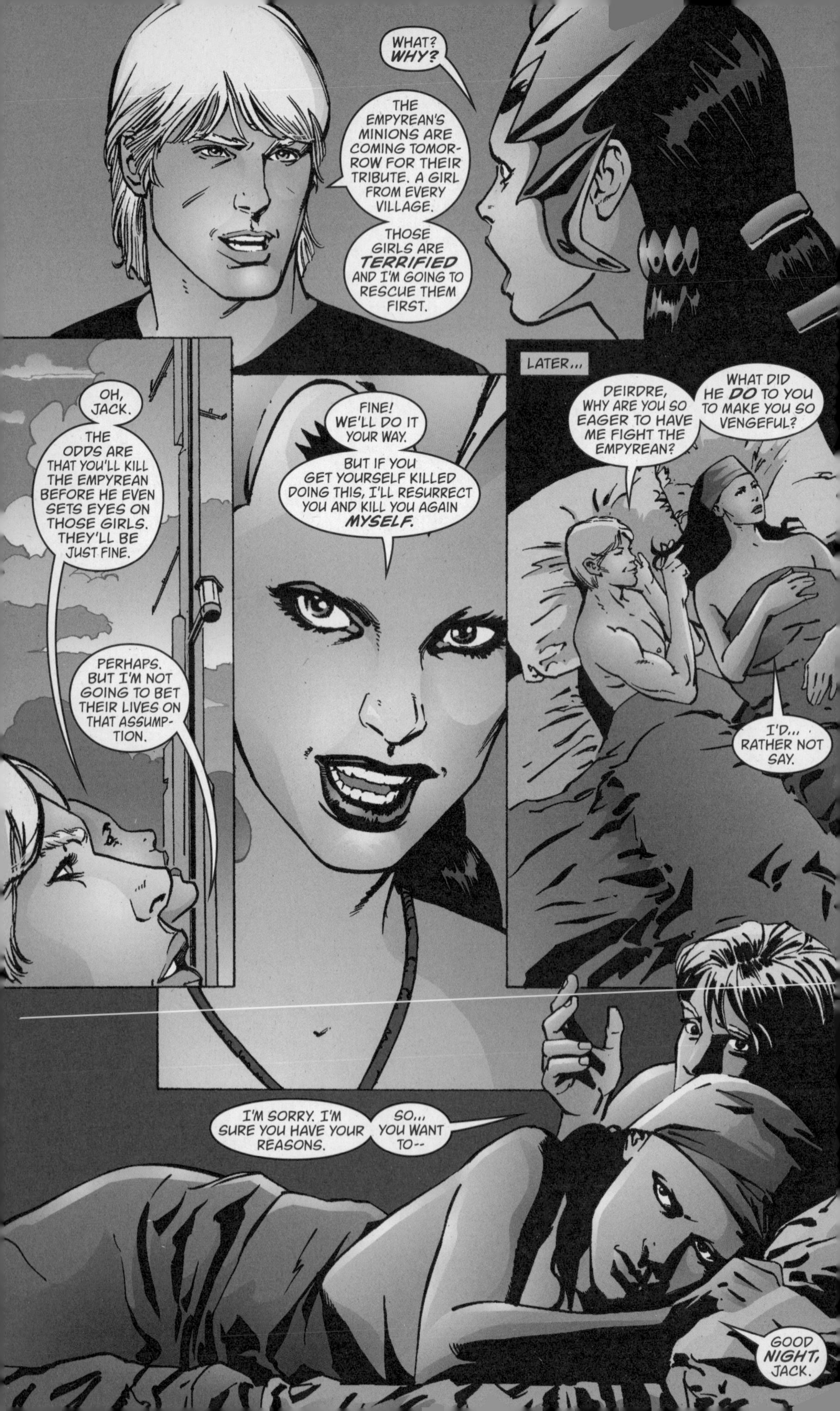
WHAT? WHY?
THE EMPYREAN'S MINIONS ARE COMING TOMORROW FOR THEIR TRIBUTE. A GIRL FROM EVERY VILLAGE.
THOSE GIRLS ARE TERRIFIED AND I'M GOING TO RESCUE THEM FIRST.
OH, JACK.
THE ODDS ARE THAT YOU'LL KILL THE EMPYREAN BEFORE HE EVEN SETS EYES ON THOSE GIRLS. THEY'LL BE JUST FINE.
PERHAPS. BUT I'M NOT GOING TO BET THEIR LIVES ON THAT ASSUMPTION.
FINE! WE'LL DO IT YOUR WAY.
BUT IF YOU GET YOURSELF KILLED DOING THIS, I'LL RESURRECT YOU AND KILL YOU AGAIN MYSELF.
LATER...
DEIRDRE, WHY ARE YOU SO EAGER TO HAVE ME FIGHT THE EMPYREAN?
WHAT DID HE DO TO YOU TO MAKE YOU SO VENGEFUL?
I'D... RATHER NOT SAY.
I'M SORRY. I'M SURE YOU HAVE YOUR REASONS.
SO... YOU WANT TO--
GOOD NIGHT, JACK.

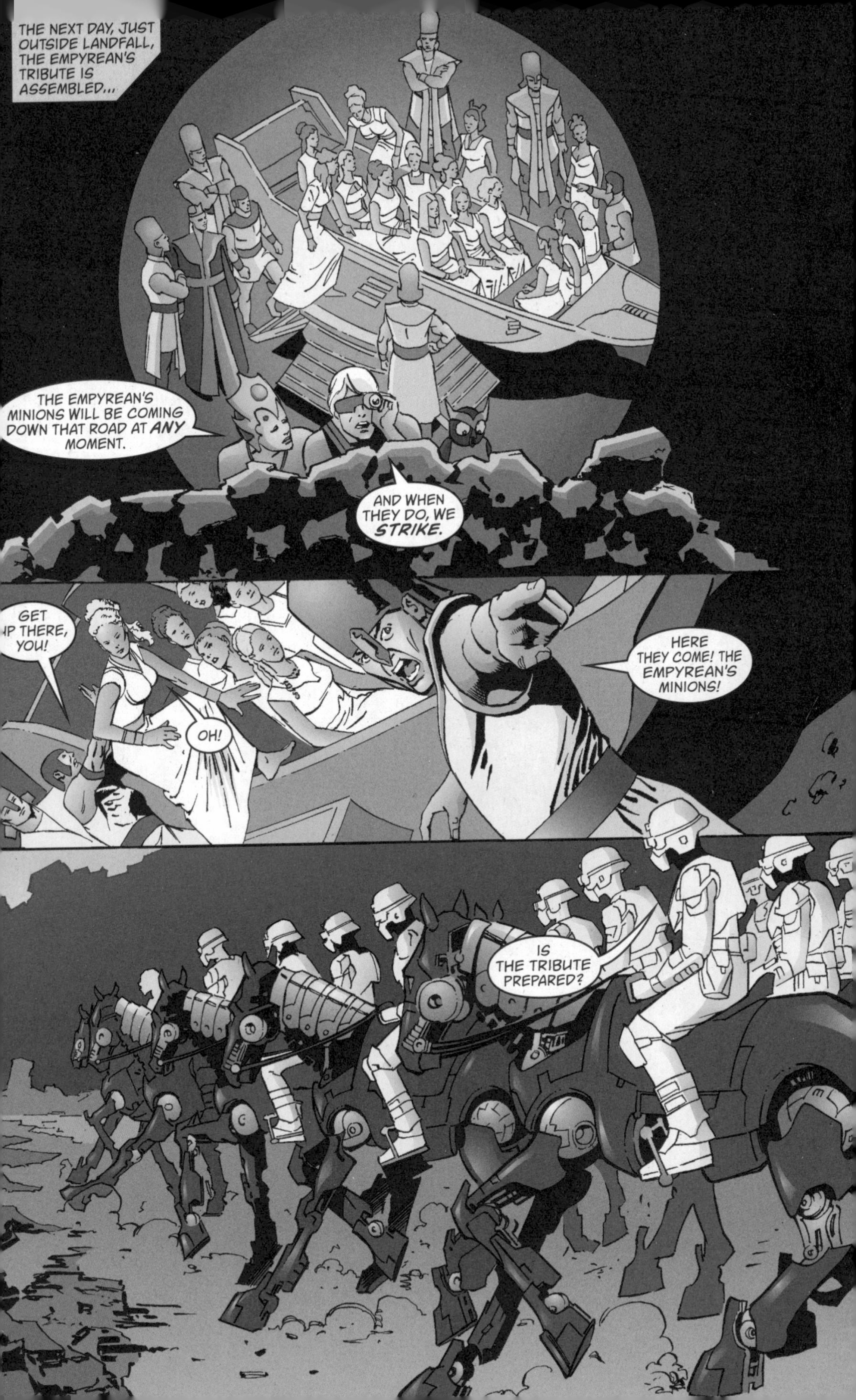
THE NEXT DAY, JUST OUTSIDE LANDFALL, THE EMPYREAN'S TRIBUTE IS ASSEMBLED...
THE EMPYREAN'S MINIONS WILL BE COMING DOWN THAT ROAD AT ANY MOMENT.
AND WHEN THEY DO, WE STRIKE.
GET UP THERE, YOU!
OH!
HERE THEY COME! THE EMPYREAN'S MINIONS!
IS THE TRIBUTE PREPARED?

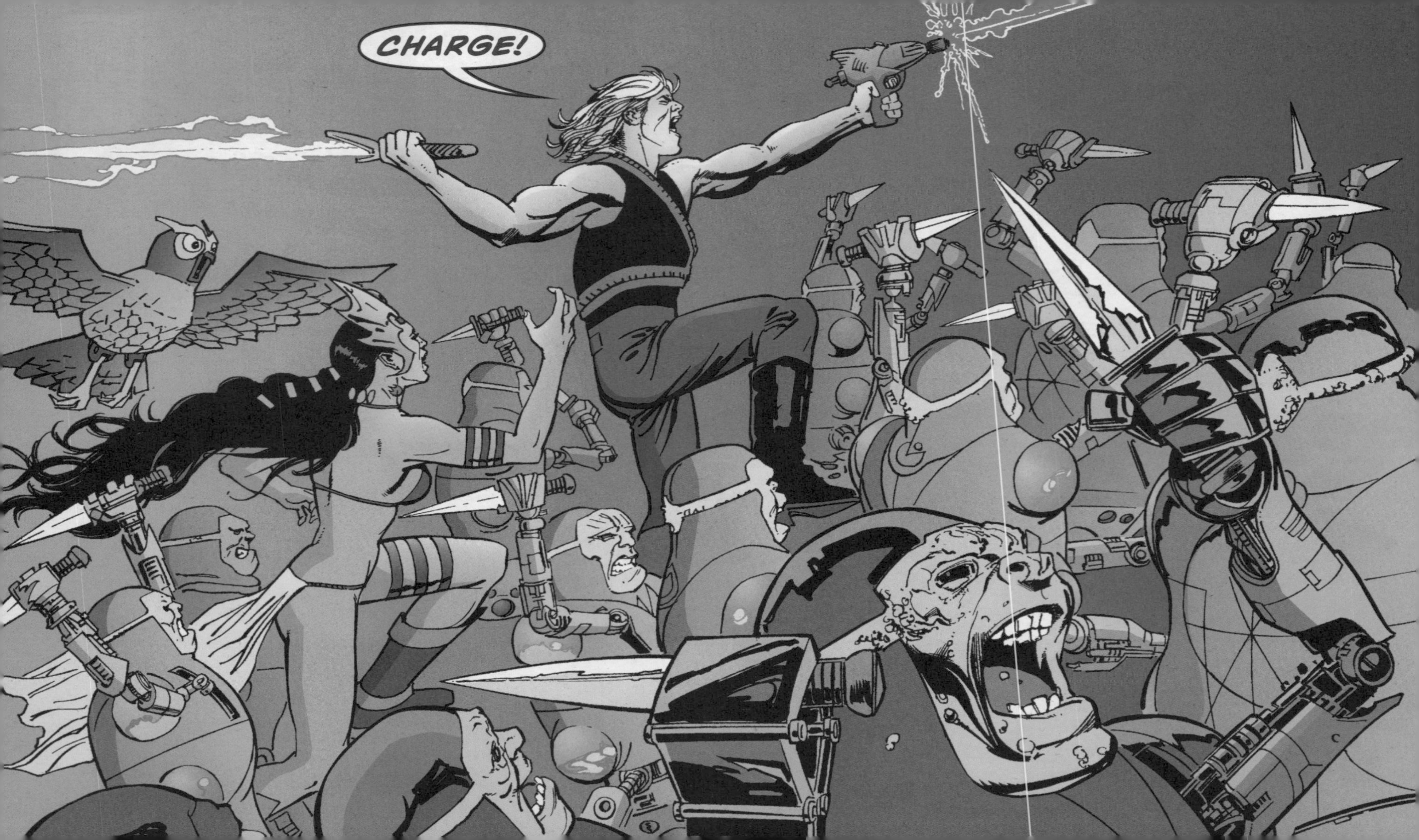
CHARGE!

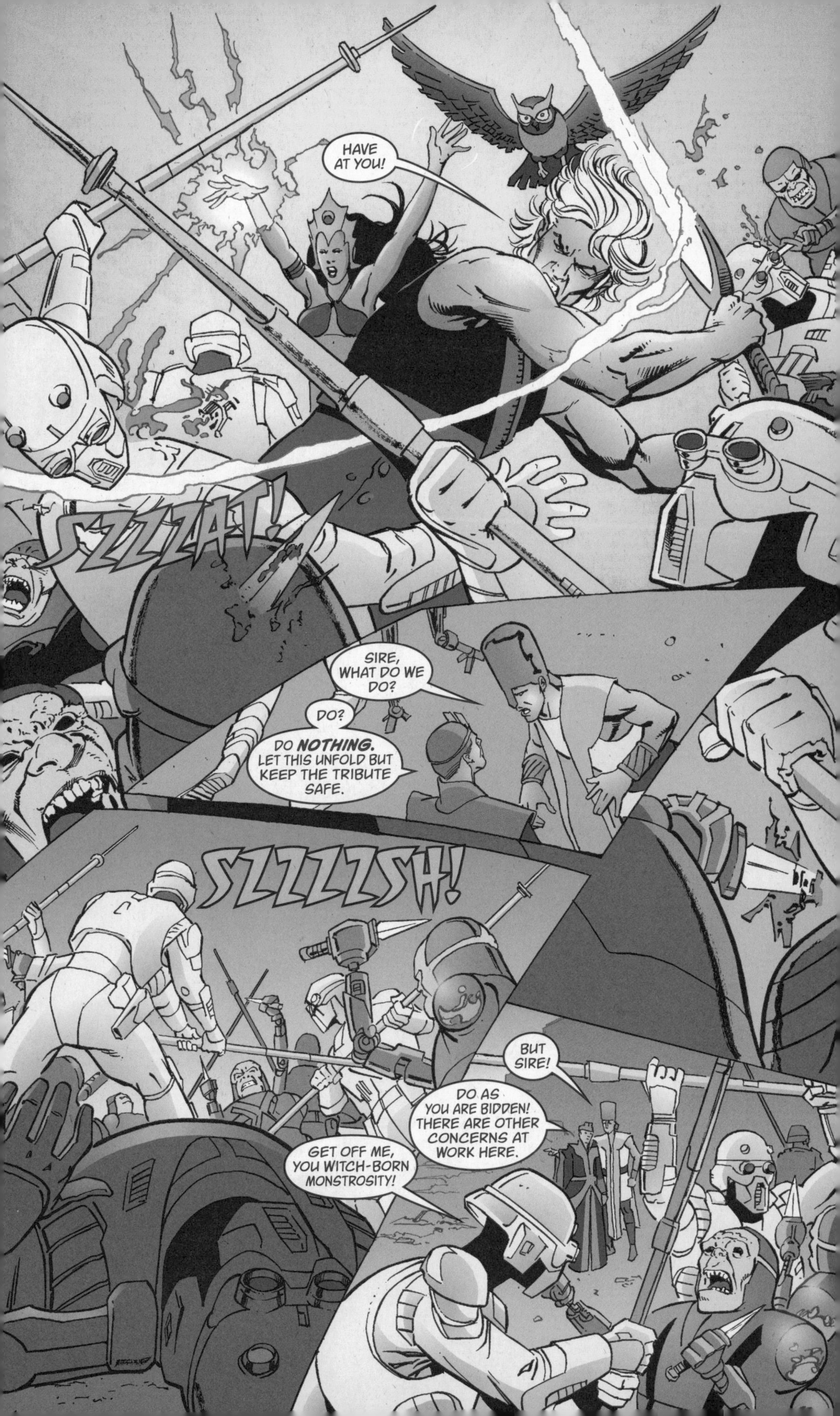
HAVE AT YOU!
SZZZZAT!
SIRE, WHAT DO WE DO?
DO?
DO **NOTHING.** LET THIS UNFOLD BUT KEEP THE TRIBUTE SAFE.
SZZZZSH!
BUT SIRE!
DO AS YOU ARE BIDDEN! THERE ARE OTHER CONCERNS AT WORK HERE.
GET OFF ME, YOU WITCH-BORN MONSTROSITY!

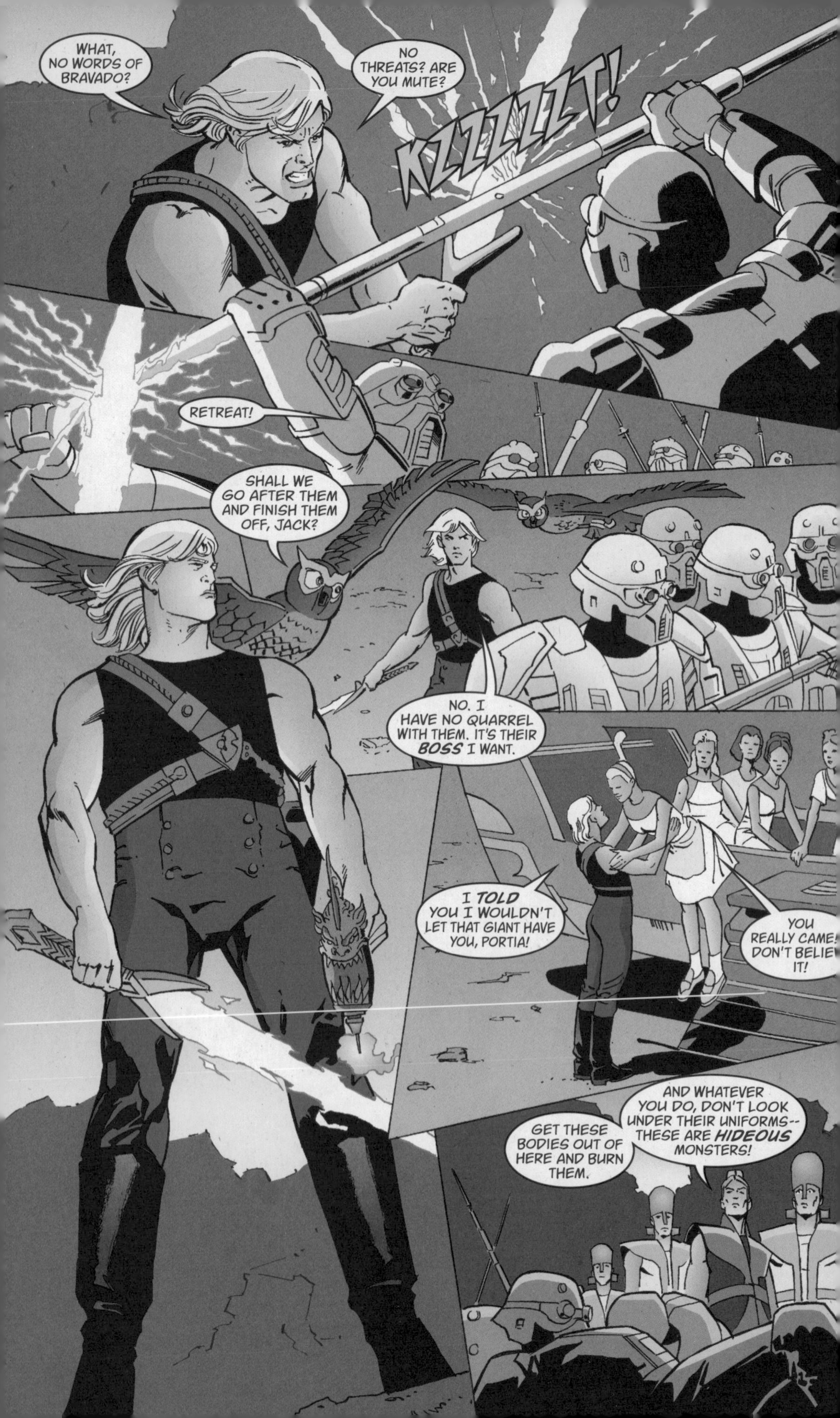
WHAT, NO WORDS OF BRAVADO?
NO THREATS? ARE YOU MUTE?
KZZZZZZT!
RETREAT!
SHALL WE GO AFTER THEM AND FINISH THEM OFF, JACK?
NO. I HAVE NO QUARREL WITH THEM. IT'S THEIR BOSS I WANT.
I TOLD YOU I WOULDN'T LET THAT GIANT HAVE YOU, PORTIA!
YOU REALLY CAME! DON'T BELIE IT!
GET THESE BODIES OUT OF HERE AND BURN THEM.
AND WHATEVER YOU DO, DON'T LOOK UNDER THEIR UNIFORMS-- THESE ARE HIDEOUS MONSTERS!

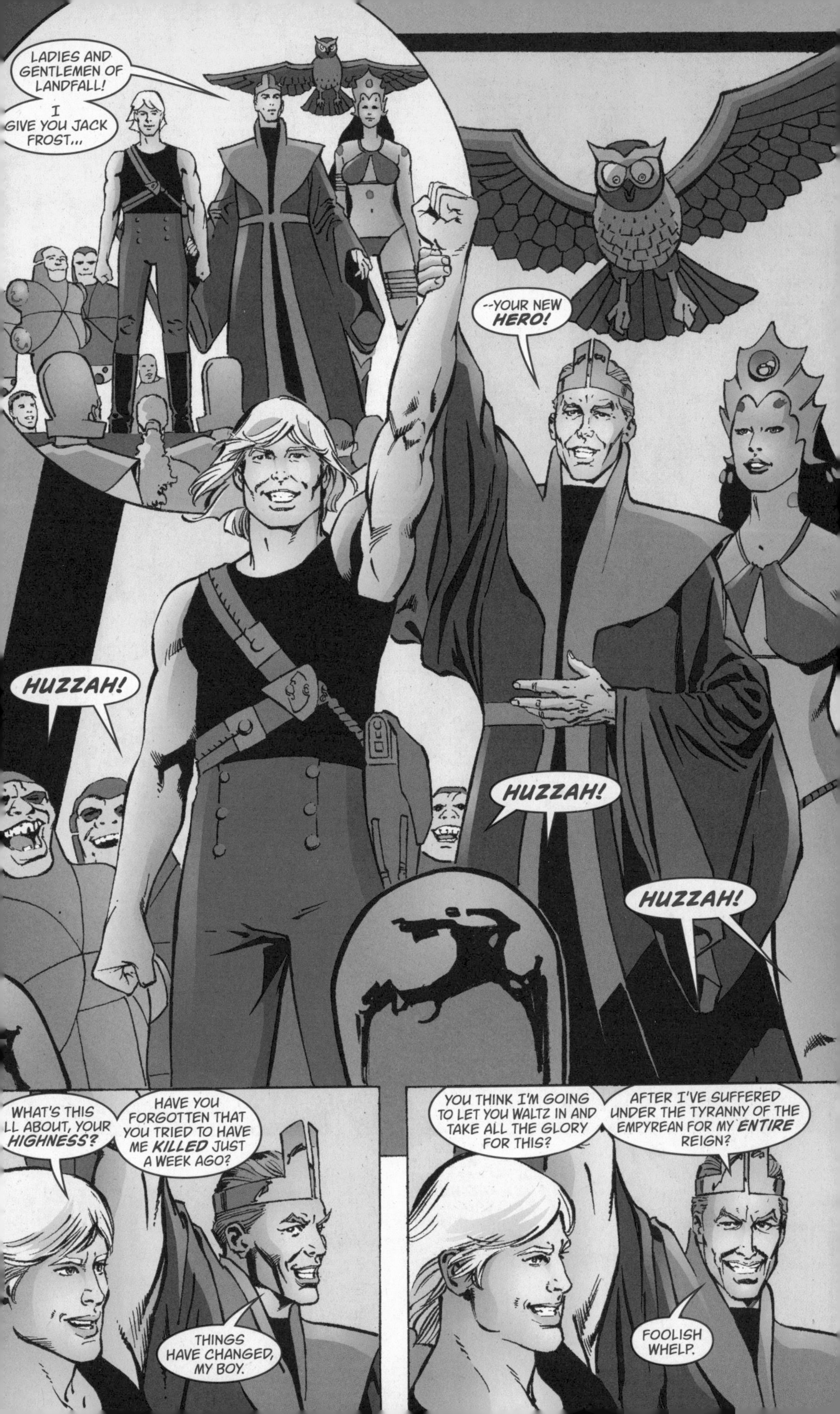
LADIES AND GENTLEMEN OF LANDFALL!
I GIVE YOU JACK FROST...
--YOUR NEW HERO!
HUZZAH!
HUZZAH!
HUZZAH!
WHAT'S THIS ...LL ABOUT, YOUR HIGHNESS?
HAVE YOU FORGOTTEN THAT YOU TRIED TO HAVE ME KILLED JUST A WEEK AGO?
THINGS HAVE CHANGED, MY BOY.
YOU THINK I'M GOING TO LET YOU WALTZ IN AND TAKE ALL THE GLORY FOR THIS?
AFTER I'VE SUFFERED UNDER THE TYRANNY OF THE EMPYREAN FOR MY ENTIRE REIGN?
FOOLISH WHELP.

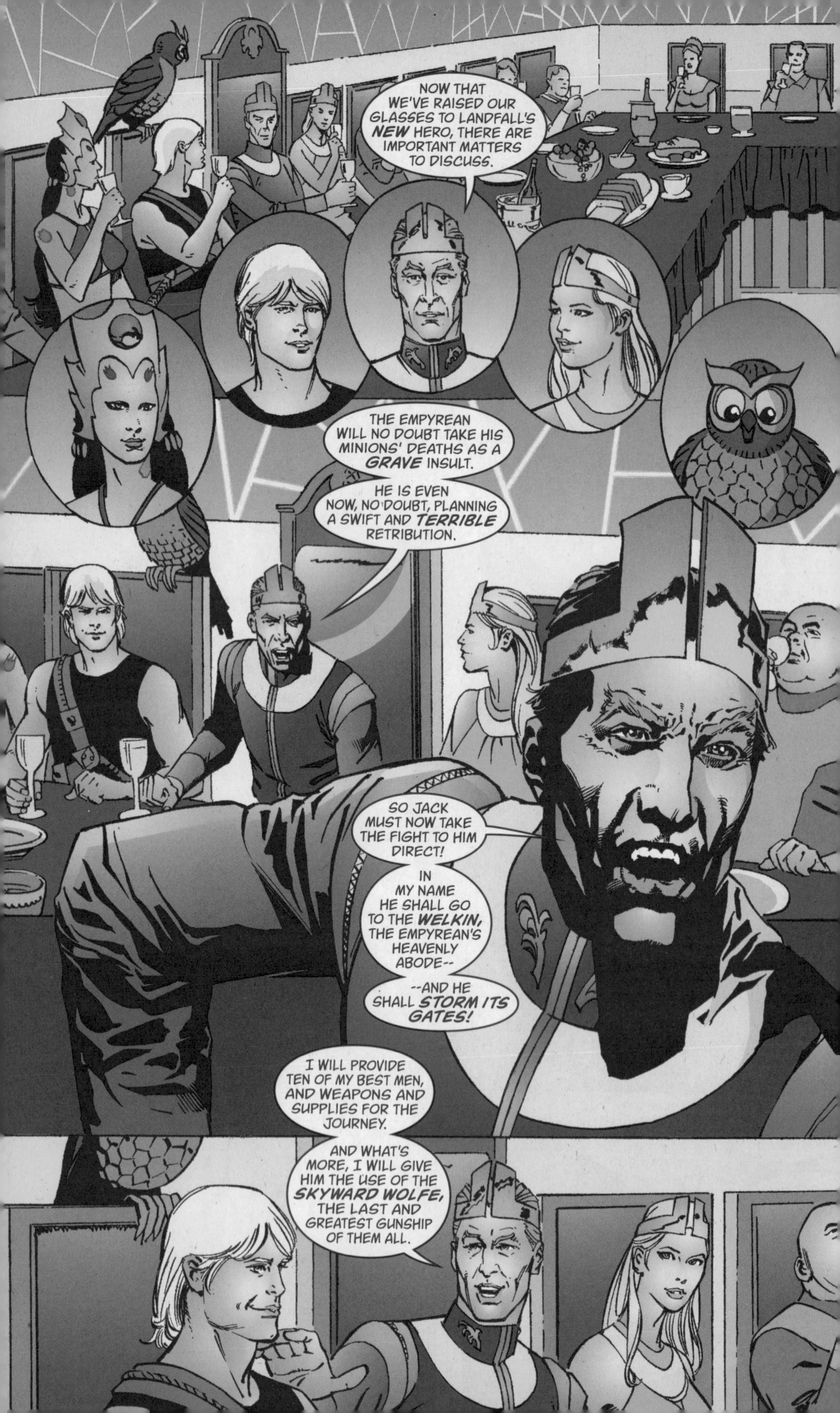

NOW THAT WE'VE RAISED OUR GLASSES TO LANDFALL'S NEW HERO, THERE ARE IMPORTANT MATTERS TO DISCUSS.
THE EMPYREAN WILL NO DOUBT TAKE HIS MINIONS' DEATHS AS A GRAVE INSULT.
HE IS EVEN NOW, NO DOUBT, PLANNING A SWIFT AND TERRIBLE RETRIBUTION.
SO JACK MUST NOW TAKE THE FIGHT TO HIM DIRECT!
IN MY NAME HE SHALL GO TO THE WELKIN, THE EMPYREAN'S HEAVENLY ABODE--
--AND HE SHALL STORM ITS GATES!
I WILL PROVIDE TEN OF MY BEST MEN, AND WEAPONS AND SUPPLIES FOR THE JOURNEY.
AND WHAT'S MORE, I WILL GIVE HIM THE USE OF THE SKYWARD WOLFE, THE LAST AND GREATEST GUNSHIP OF THEM ALL.

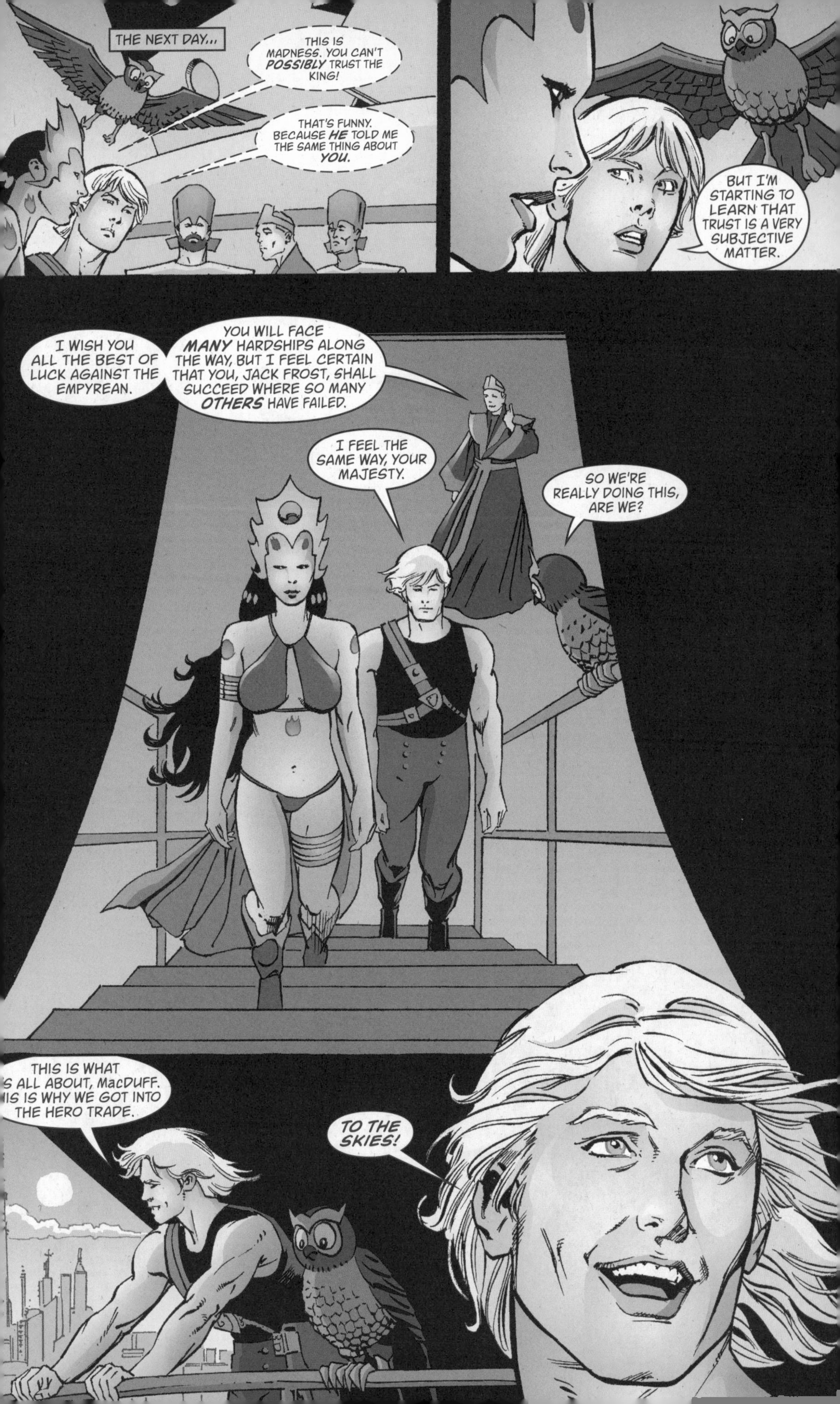

THE NEXT DAY...
THIS IS MADNESS. YOU CAN'T POSSIBLY TRUST THE KING!
THAT'S FUNNY. BECAUSE HE TOLD ME THE SAME THING ABOUT YOU.
BUT I'M STARTING TO LEARN THAT TRUST IS A VERY SUBJECTIVE MATTER.
I WISH YOU ALL THE BEST OF LUCK AGAINST THE EMPYREAN.
YOU WILL FACE MANY HARDSHIPS ALONG THE WAY, BUT I FEEL CERTAIN THAT YOU, JACK FROST, SHALL SUCCEED WHERE SO MANY OTHERS HAVE FAILED.
I FEEL THE SAME WAY, YOUR MAJESTY.
SO WE'RE REALLY DOING THIS, ARE WE?
THIS IS WHAT
S ALL ABOUT, MacDUFF.
IS IS WHY WE GOT INTO
THE HERO TRADE.
TO THE SKIES!

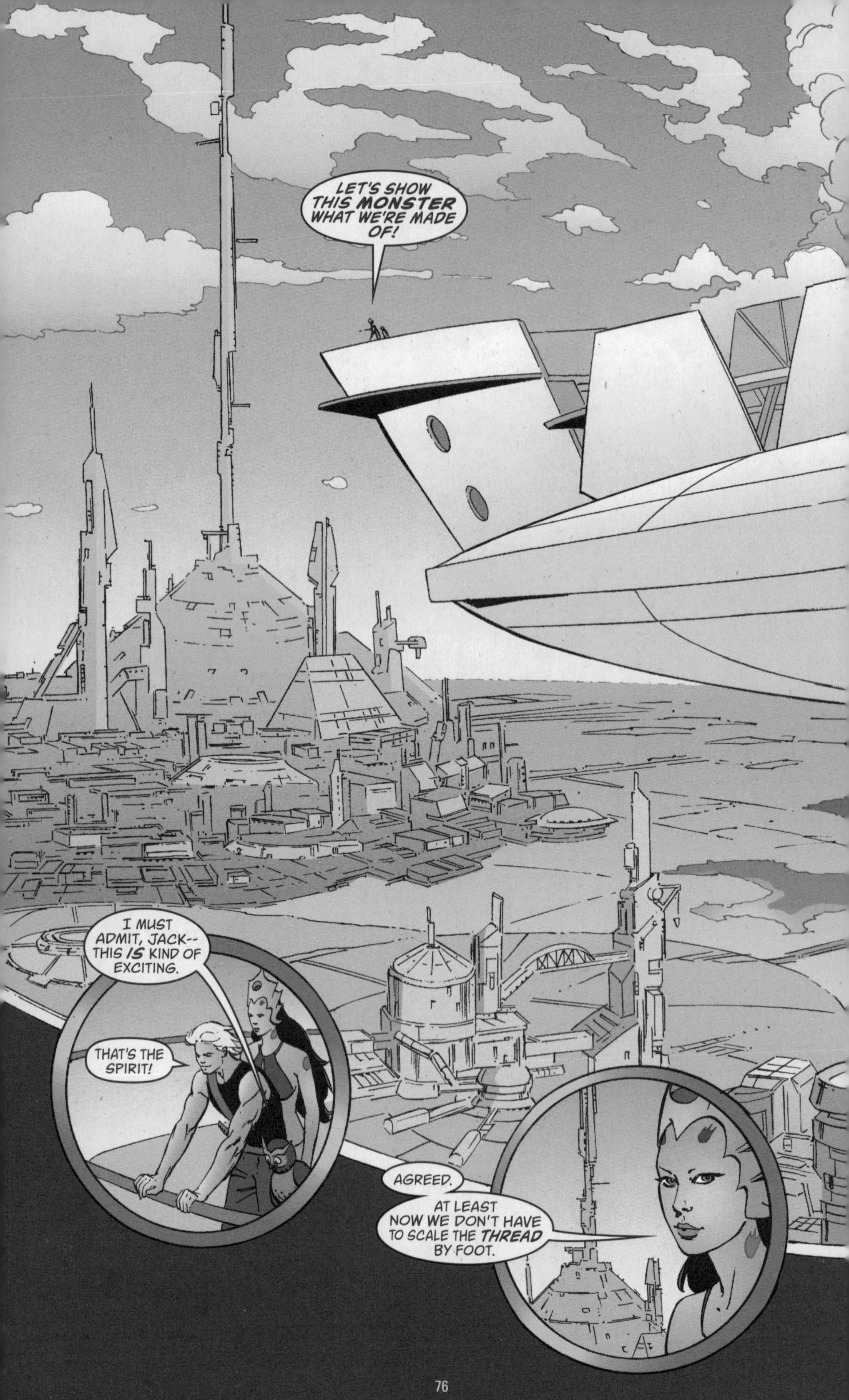
LET'S SHOW THIS MONSTER WHAT WE'RE MADE OF!
I MUST ADMIT, JACK-- THIS IS KIND OF EXCITING.
THAT'S THE SPIRIT!
AGREED.
AT LEAST NOW WE DON'T HAVE TO SCALE THE THREAD BY FOOT.

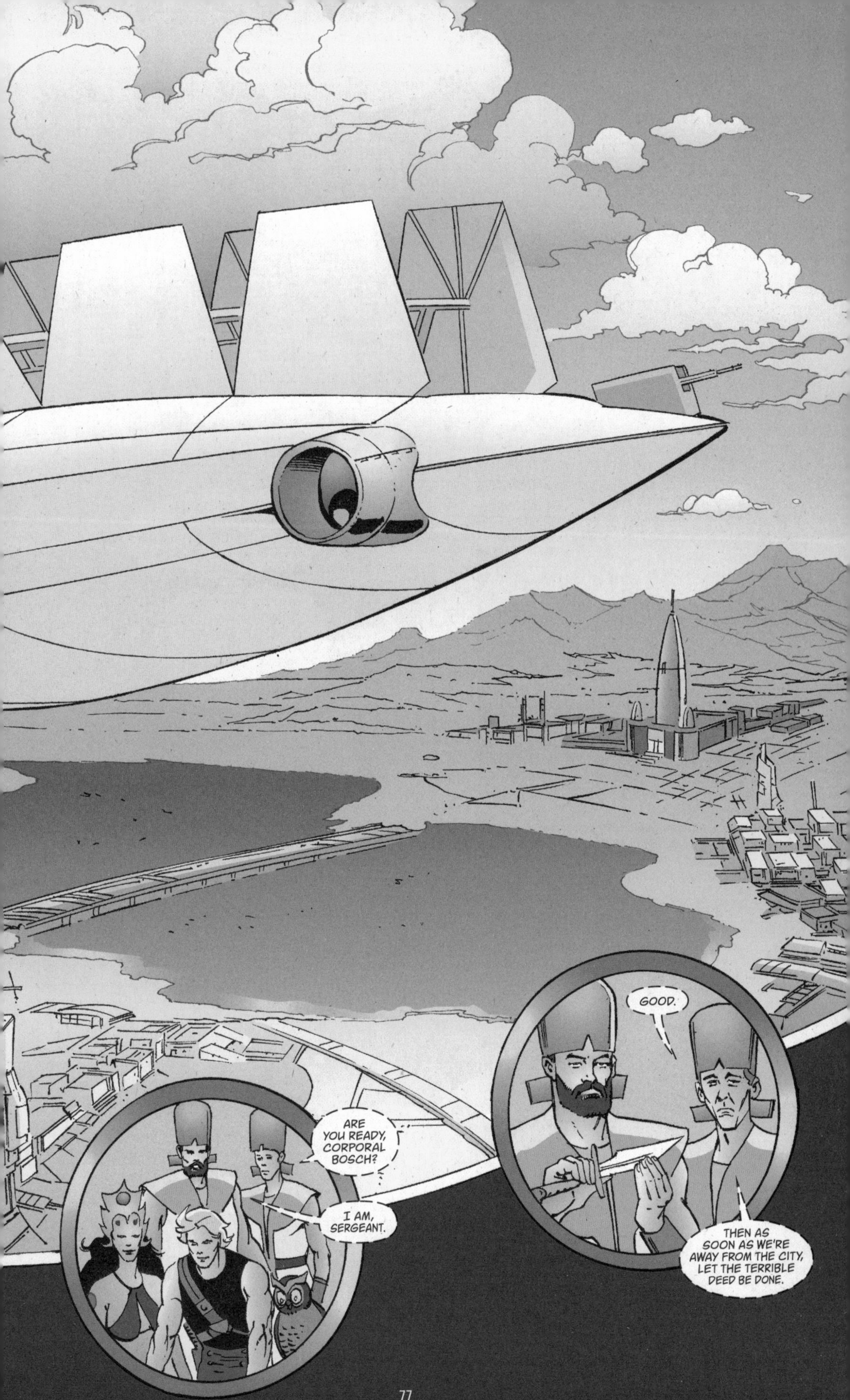

ARE YOU READY, CORPORAL BOSCH?
I AM, SERGEANT.
GOOD.
THEN AS SOON AS WE'RE AWAY FROM THE CITY, LET THE TERRIBLE DEED BE DONE.

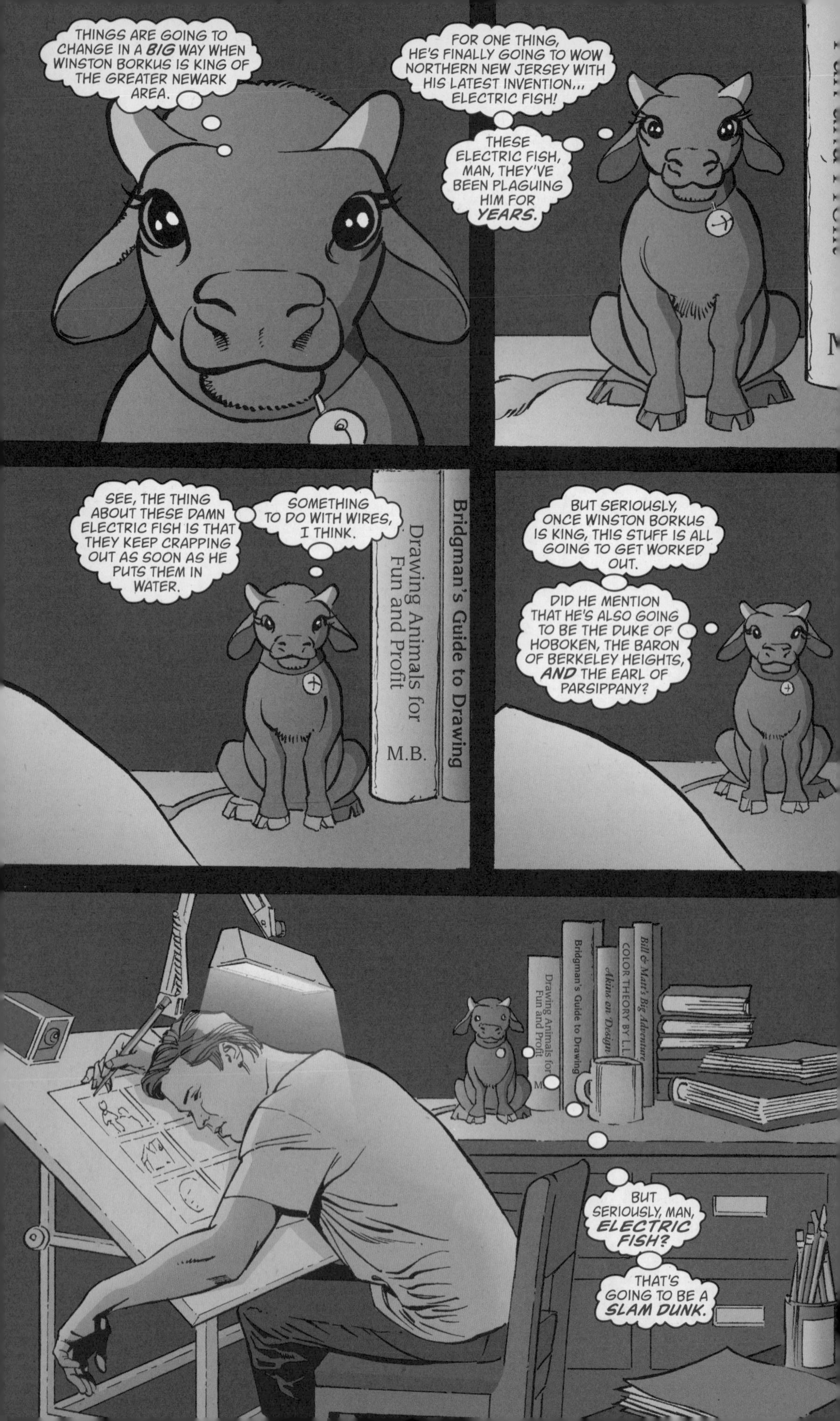
THINGS ARE GOING TO CHANGE IN A BIG WAY WHEN WINSTON BORKUS IS KING OF THE GREATER NEWARK AREA.
FOR ONE THING, HE'S FINALLY GOING TO WOW NORTHERN NEW JERSEY WITH HIS LATEST INVENTION... ELECTRIC FISH!
THESE ELECTRIC FISH, MAN, THEY'VE BEEN PLAGUING HIM FOR YEARS.
SEE, THE THING ABOUT THESE DAMN ELECTRIC FISH IS THAT THEY KEEP CRAPPING OUT AS SOON AS HE PUTS THEM IN WATER.
SOMETHING TO DO WITH WIRES, I THINK.
Drawing Animals for Fun and Profit
M.B.
Bridgman's Guide to Drawing
BUT SERIOUSLY, ONCE WINSTON BORKUS IS KING, THIS STUFF IS ALL GOING TO GET WORKED OUT.
DID HE MENTION THAT HE'S ALSO GOING TO BE THE DUKE OF HOBOKEN, THE BARON OF BERKELEY HEIGHTS, AND THE EARL OF PARSIPPANY?
Drawing Animals for Fun and Profit
Bridgman's Guide to Drawing
Akins on Design
COLOR THEORY BY L.L.
Bill & Matt's Big Adventure
BUT SERIOUSLY, MAN, ELECTRIC FISH?
THAT'S GOING TO BE A SLAM DUNK.

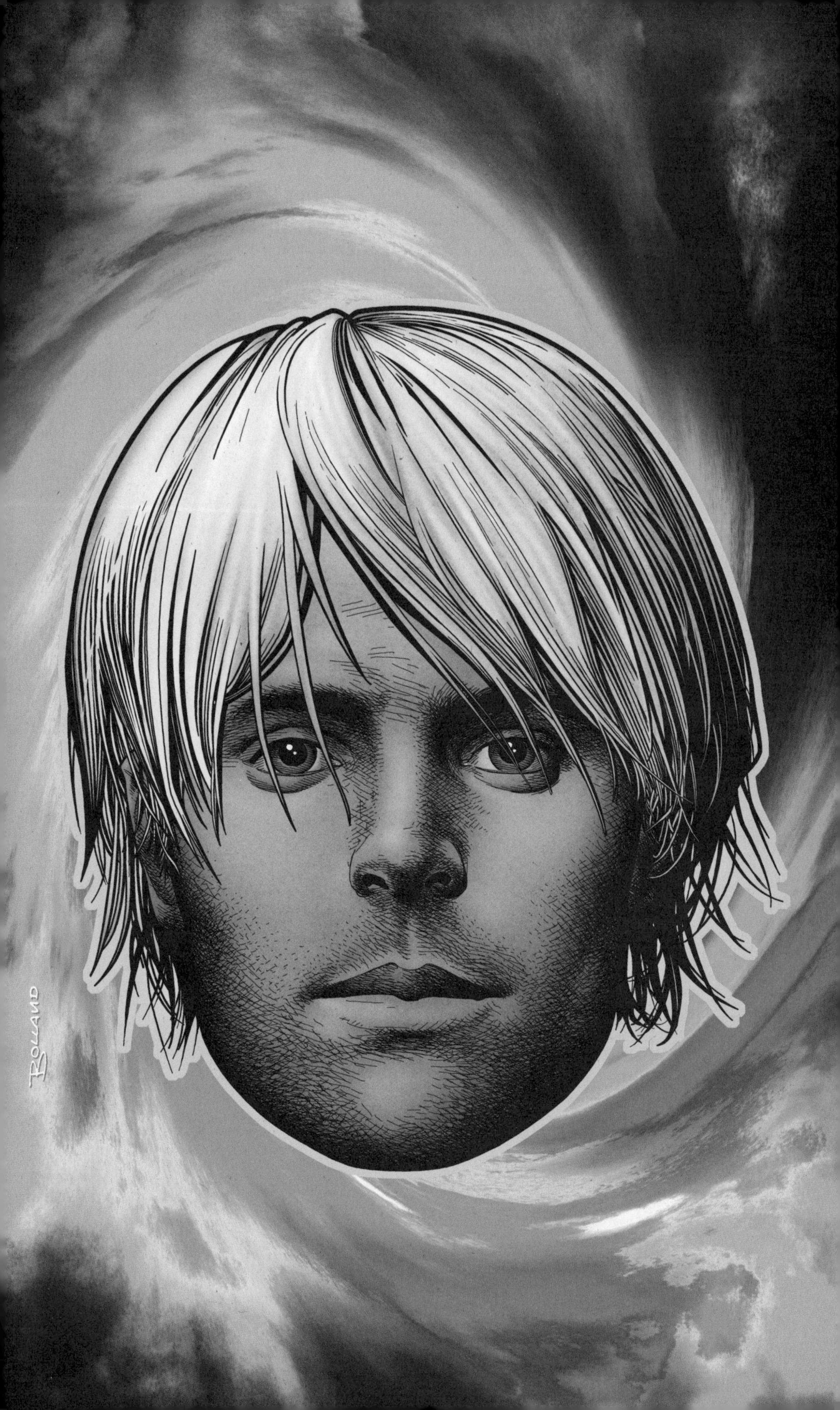
BOLLAND

*"I must be the luckiest person
in this world!"*

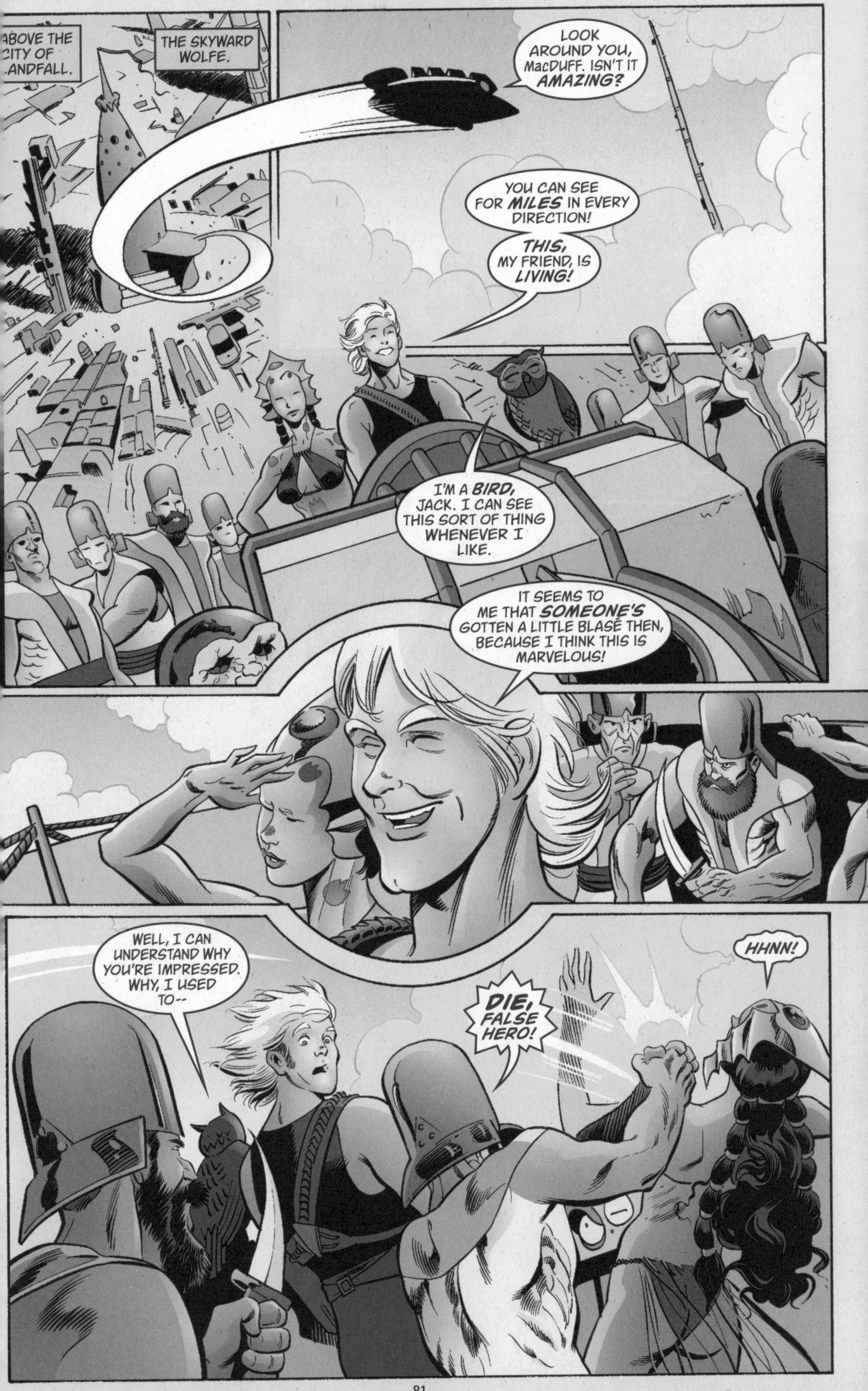
ABOVE THE
CITY OF
LANDFALL.
THE SKYWARD
WOLFE.
LOOK AROUND YOU, MacDUFF. ISN'T IT AMAZING?
YOU CAN SEE FOR MILES IN EVERY DIRECTION!
THIS, MY FRIEND, IS LIVING!
I'M A BIRD, JACK. I CAN SEE THIS SORT OF THING WHENEVER I LIKE.
IT SEEMS TO ME THAT SOMEONE'S GOTTEN A LITTLE BLASÉ THEN, BECAUSE I THINK THIS IS MARVELOUS!
WELL, I CAN UNDERSTAND WHY YOU'RE IMPRESSED. WHY, I USED TO--
DIE, FALSE HERO!
HHNN!

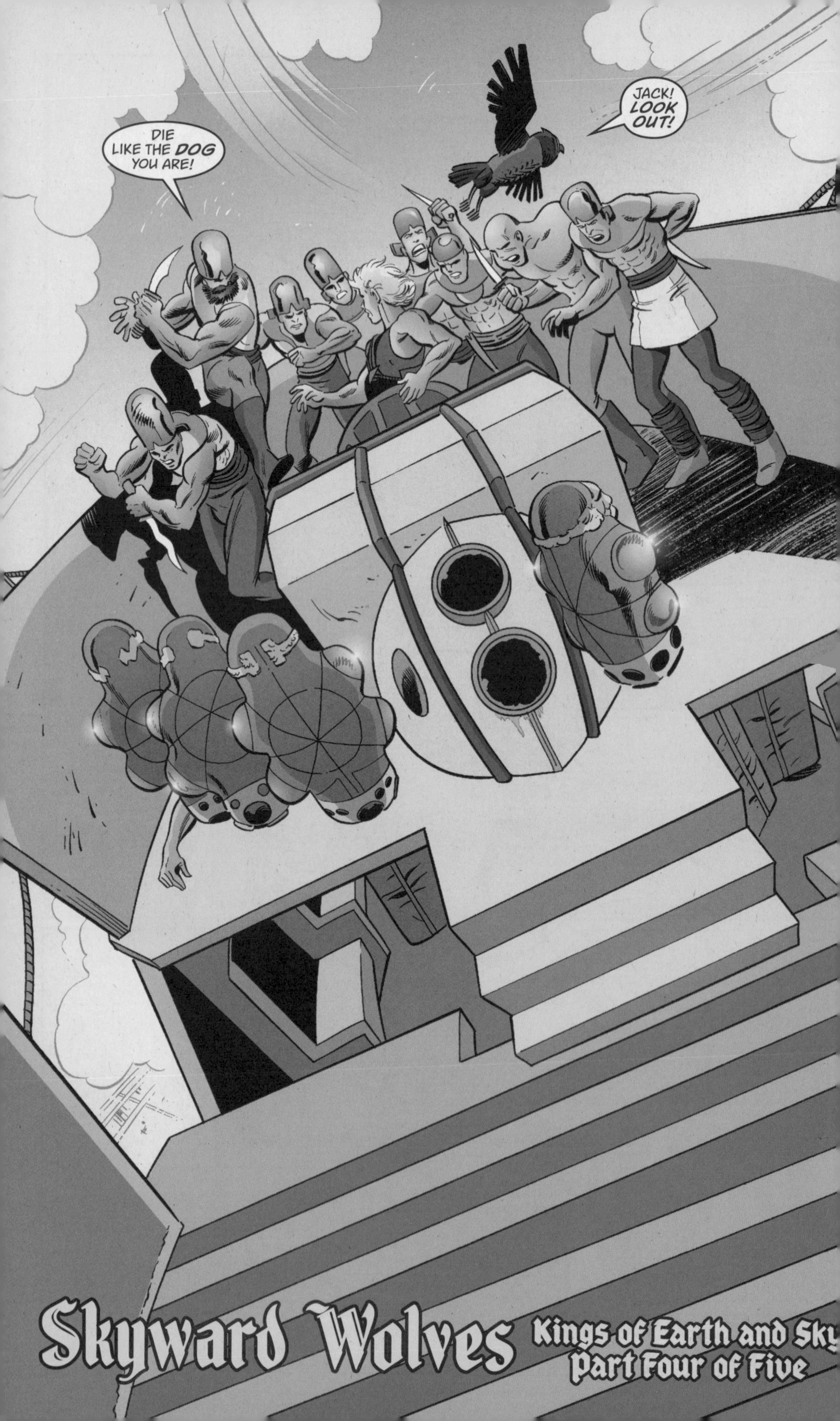
DIE LIKE THE DOG YOU ARE!
JACK! LOOK OUT!
Skyward Wolves
Kings of Earth and Sky
Part Four of Five

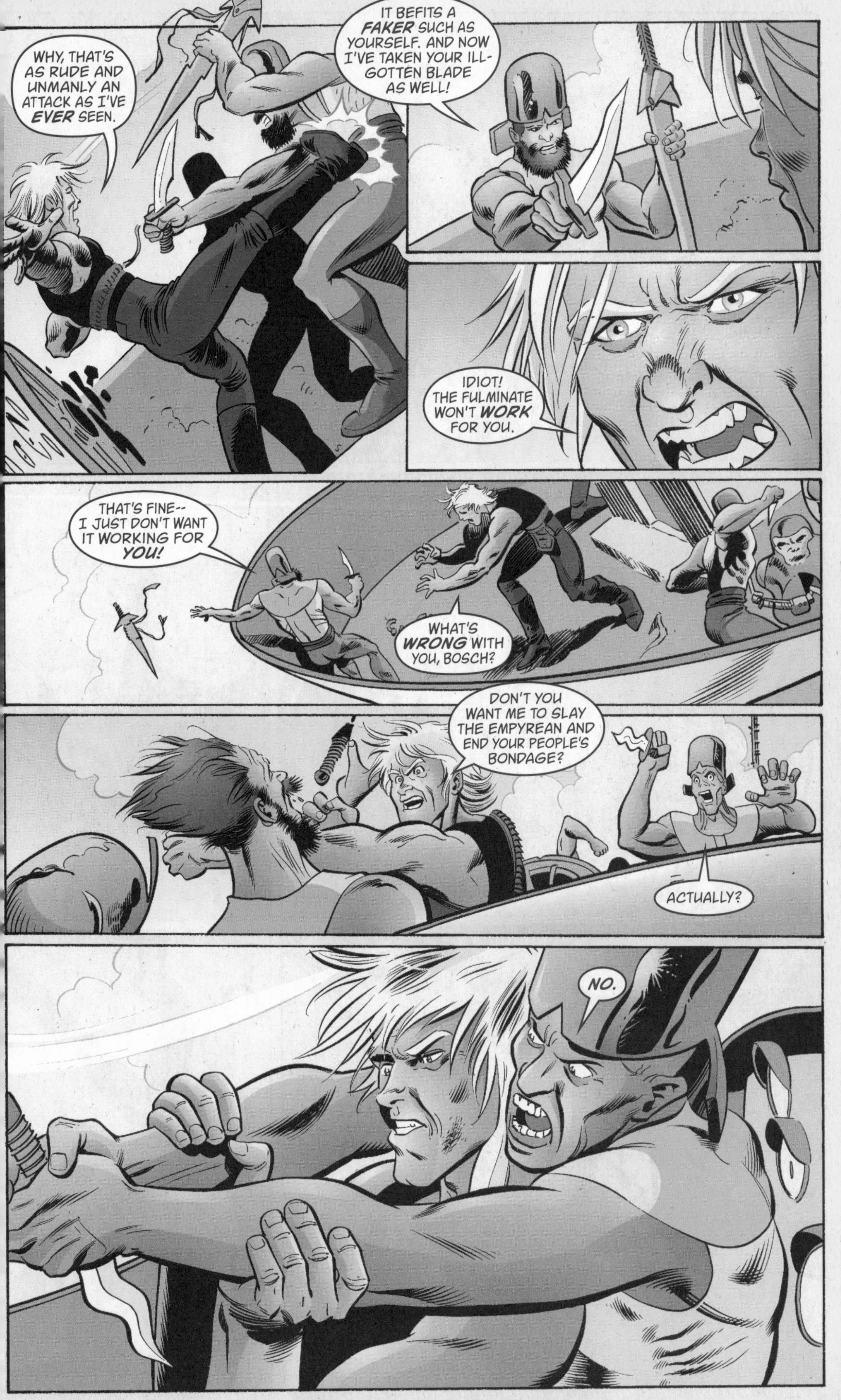
WHY, THAT'S AS RUDE AND UNMANLY AN ATTACK AS I'VE EVER SEEN.
IT BEFITS A FAKER SUCH AS YOURSELF. AND NOW I'VE TAKEN YOUR ILL-GOTTEN BLADE AS WELL!
IDIOT! THE FULMINATE WON'T WORK FOR YOU.
THAT'S FINE-- I JUST DON'T WANT IT WORKING FOR YOU!
WHAT'S WRONG WITH YOU, BOSCH?
DON'T YOU WANT ME TO SLAY THE EMPYREAN AND END YOUR PEOPLE'S BONDAGE?
ACTUALLY?
NO.

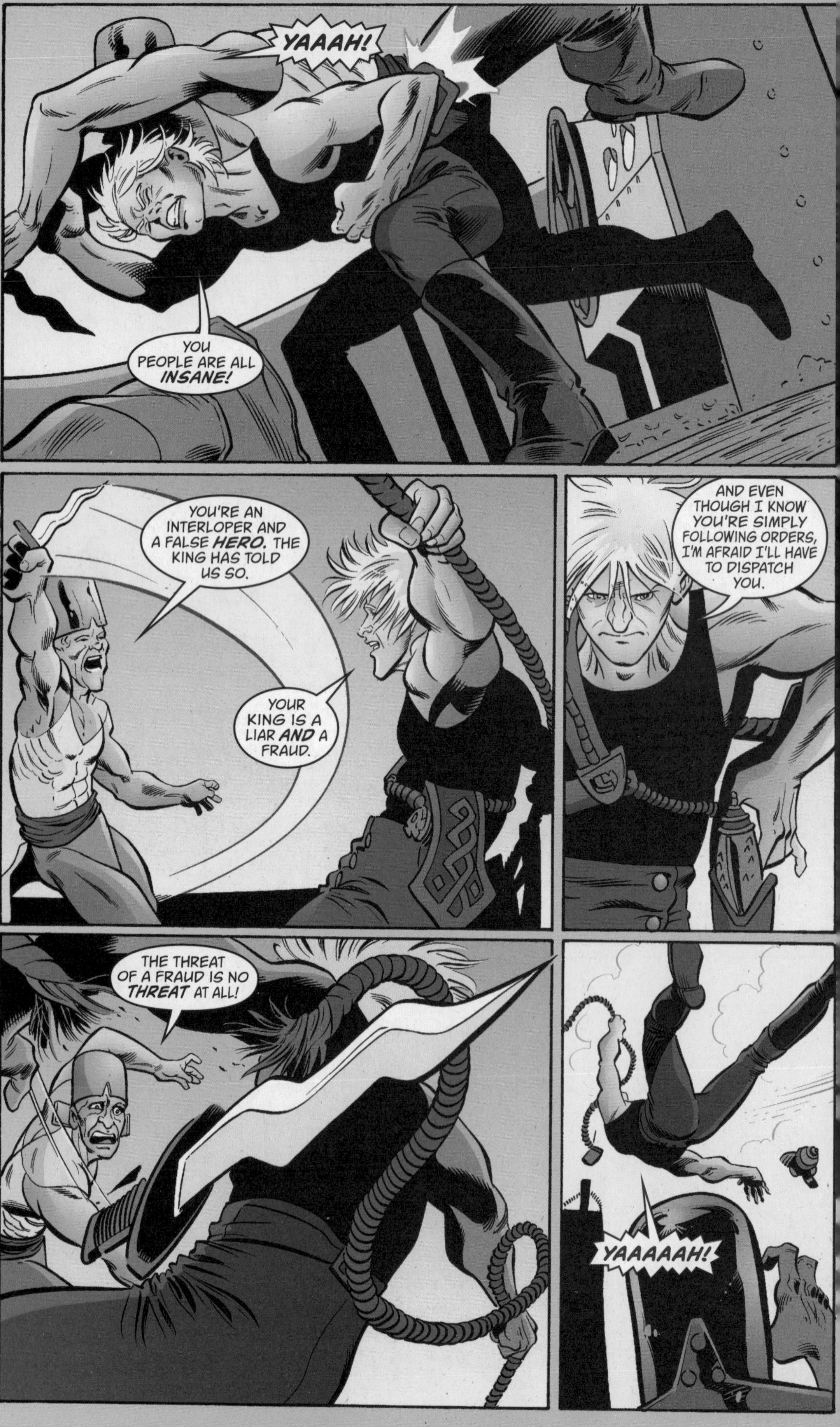
YAAAH!
YOU PEOPLE ARE ALL INSANE!
YOU'RE AN INTERLOPER AND A FALSE HERO. THE KING HAS TOLD US SO.
YOUR KING IS A LIAR AND A FRAUD.
AND EVEN THOUGH I KNOW YOU'RE SIMPLY FOLLOWING ORDERS, I'M AFRAID I'LL HAVE TO DISPATCH YOU.
THE THREAT OF A FRAUD IS NO THREAT AT ALL!
YAAAAAH!

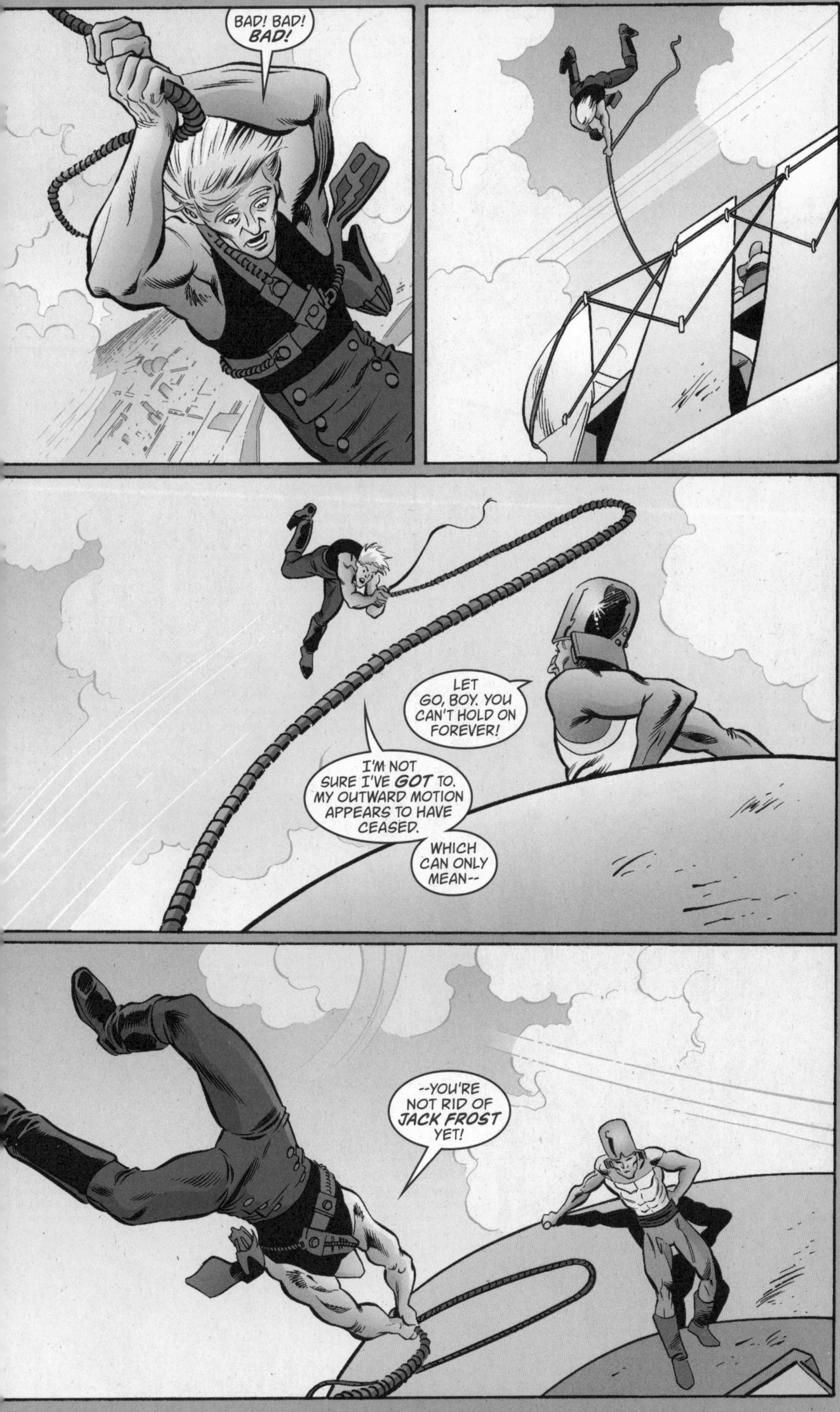
BAD! BAD! BAD!
LET GO, BOY. YOU CAN'T HOLD ON FOREVER!
I'M NOT SURE I'VE GOT TO. MY OUTWARD MOTION APPEARS TO HAVE CEASED.
WHICH CAN ONLY MEAN--
--YOU'RE NOT RID OF JACK FROST YET!

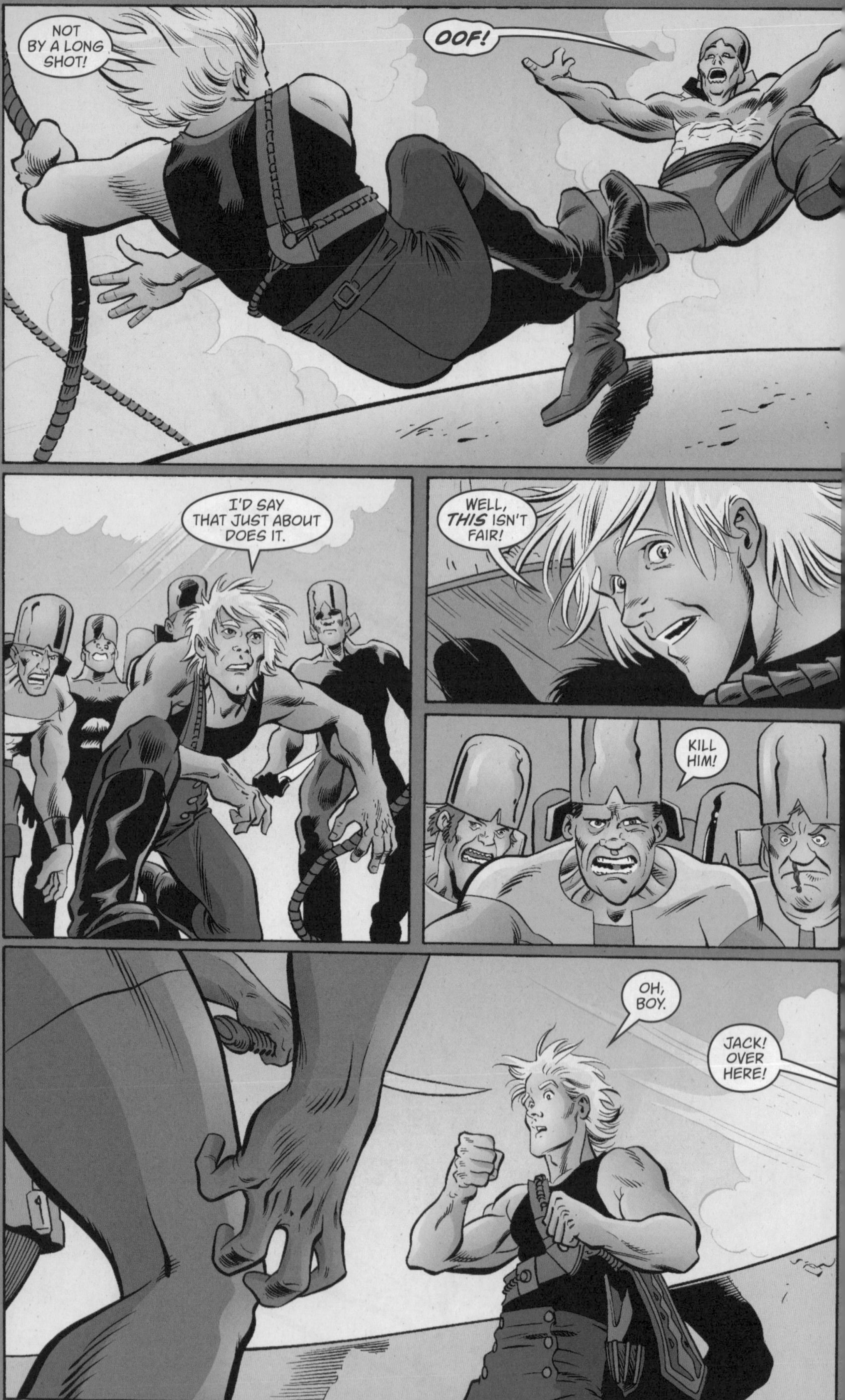
NOT BY A LONG SHOT!
OOF!
I'D SAY THAT JUST ABOUT DOES IT.
WELL, THIS ISN'T FAIR!
KILL HIM!
OH, BOY.
JACK! OVER HERE!

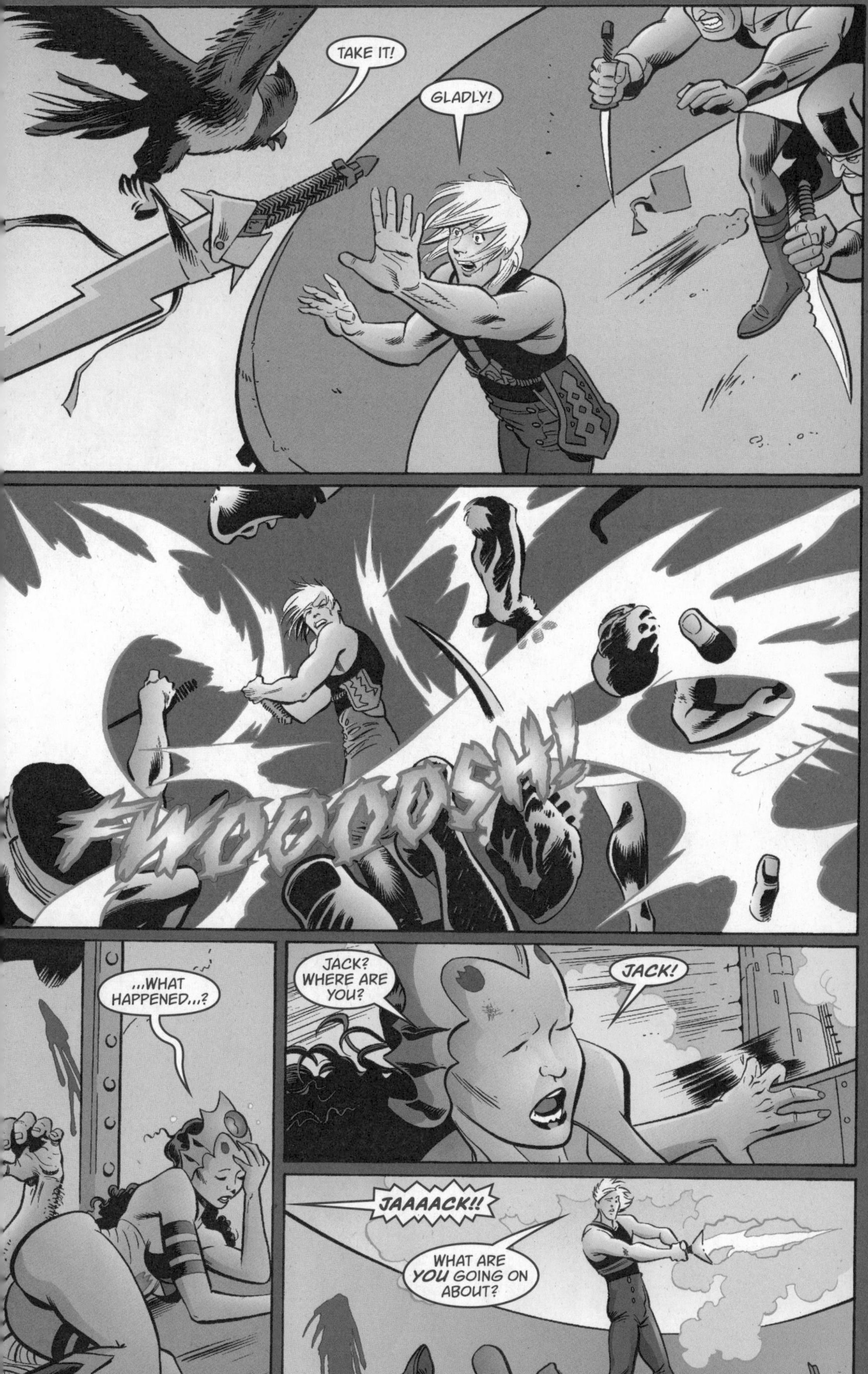
TAKE IT!
GLADLY!
FWOOOOSH!
...WHAT HAPPENED...?
JACK? WHERE ARE YOU?
JACK!
JAAAACK!!
WHAT ARE YOU GOING ON ABOUT?

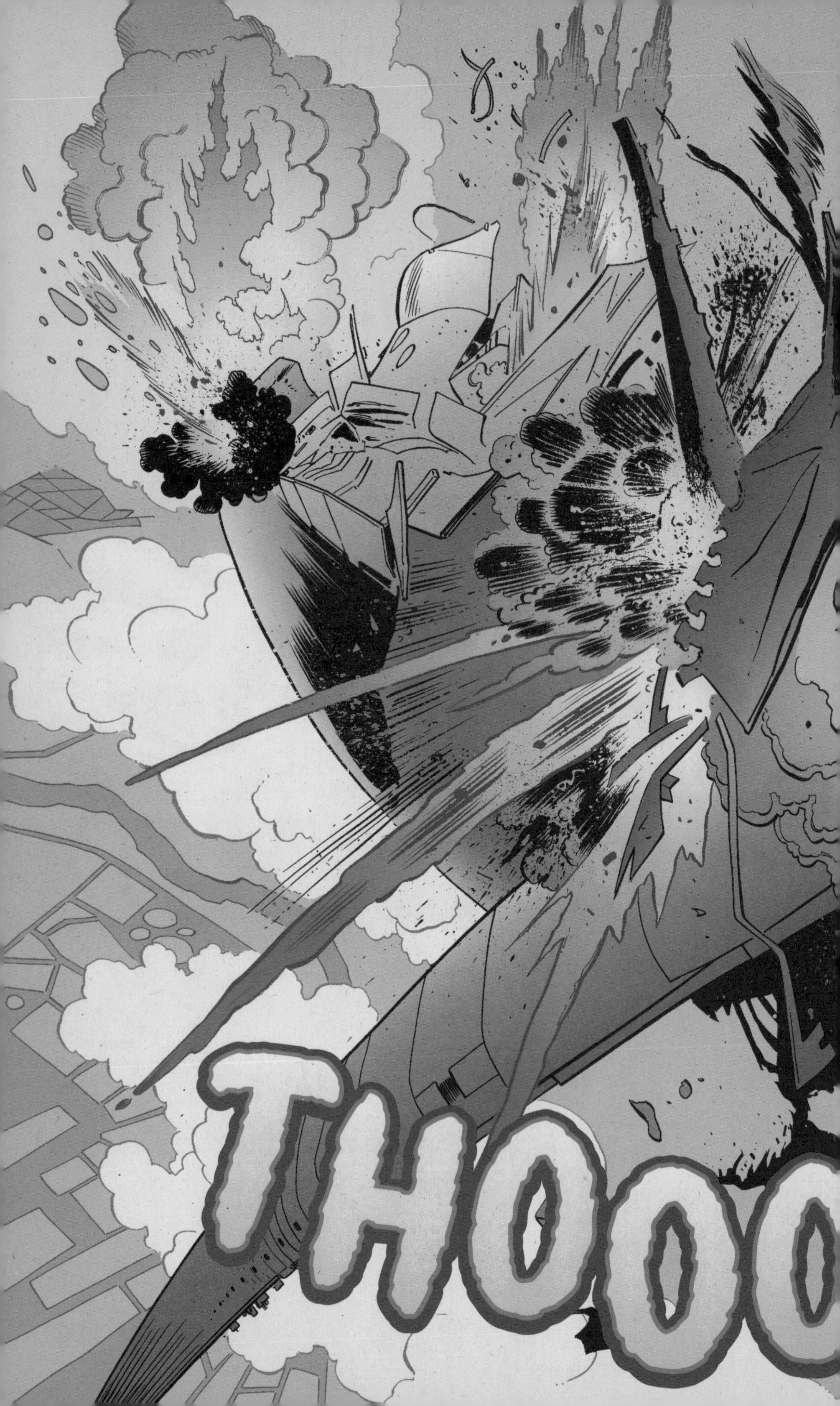
THOOO

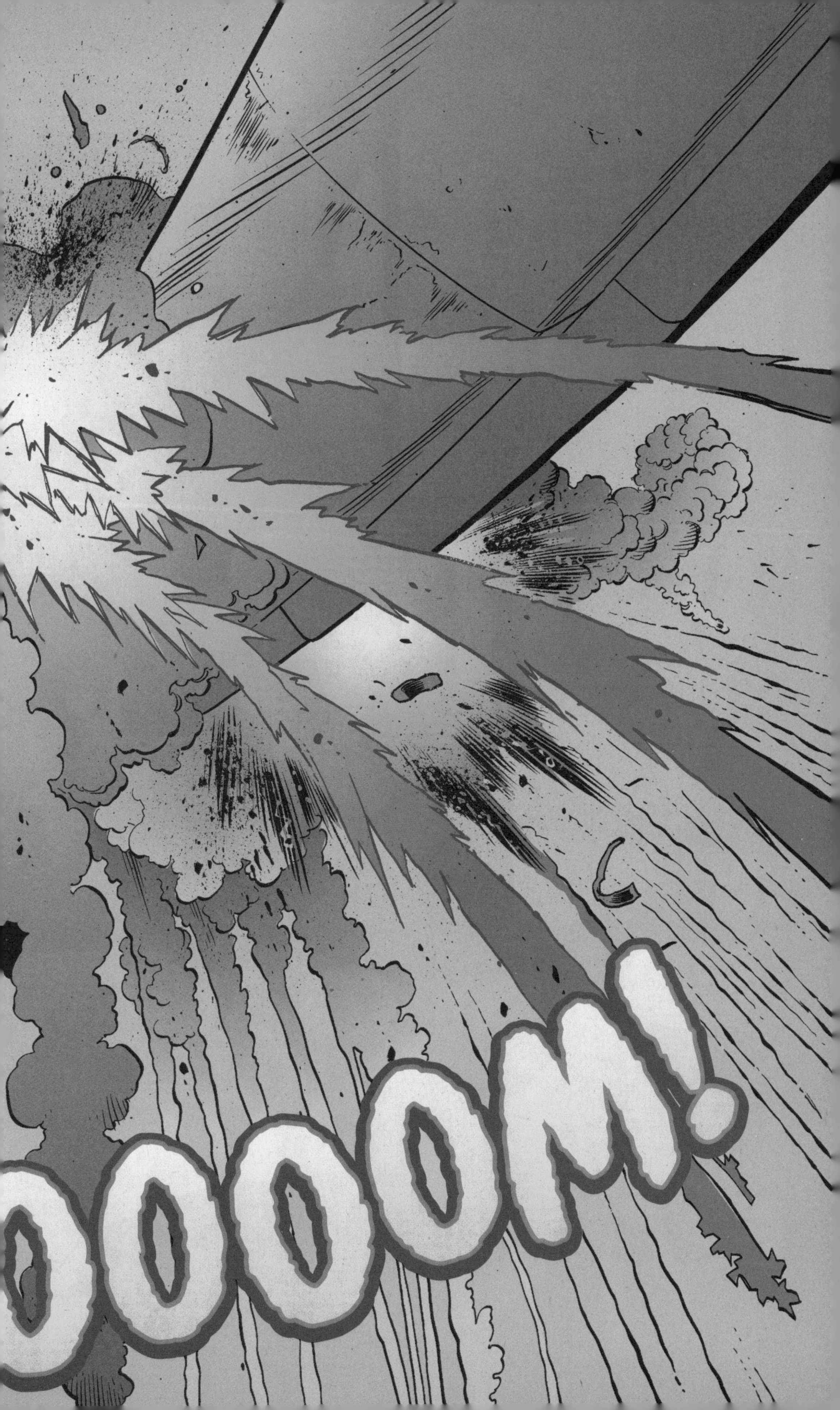
OOOOOM!

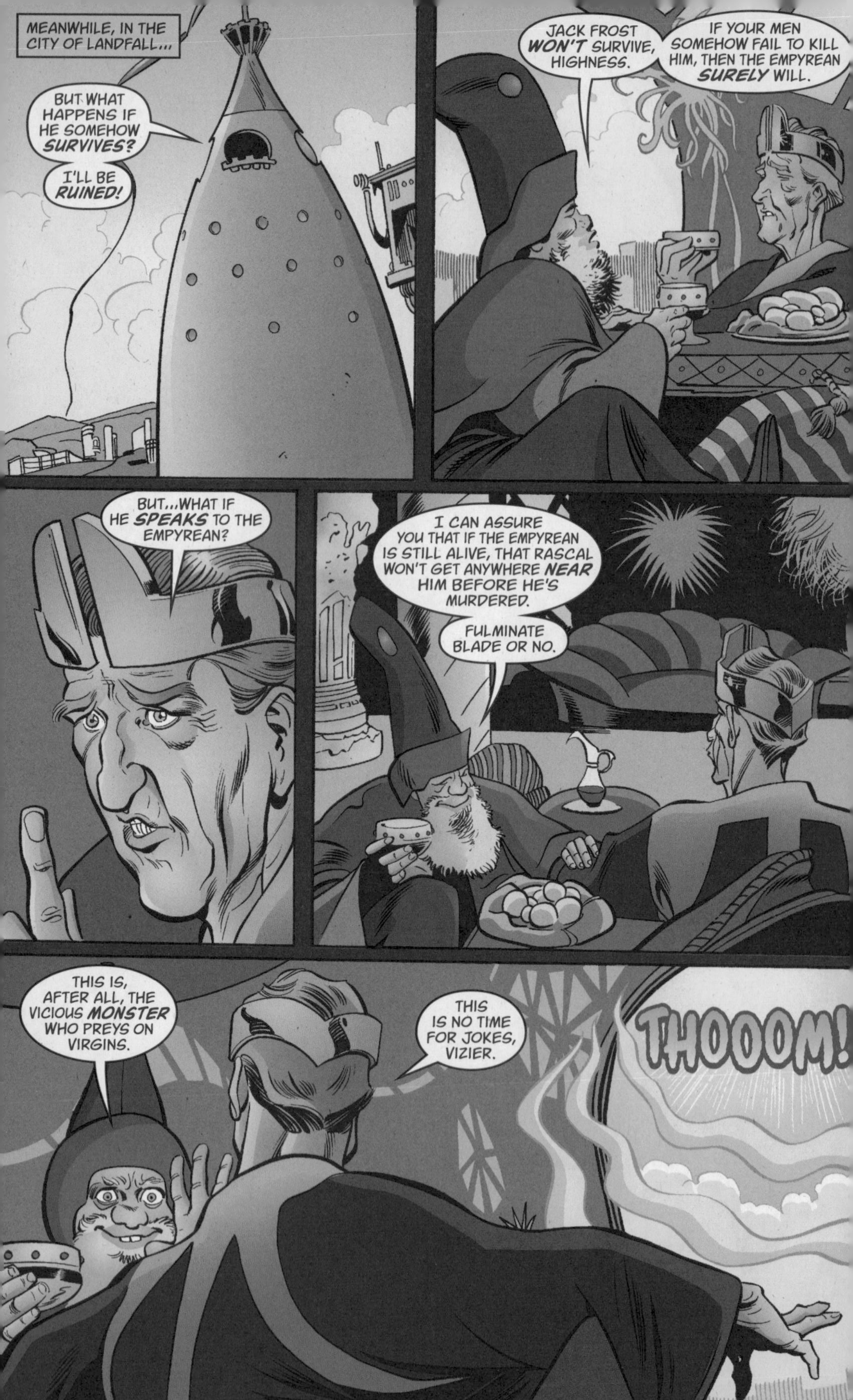

MEANWHILE, IN THE CITY OF LANDFALL...
BUT WHAT HAPPENS IF HE SOMEHOW SURVIVES?
I'LL BE RUINED!
JACK FROST WON'T SURVIVE, HIGHNESS.
IF YOUR MEN SOMEHOW FAIL TO KILL HIM, THEN THE EMPYREAN SURELY WILL.
BUT...WHAT IF HE SPEAKS TO THE EMPYREAN?
I CAN ASSURE YOU THAT IF THE EMPYREAN IS STILL ALIVE, THAT RASCAL WON'T GET ANYWHERE NEAR HIM BEFORE HE'S MURDERED.
FULMINATE BLADE OR NO.
THIS IS, AFTER ALL, THE VICIOUS MONSTER WHO PREYS ON VIRGINS.
THIS IS NO TIME FOR JOKES, VIZIER.
THOOOM!

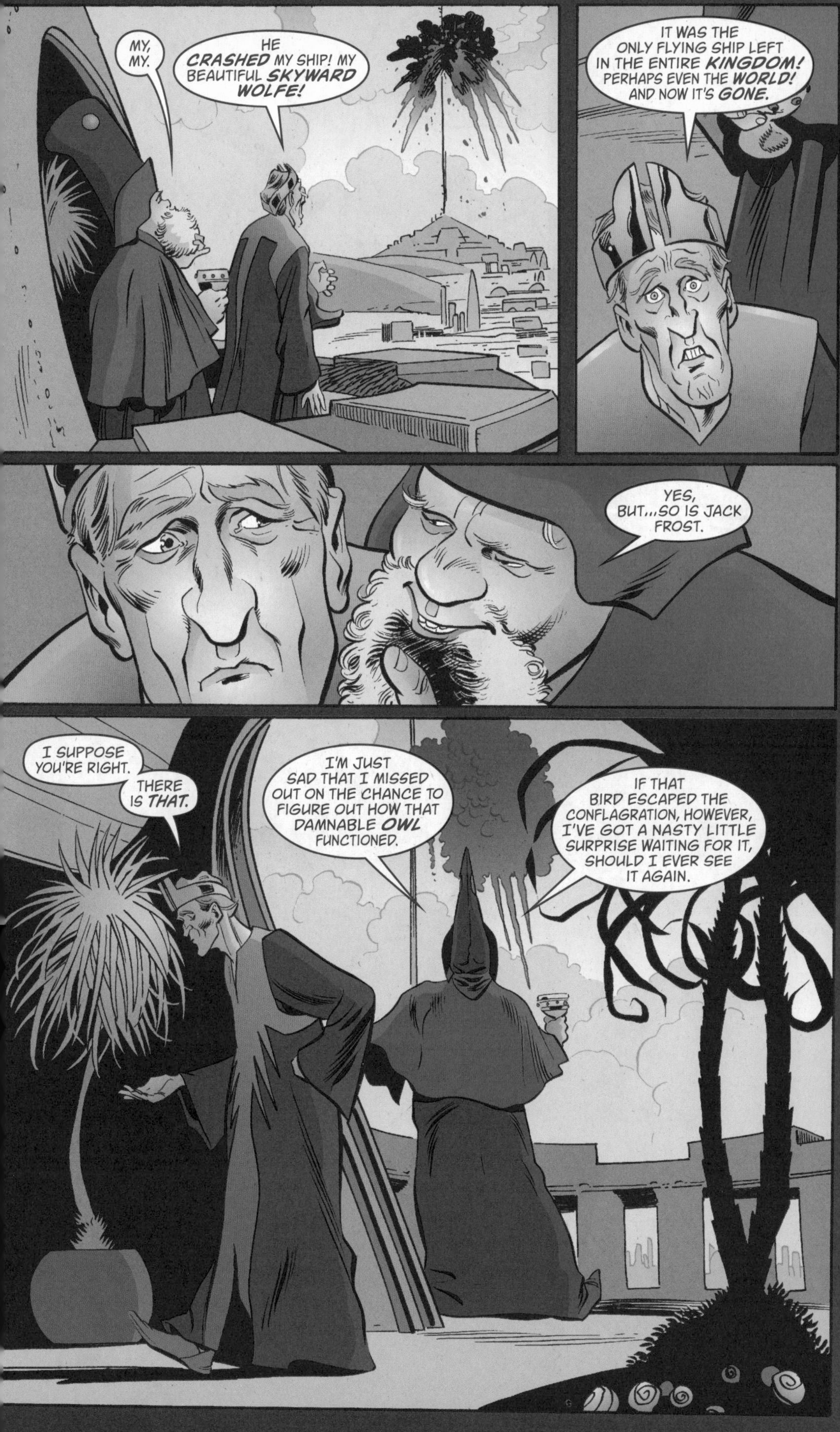
MY, MY.
HE CRASHED MY SHIP! MY BEAUTIFUL SKYWARD WOLFE!
IT WAS THE ONLY FLYING SHIP LEFT IN THE ENTIRE KINGDOM! PERHAPS EVEN THE WORLD! AND NOW IT'S GONE.
YES, BUT...SO IS JACK FROST.
I SUPPOSE YOU'RE RIGHT.
THERE IS THAT.
I'M JUST SAD THAT I MISSED OUT ON THE CHANCE TO FIGURE OUT HOW THAT DAMNABLE OWL FUNCTIONED.
IF THAT BIRD ESCAPED THE CONFLAGRATION, HOWEVER, I'VE GOT A NASTY LITTLE SURPRISE WAITING FOR IT, SHOULD I EVER SEE IT AGAIN.

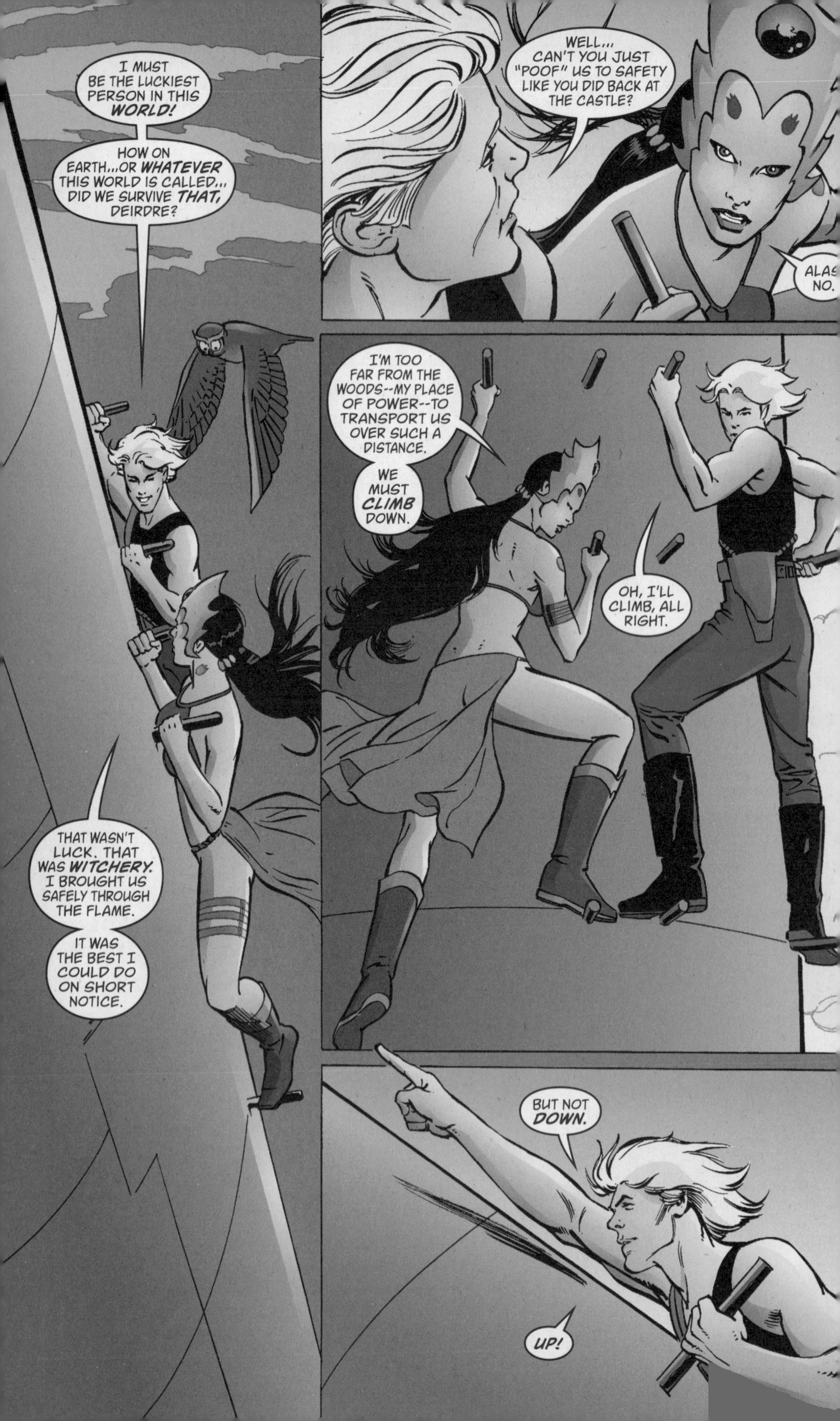

I MUST BE THE LUCKIEST PERSON IN THIS **WORLD!**
HOW ON EARTH...OR **WHATEVER** THIS WORLD IS CALLED... DID WE SURVIVE **THAT,** DEIRDRE?
THAT WASN'T LUCK. THAT WAS **WITCHERY.** I BROUGHT US SAFELY THROUGH THE FLAME.
IT WAS THE BEST I COULD DO ON SHORT NOTICE.
WELL... CAN'T YOU JUST "POOF" US TO SAFETY LIKE YOU DID BACK AT THE CASTLE?
ALAS NO.
I'M TOO FAR FROM THE WOODS--MY PLACE OF POWER--TO TRANSPORT US OVER SUCH A DISTANCE.
WE MUST **CLIMB** DOWN.
OH, I'LL CLIMB, ALL RIGHT.
BUT NOT **DOWN.**
UP!

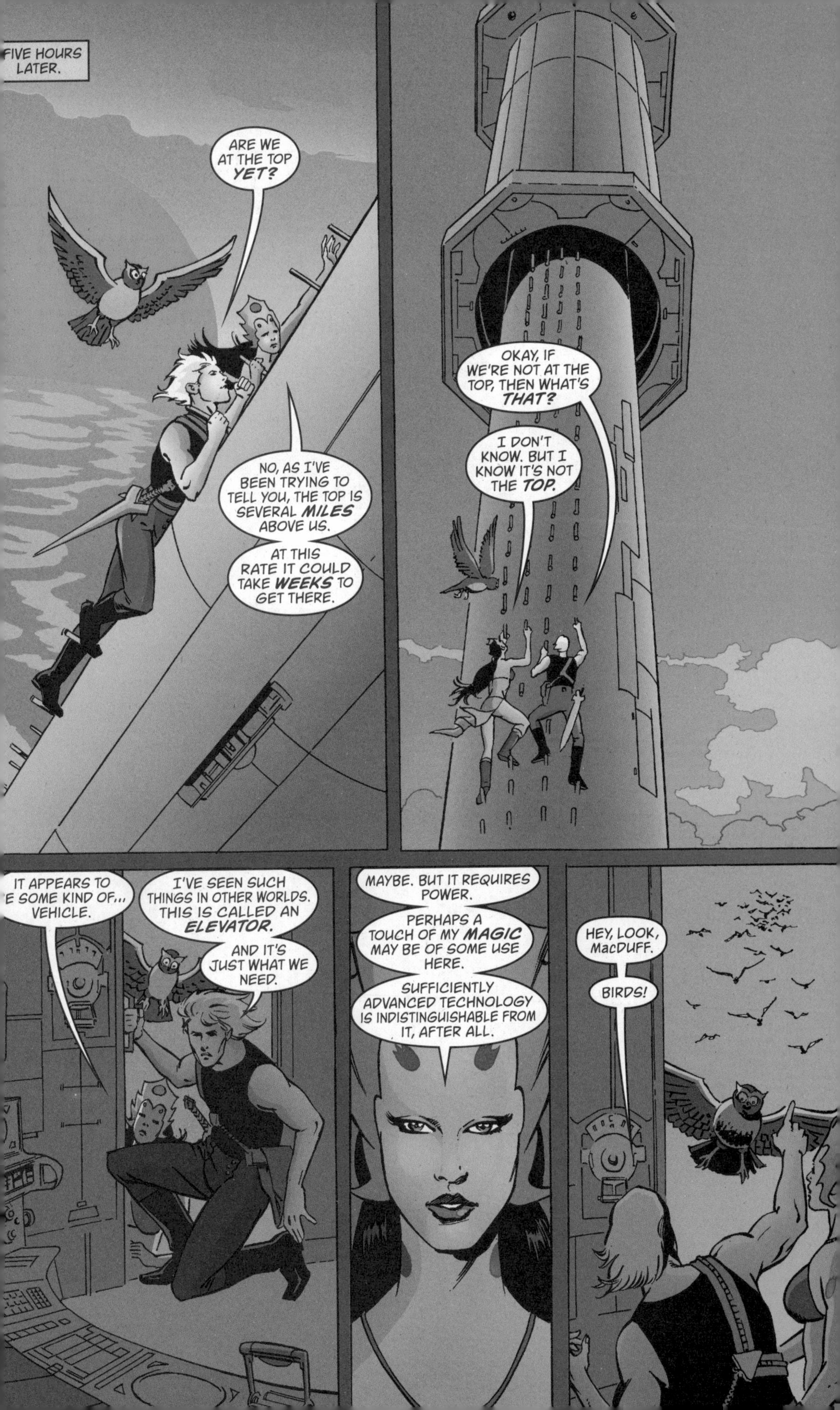
FIVE HOURS LATER.
ARE WE AT THE TOP YET?
NO, AS I'VE BEEN TRYING TO TELL YOU, THE TOP IS SEVERAL MILES ABOVE US.
AT THIS RATE IT COULD TAKE WEEKS TO GET THERE.
OKAY, IF WE'RE NOT AT THE TOP, THEN WHAT'S THAT?
I DON'T KNOW. BUT I KNOW IT'S NOT THE TOP.
IT APPEARS TO E SOME KIND OF... VEHICLE.
I'VE SEEN SUCH THINGS IN OTHER WORLDS. THIS IS CALLED AN ELEVATOR.
AND IT'S JUST WHAT WE NEED.
MAYBE. BUT IT REQUIRES POWER.
PERHAPS A TOUCH OF MY MAGIC MAY BE OF SOME USE HERE.
SUFFICIENTLY ADVANCED TECHNOLOGY IS INDISTINGUISHABLE FROM IT, AFTER ALL.
HEY, LOOK, MacDUFF.
BIRDS!

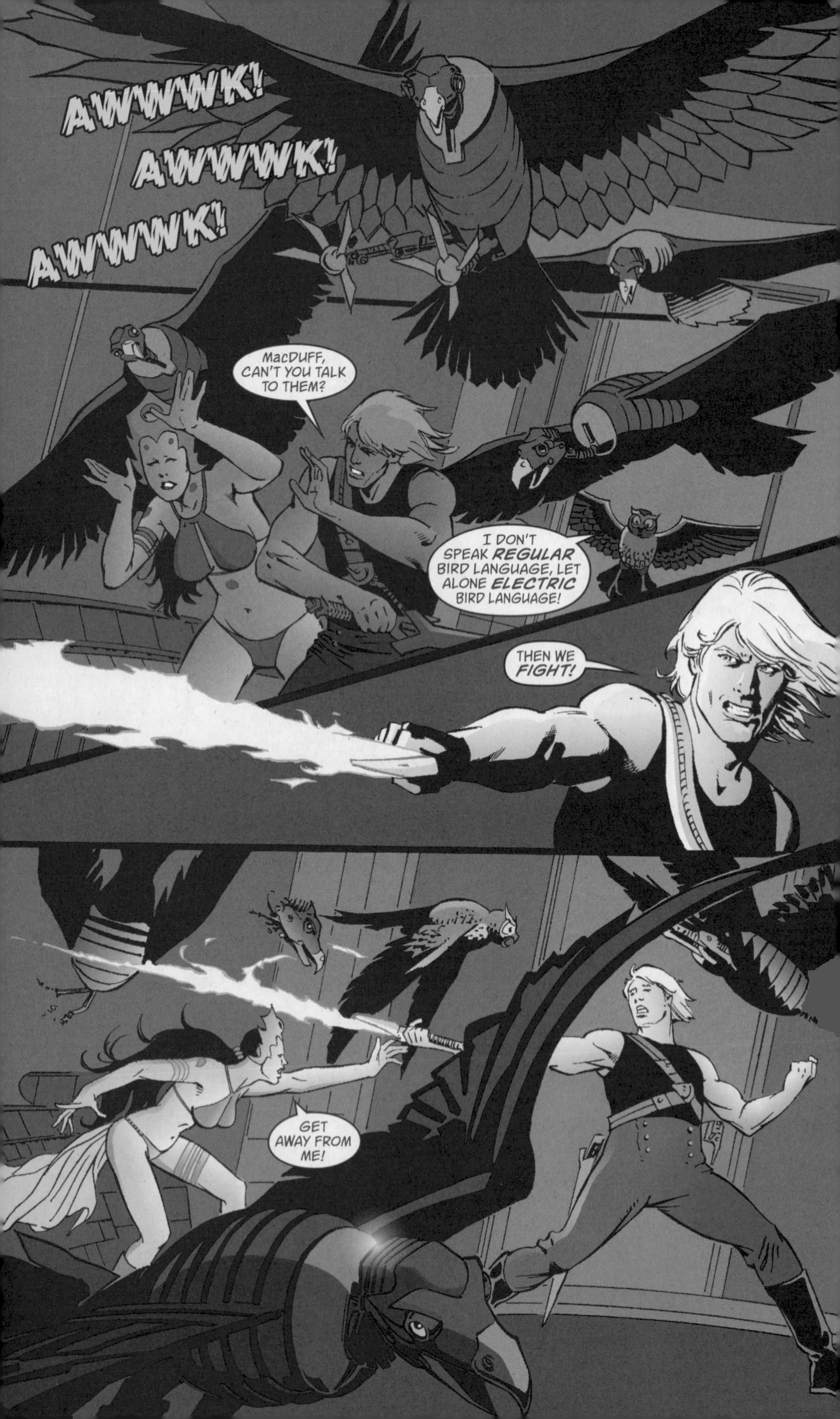
AWWWK!
AWWWK!
AWWWK!
MacDUFF, CAN'T YOU TALK TO THEM?
I DON'T SPEAK REGULAR BIRD LANGUAGE, LET ALONE ELECTRIC BIRD LANGUAGE!
THEN WE FIGHT!
GET AWAY FROM ME!

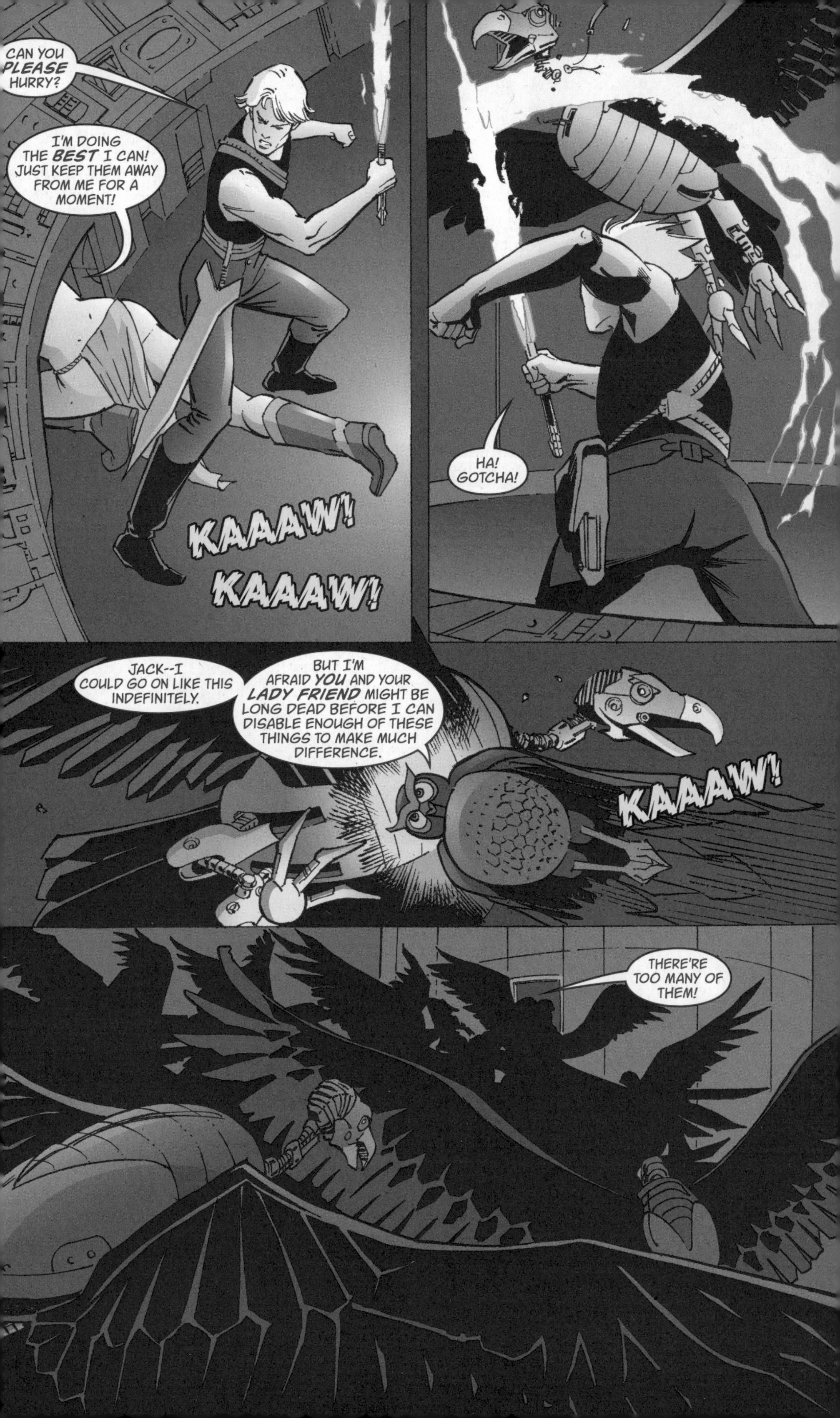
CAN YOU PLEASE HURRY?
I'M DOING THE BEST I CAN! JUST KEEP THEM AWAY FROM ME FOR A MOMENT!
KAAAW!
KAAAW!
HA! GOTCHA!
JACK--I COULD GO ON LIKE THIS INDEFINITELY.
BUT I'M AFRAID YOU AND YOUR LADY FRIEND MIGHT BE LONG DEAD BEFORE I CAN DISABLE ENOUGH OF THESE THINGS TO MAKE MUCH DIFFERENCE.
KAAAW!
THERE'RE TOO MANY OF THEM!

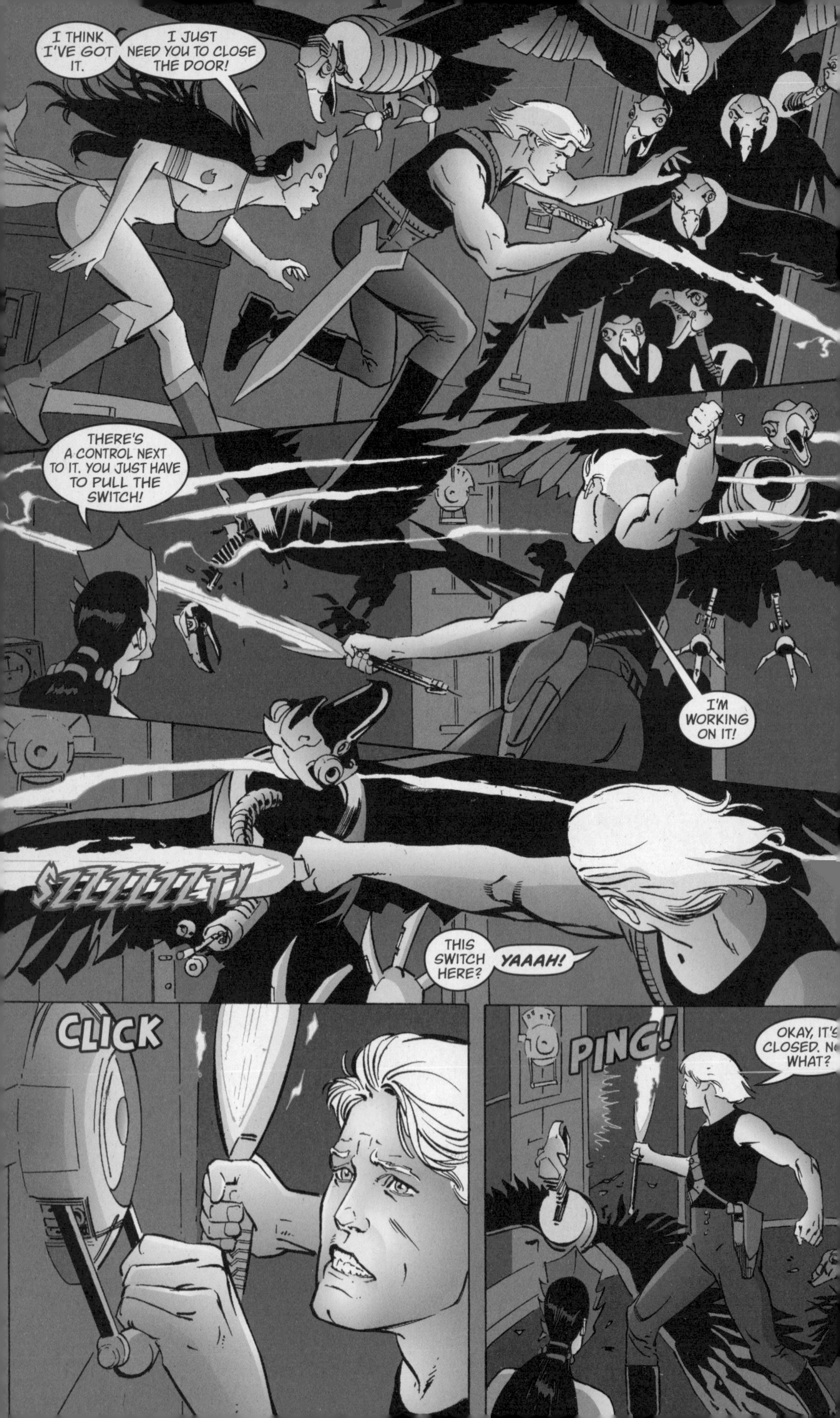
I THINK I'VE GOT IT.
I JUST NEED YOU TO CLOSE THE DOOR!
THERE'S A CONTROL NEXT TO IT. YOU JUST HAVE TO PULL THE SWITCH!
I'M WORKING ON IT!
SZZZZZZZT!
THIS SWITCH HERE?
YAAAH!
CLICK
PING!
OKAY, IT'S CLOSED. NOW WHAT?

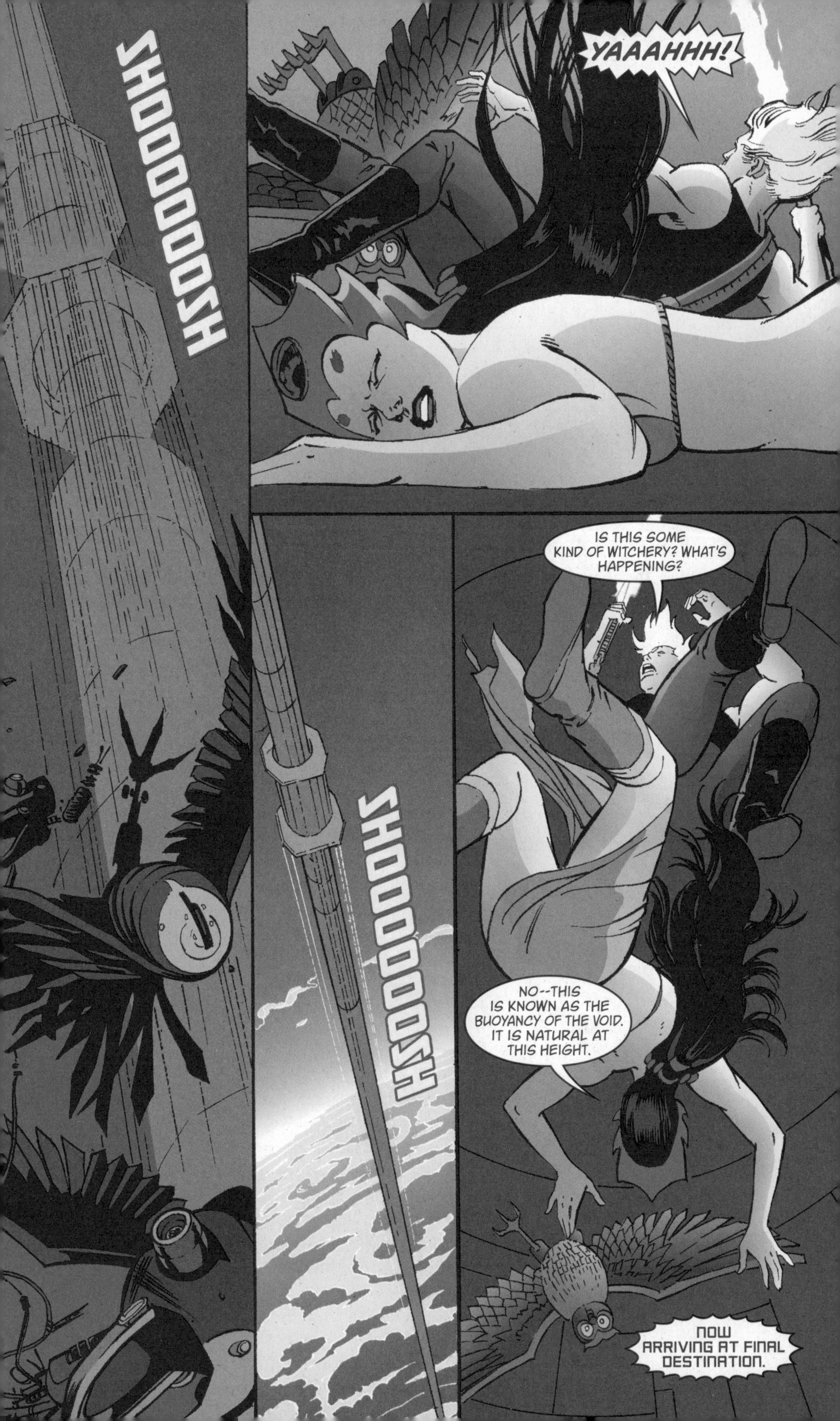
SHOOOOOOSH
YAAAHHH!
SHOOOOOOSH
IS THIS SOME KIND OF WITCHERY? WHAT'S HAPPENING?
NO--THIS IS KNOWN AS THE BUOYANCY OF THE VOID. IT IS NATURAL AT THIS HEIGHT.
NOW ARRIVING AT FINAL DESTINATION.

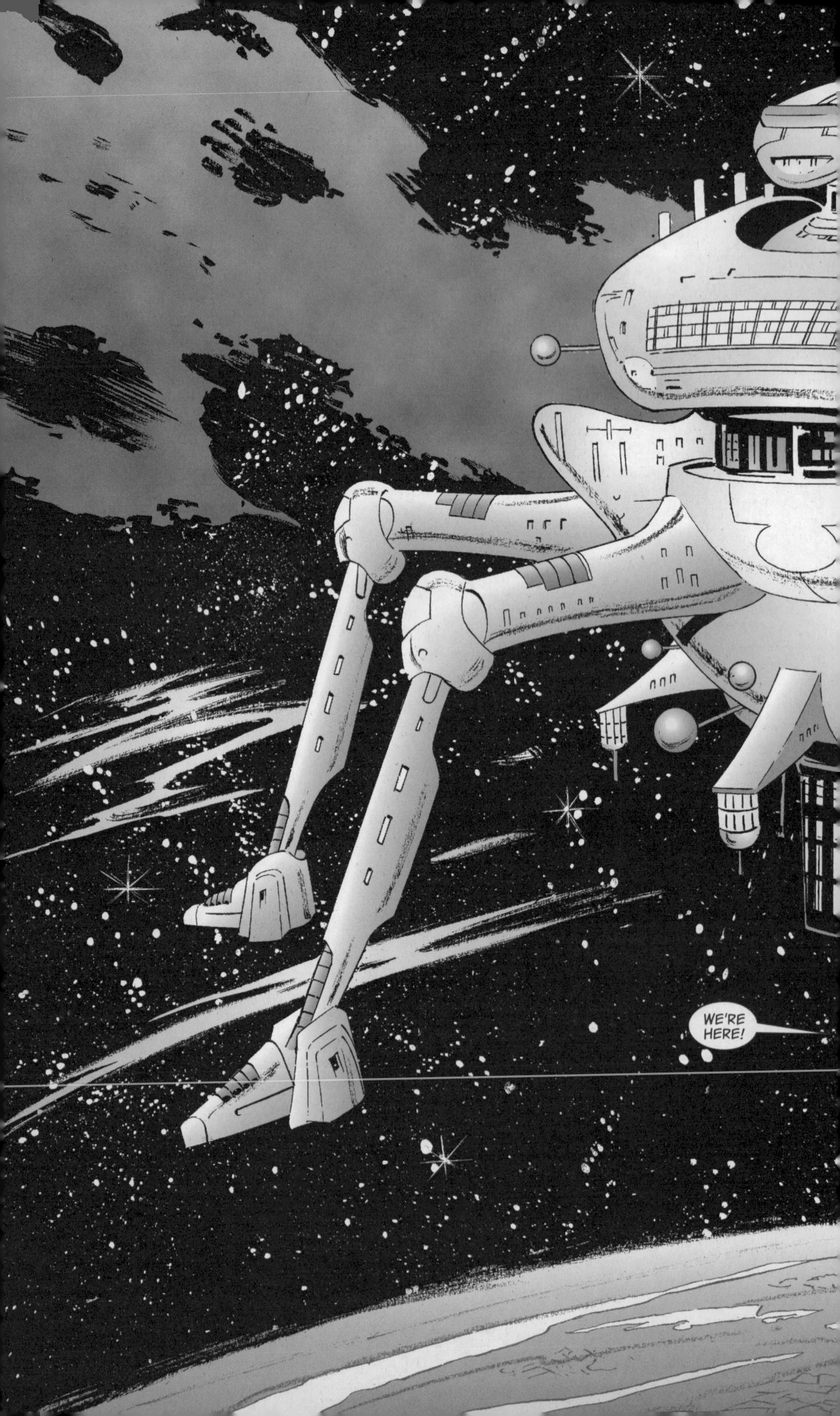
WE'RE HERE!

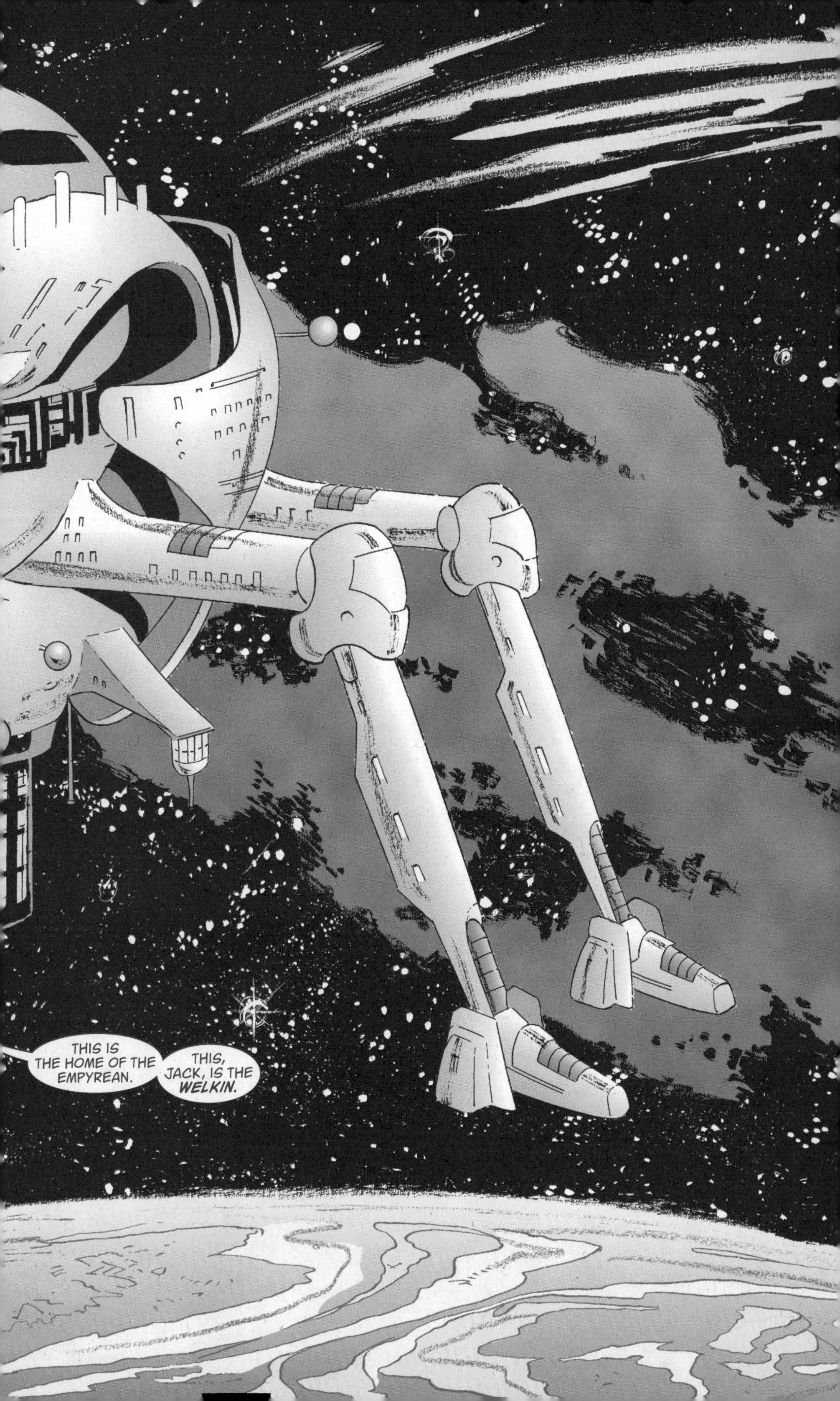
THIS IS THE HOME OF THE EMPYREAN.
THIS, JACK, IS THE WELKIN.

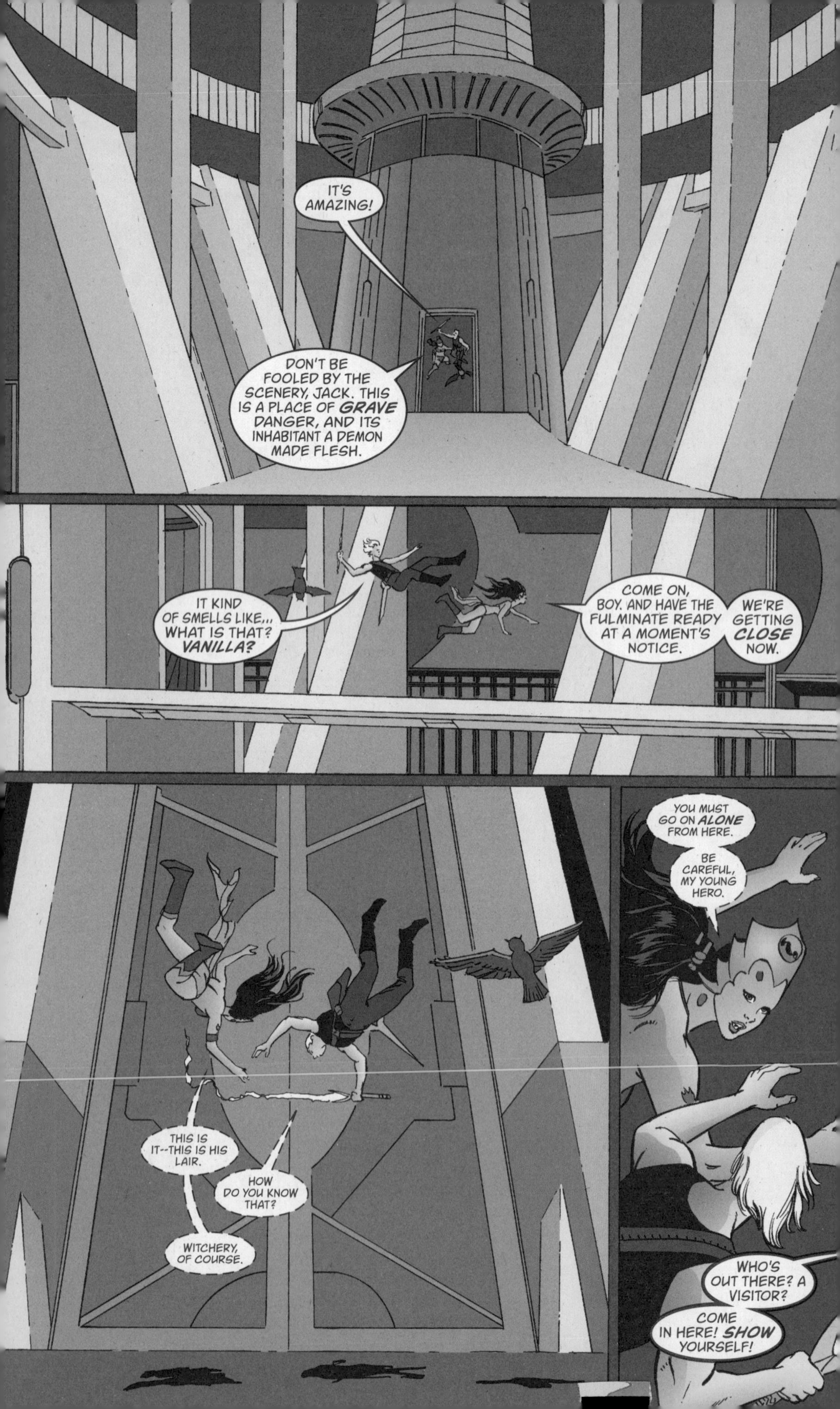
IT'S AMAZING!
DON'T BE FOOLED BY THE SCENERY, JACK. THIS IS A PLACE OF GRAVE DANGER, AND ITS INHABITANT A DEMON MADE FLESH.
IT KIND OF SMELLS LIKE... WHAT IS THAT? VANILLA?
COME ON, BOY. AND HAVE THE FULMINATE READY AT A MOMENT'S NOTICE.
WE'RE GETTING CLOSE NOW.
THIS IS IT--THIS IS HIS LAIR.
HOW DO YOU KNOW THAT?
WITCHERY, OF COURSE.
YOU MUST GO ON ALONE FROM HERE.
BE CAREFUL, MY YOUNG HERO.
WHO'S OUT THERE? A VISITOR?
COME IN HERE! SHOW YOURSELF!

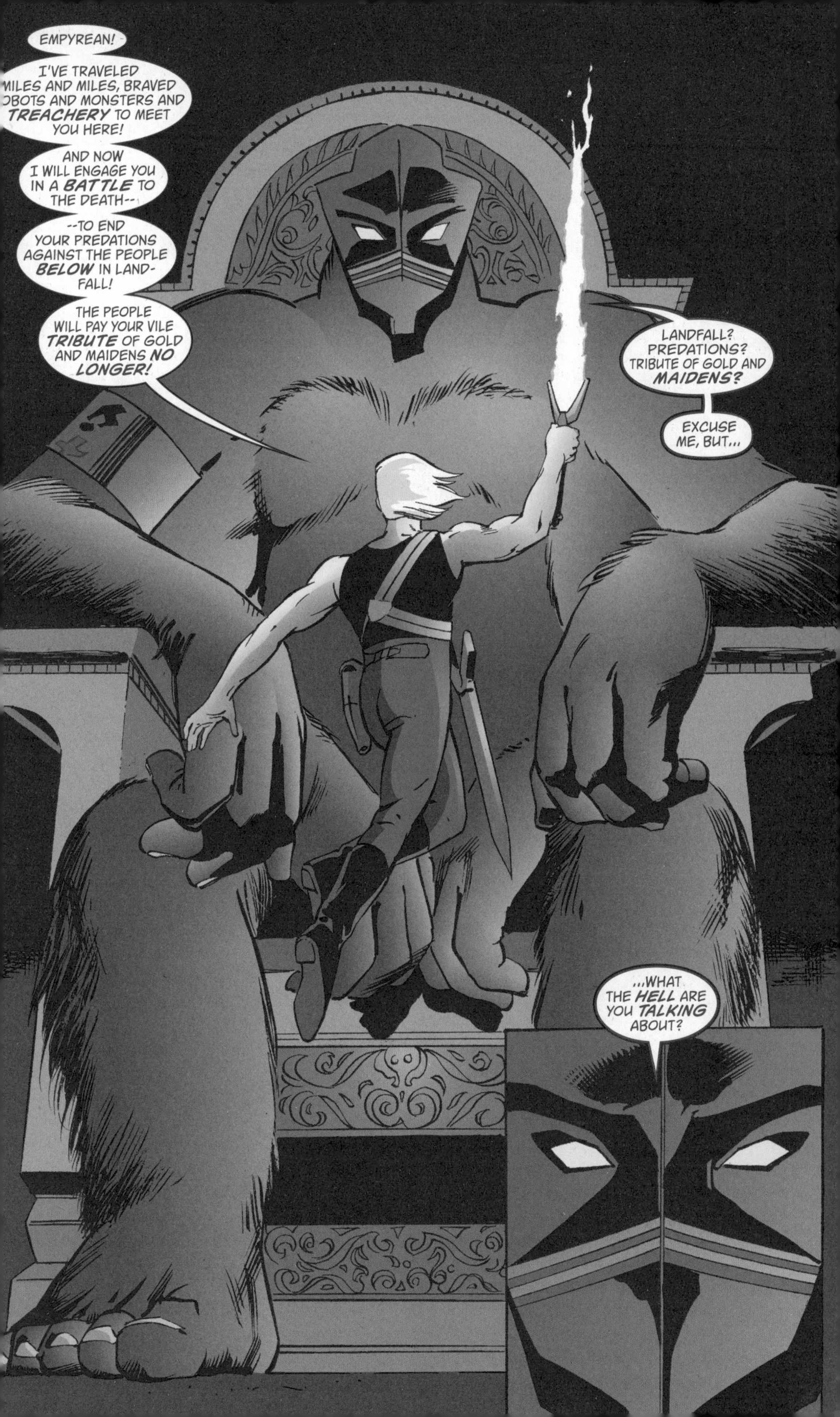
EMPYREAN!
I'VE TRAVELED MILES AND MILES, BRAVED ROBOTS AND MONSTERS AND TREACHERY TO MEET YOU HERE!
AND NOW I WILL ENGAGE YOU IN A BATTLE TO THE DEATH--
--TO END YOUR PREDATIONS AGAINST THE PEOPLE BELOW IN LAND-FALL!
THE PEOPLE WILL PAY YOUR VILE TRIBUTE OF GOLD AND MAIDENS NO LONGER!
LANDFALL? PREDATIONS? TRIBUTE OF GOLD AND MAIDENS?
EXCUSE ME, BUT...
...WHAT THE HELL ARE YOU TALKING ABOUT?

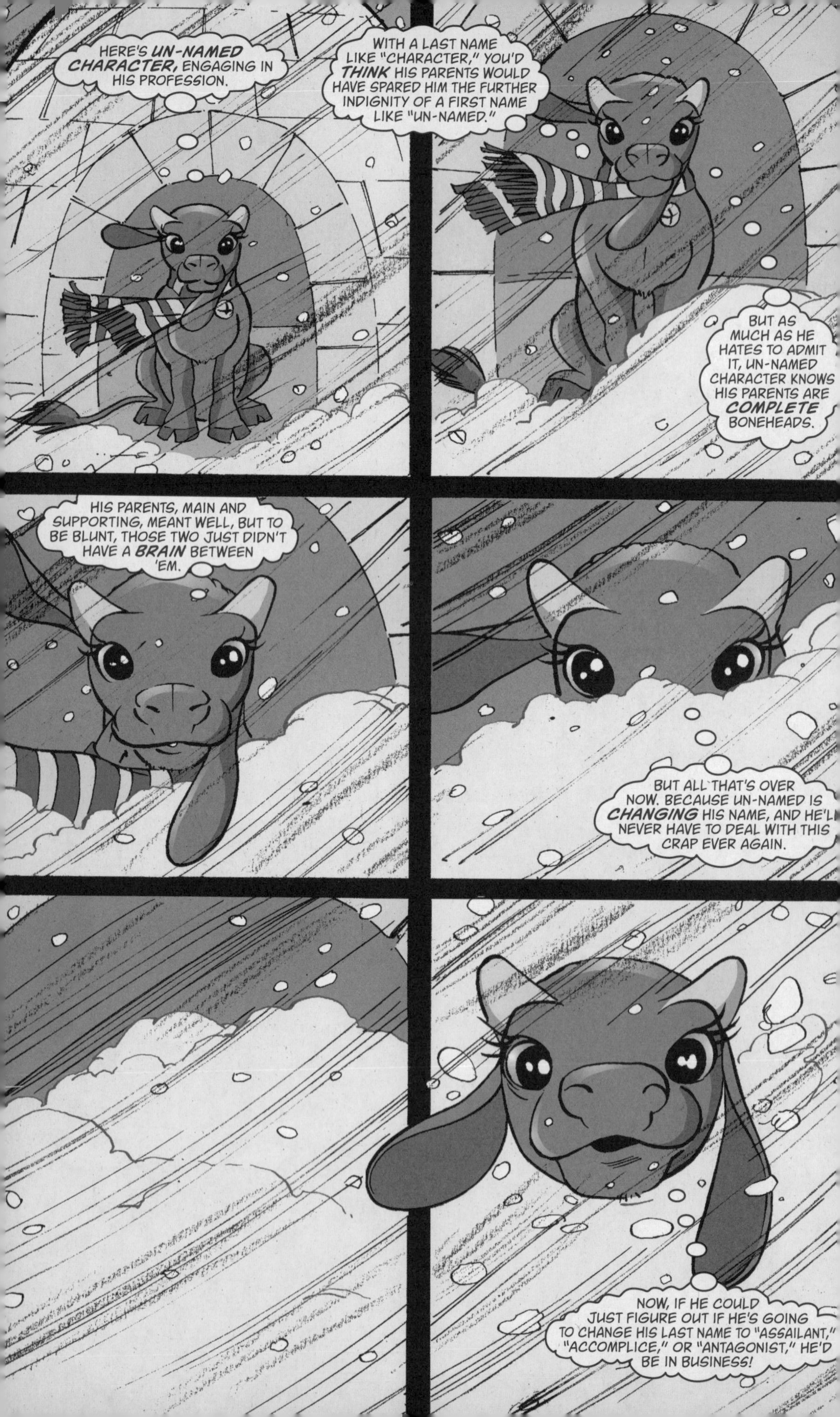
HERE'S UN-NAMED CHARACTER, ENGAGING IN HIS PROFESSION.
WITH A LAST NAME LIKE "CHARACTER," YOU'D THINK HIS PARENTS WOULD HAVE SPARED HIM THE FURTHER INDIGNITY OF A FIRST NAME LIKE "UN-NAMED."
BUT AS MUCH AS HE HATES TO ADMIT IT, UN-NAMED CHARACTER KNOWS HIS PARENTS ARE COMPLETE BONEHEADS.
HIS PARENTS, MAIN AND SUPPORTING, MEANT WELL, BUT TO BE BLUNT, THOSE TWO JUST DIDN'T HAVE A BRAIN BETWEEN 'EM.
BUT ALL THAT'S OVER NOW. BECAUSE UN-NAMED IS CHANGING HIS NAME, AND HE'LL NEVER HAVE TO DEAL WITH THIS CRAP EVER AGAIN.
NOW, IF HE COULD JUST FIGURE OUT IF HE'S GOING TO CHANGE HIS LAST NAME TO "ASSAILANT," "ACCOMPLICE," OR "ANTAGONIST," HE'D BE IN BUSINESS!

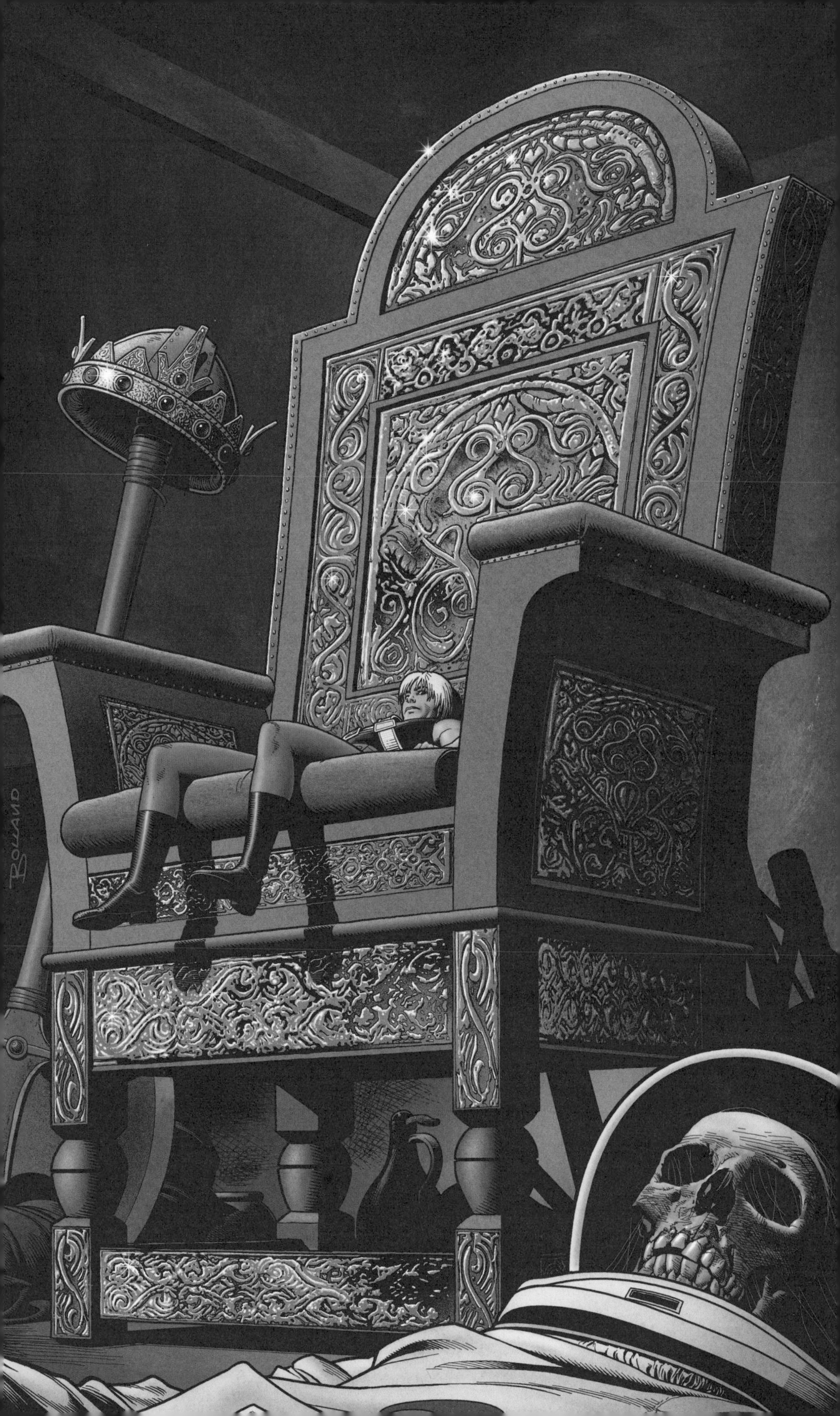
BOLLAND

"I'm not sure I've ever
been this angry. I wonder
what I'll do now?"

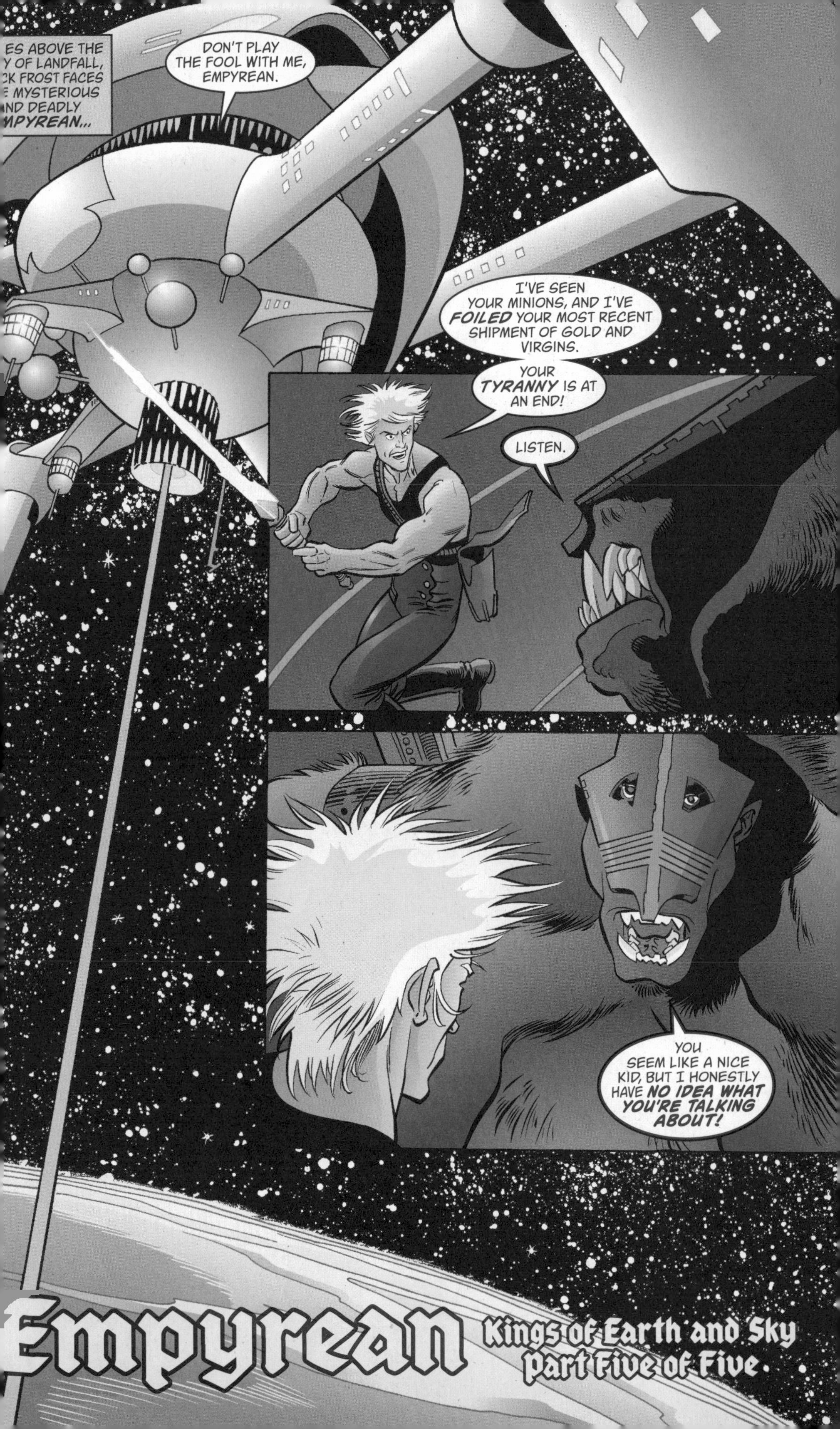
ES ABOVE THE Y OF LANDFALL, CK FROST FACES E MYSTERIOUS ND DEADLY MPYREAN...
DON'T PLAY THE FOOL WITH ME, EMPYREAN.
I'VE SEEN YOUR MINIONS, AND I'VE FOILED YOUR MOST RECENT SHIPMENT OF GOLD AND VIRGINS.
YOUR TYRANNY IS AT AN END!
LISTEN.
YOU SEEM LIKE A NICE KID, BUT I HONESTLY HAVE NO IDEA WHAT YOU'RE TALKING ABOUT!
Empyrean
Kings of Earth and Sky
part Five of Five

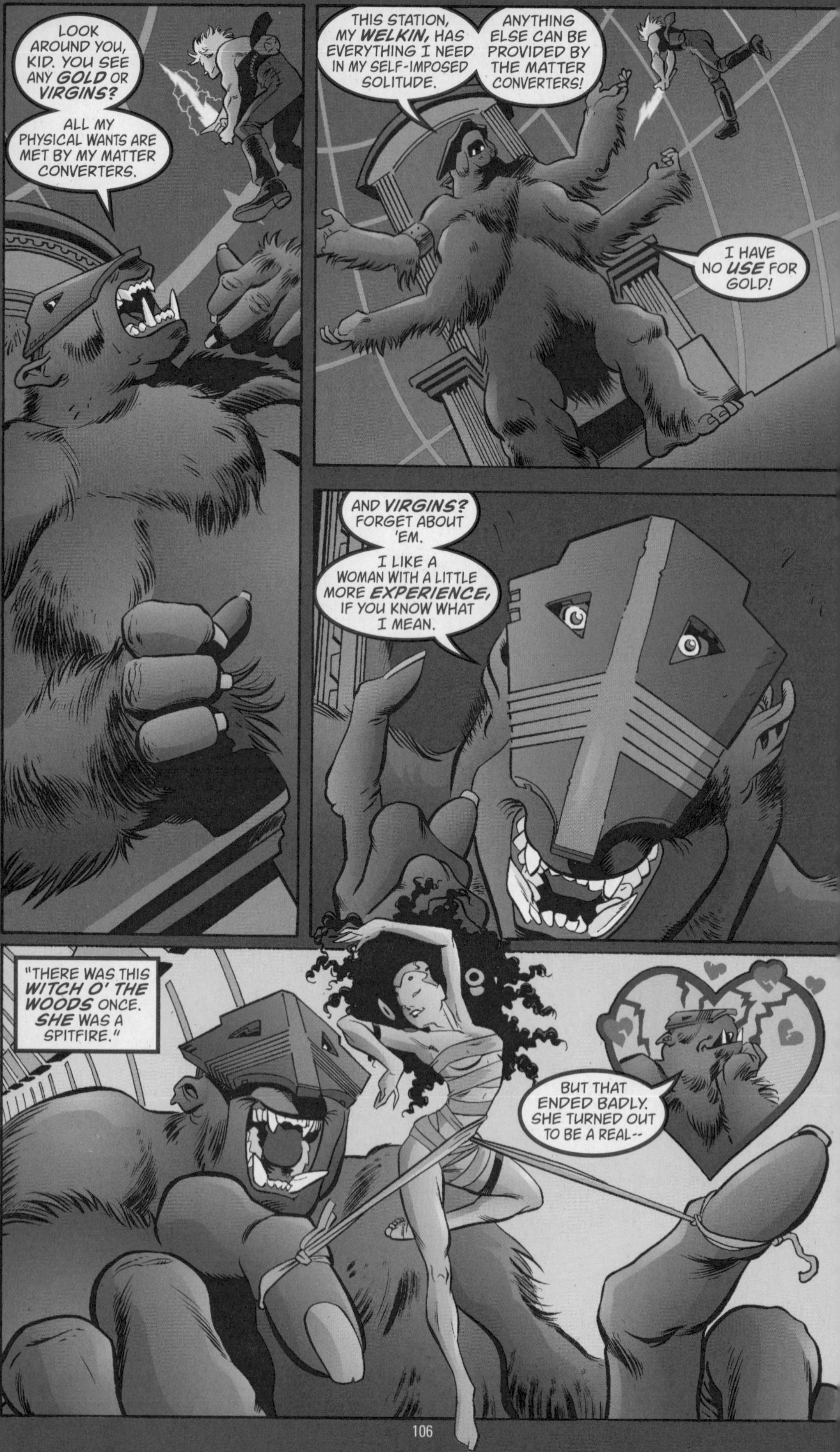
LOOK AROUND YOU, KID. YOU SEE ANY GOLD OR VIRGINS?
ALL MY PHYSICAL WANTS ARE MET BY MY MATTER CONVERTERS.
THIS STATION, MY WELKIN, HAS EVERYTHING I NEED IN MY SELF-IMPOSED SOLITUDE.
ANYTHING ELSE CAN BE PROVIDED BY THE MATTER CONVERTERS!
I HAVE NO USE FOR GOLD!
AND VIRGINS? FORGET ABOUT 'EM.
I LIKE A WOMAN WITH A LITTLE MORE EXPERIENCE, IF YOU KNOW WHAT I MEAN.
"THERE WAS THIS WITCH O' THE WOODS ONCE. SHE WAS A SPITFIRE."
BUT THAT ENDED BADLY. SHE TURNED OUT TO BE A REAL--

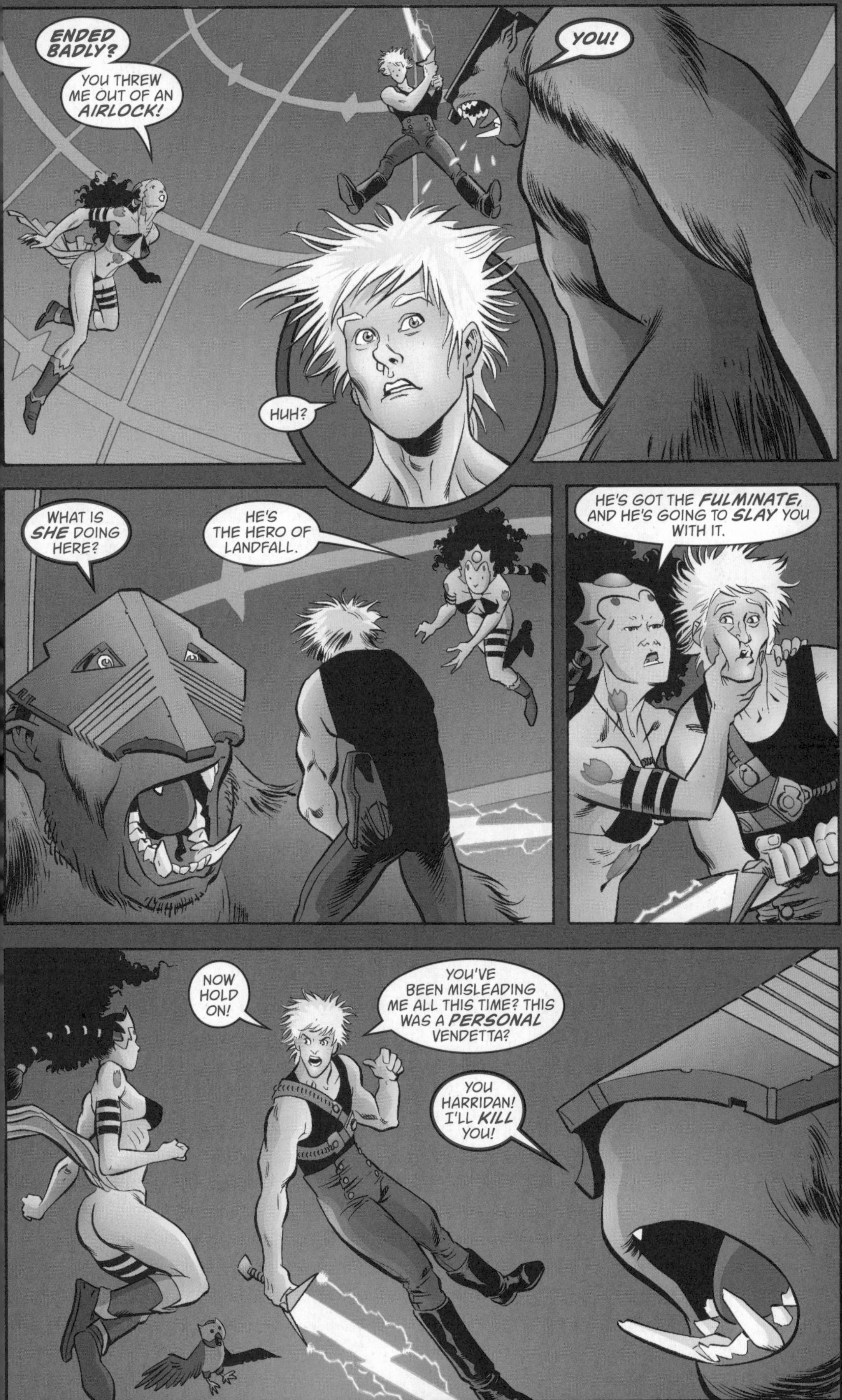
ENDED BADLY?
YOU THREW ME OUT OF AN AIRLOCK!
YOU!
HUH?
WHAT IS SHE DOING HERE?
HE'S THE HERO OF LANDFALL.
HE'S GOT THE FULMINATE, AND HE'S GOING TO SLAY YOU WITH IT.
NOW HOLD ON!
YOU'VE BEEN MISLEADING ME ALL THIS TIME? THIS WAS A PERSONAL VENDETTA?
YOU HARRIDAN! I'LL KILL YOU!

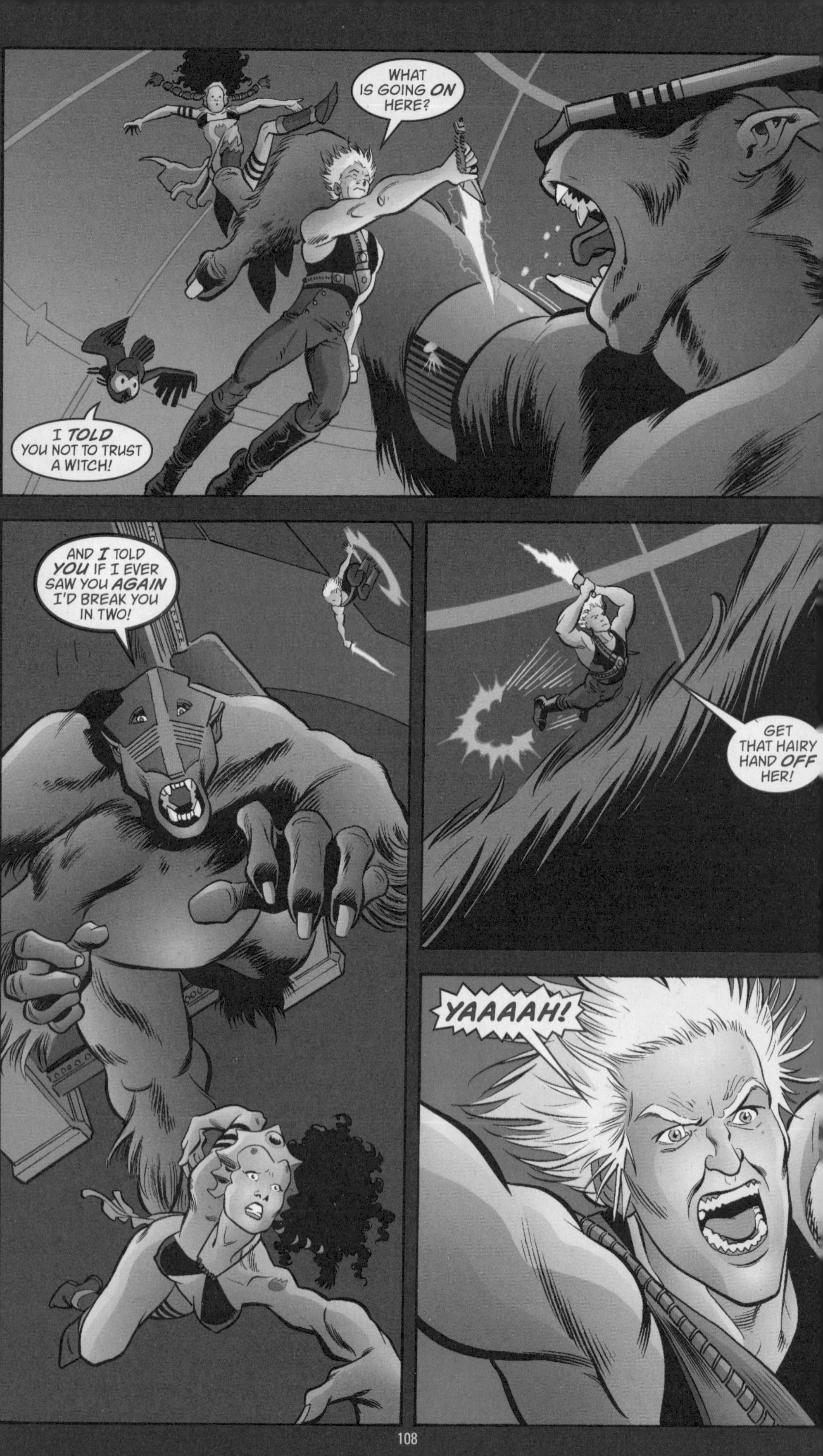
WHAT IS GOING ON HERE?
I TOLD YOU NOT TO TRUST A WITCH!
AND I TOLD YOU IF I EVER SAW YOU AGAIN I'D BREAK YOU IN TWO!
GET THAT HAIRY HAND OFF HER!
YAAAAH!

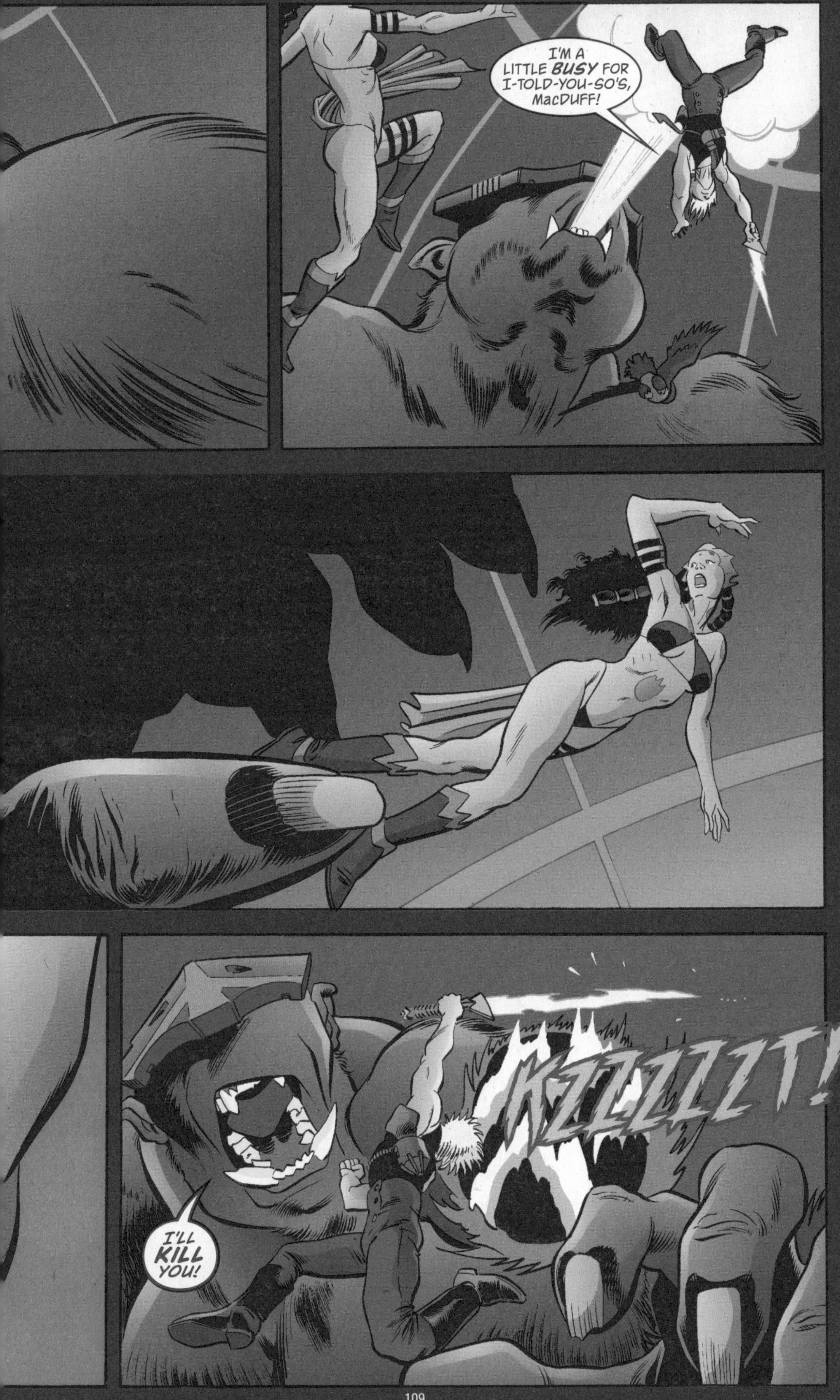
I'M A LITTLE BUSY FOR I-TOLD-YOU-SO'S, MacDUFF!
KZZZZZZT!
I'LL KILL YOU!

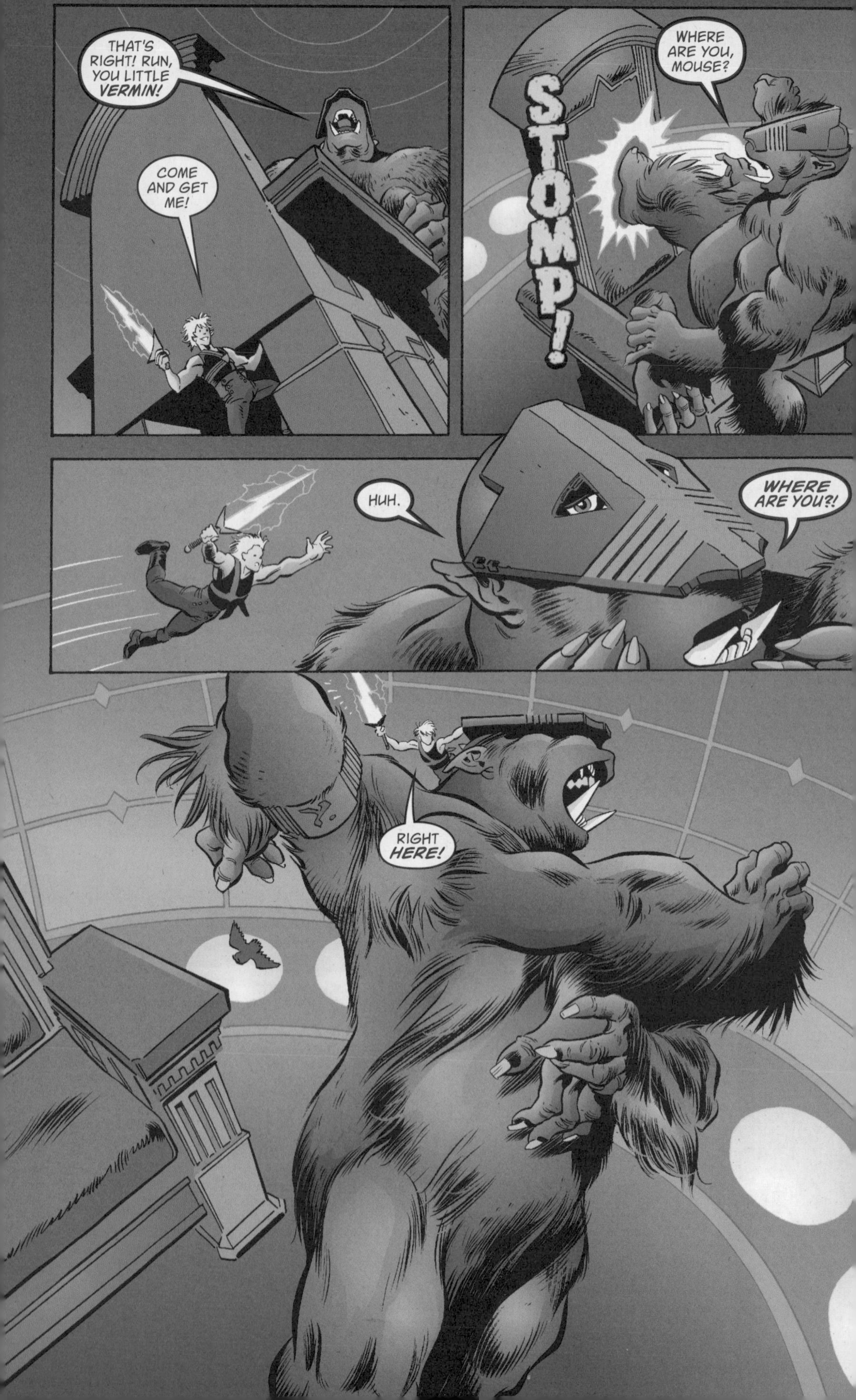

THAT'S RIGHT! RUN, YOU LITTLE VERMIN!
COME AND GET ME!
WHERE ARE YOU, MOUSE?
STOMP!
HUH.
WHERE ARE YOU?!
RIGHT HERE!

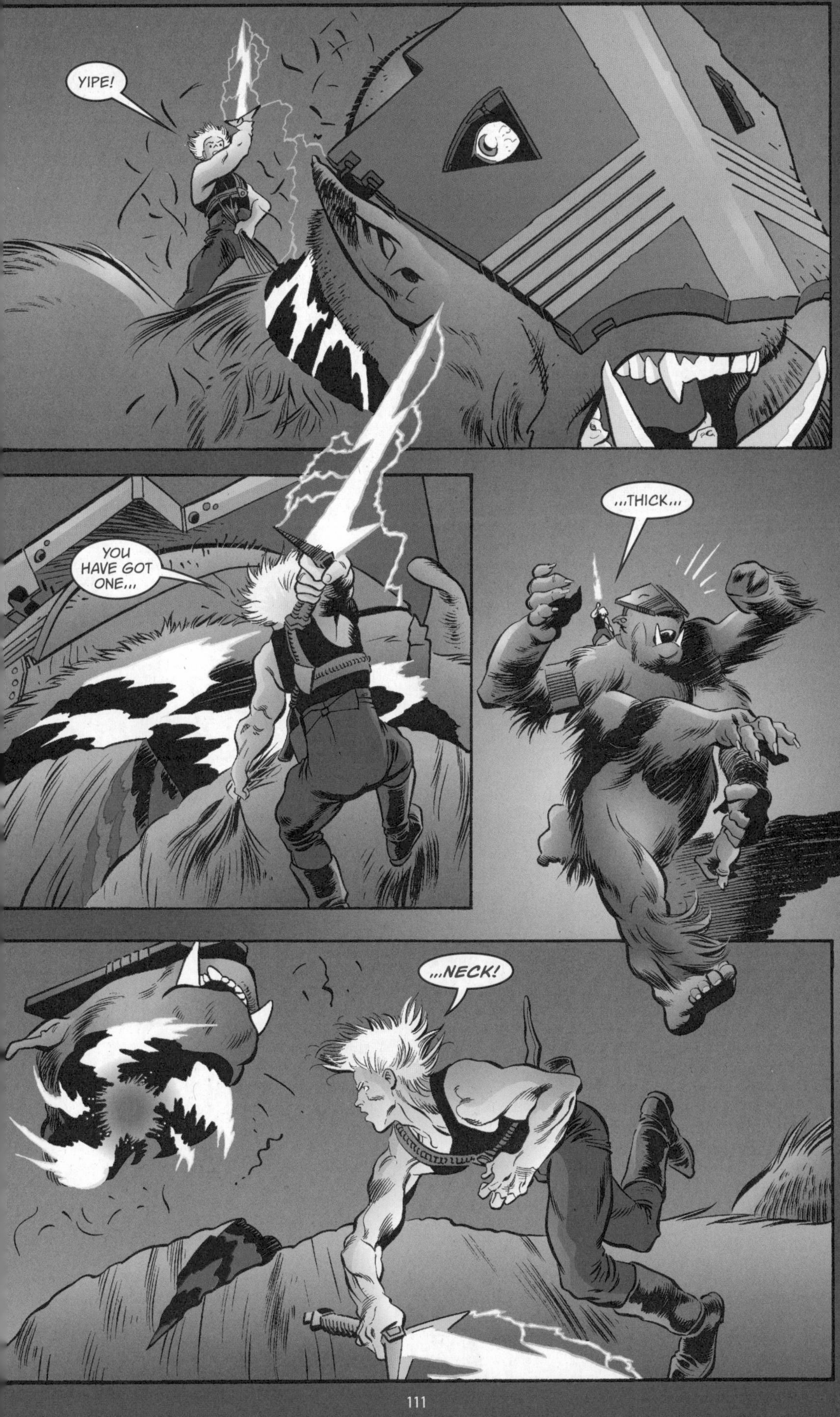
YIPE!
YOU HAVE GOT ONE...
...THICK...
...NECK!

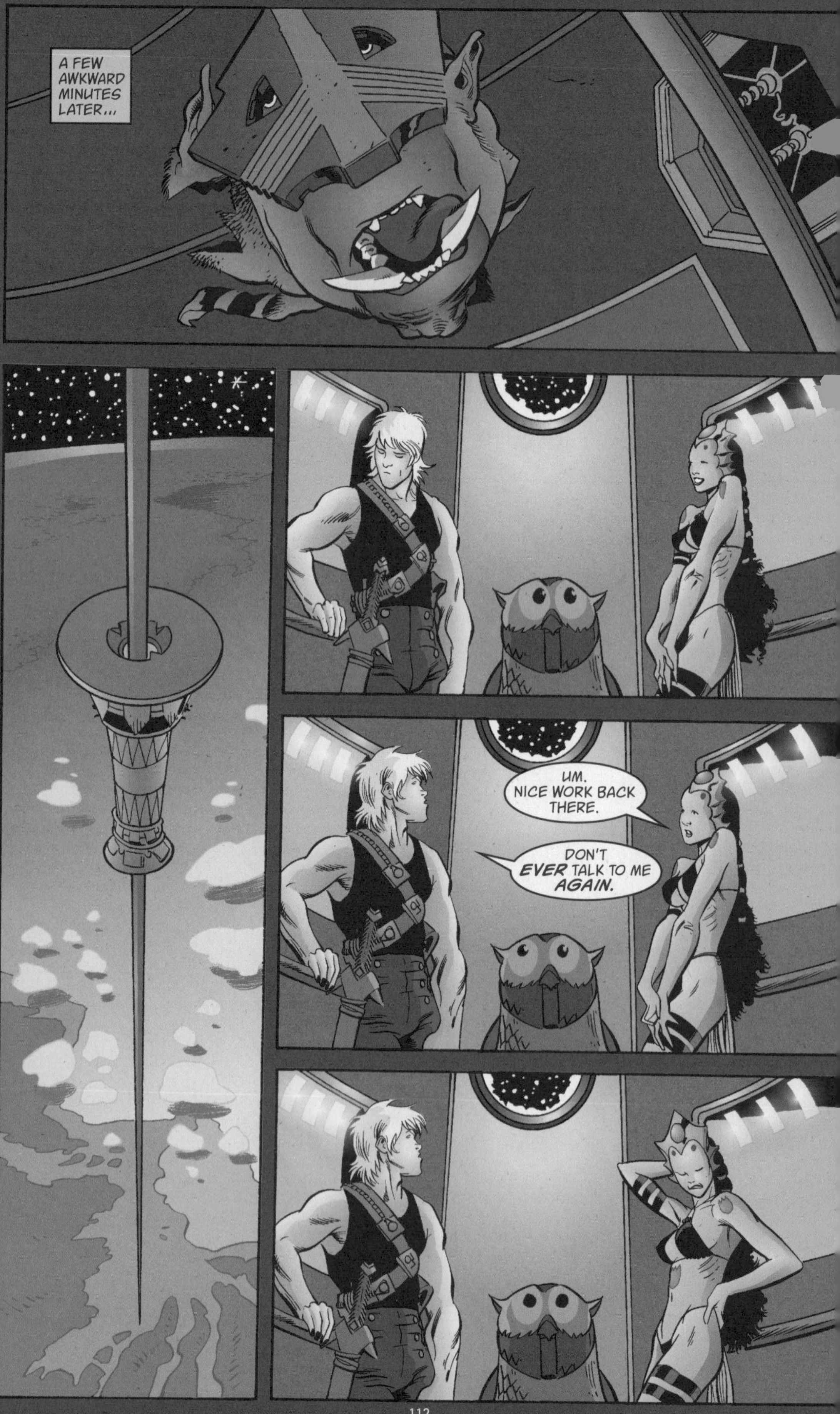
A FEW AWKWARD MINUTES LATER...
UM. NICE WORK BACK THERE.
DON'T EVER TALK TO ME AGAIN.

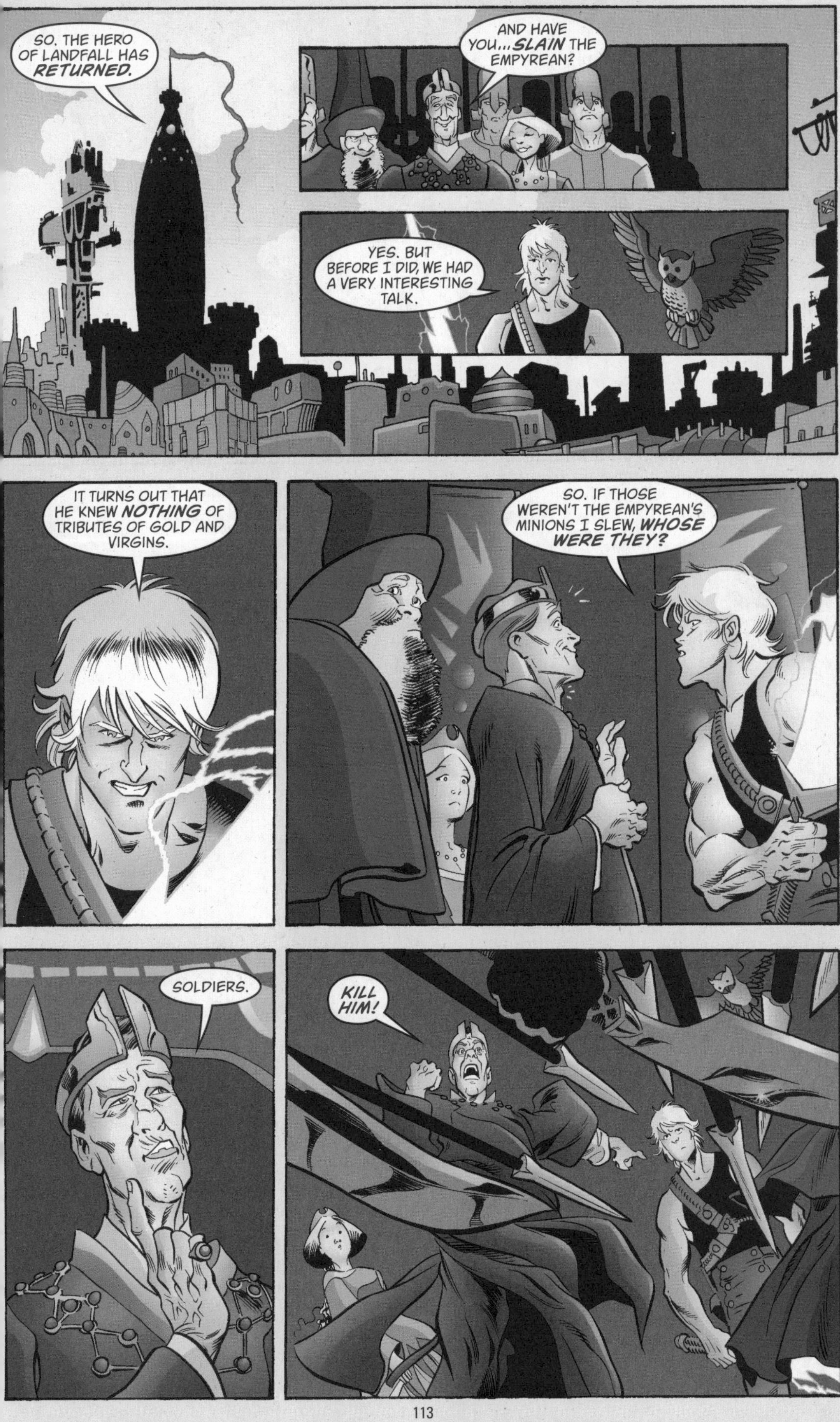
SO. THE HERO OF LANDFALL HAS RETURNED.
AND HAVE YOU... SLAIN THE EMPYREAN?
YES. BUT BEFORE I DID, WE HAD A VERY INTERESTING TALK.
IT TURNS OUT THAT HE KNEW NOTHING OF TRIBUTES OF GOLD AND VIRGINS.
SO. IF THOSE WEREN'T THE EMPYREAN'S MINIONS I SLEW, WHOSE WERE THEY?
SOLDIERS.
KILL HIM!

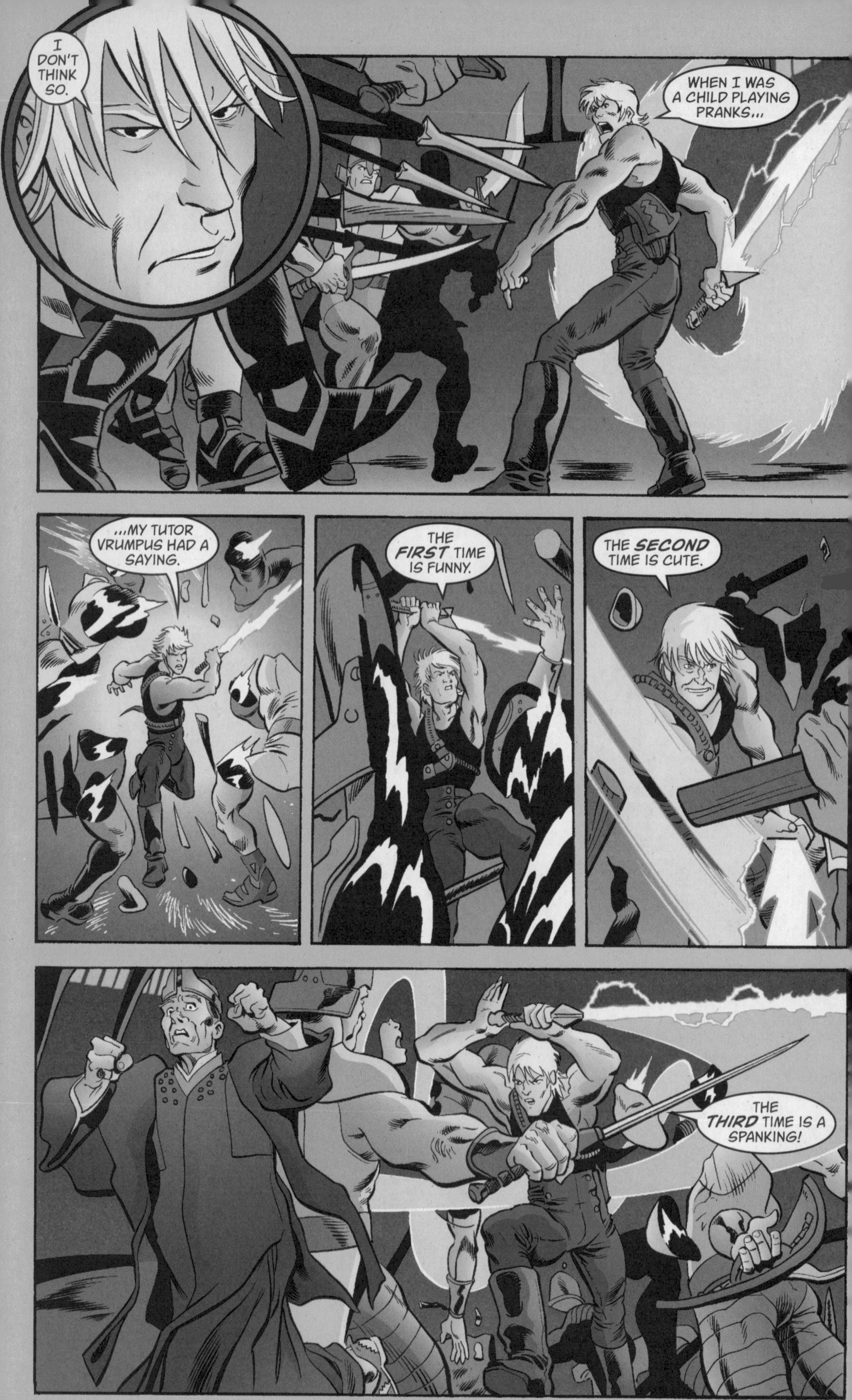
I DON'T THINK SO.
WHEN I WAS A CHILD PLAYING PRANKS...
...MY TUTOR VRUMPUS HAD A SAYING.
THE FIRST TIME IS FUNNY.
THE SECOND TIME IS CUTE.
THE THIRD TIME IS A SPANKING!

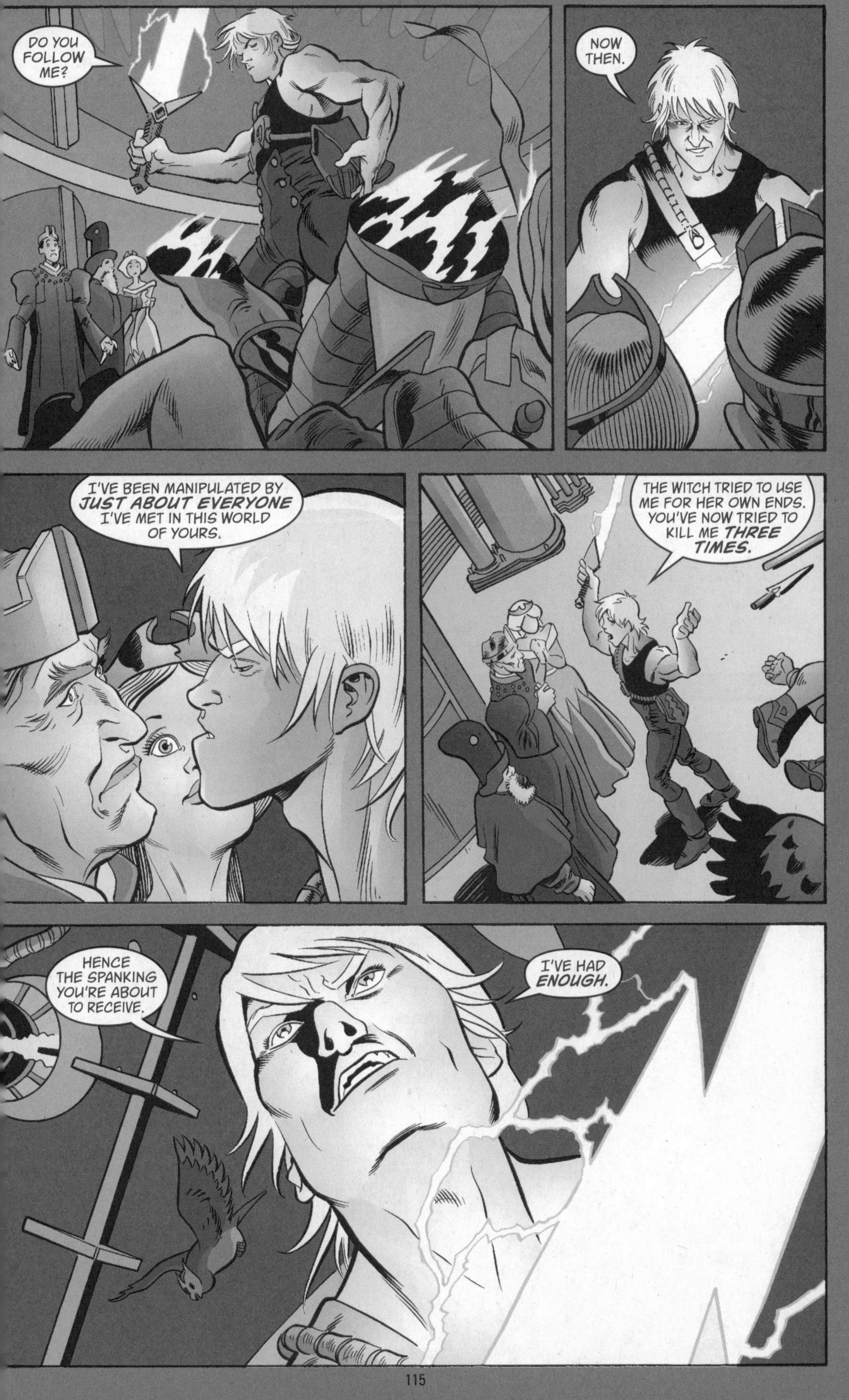

DO YOU FOLLOW ME?
NOW THEN.
I'VE BEEN MANIPULATED BY ***JUST ABOUT EVERYONE*** I'VE MET IN THIS WORLD OF YOURS.
THE WITCH TRIED TO USE ME FOR HER OWN ENDS. YOU'VE NOW TRIED TO KILL ME ***THREE TIMES.***
HENCE THE SPANKING YOU'RE ABOUT TO RECEIVE.
I'VE HAD ***ENOUGH.***

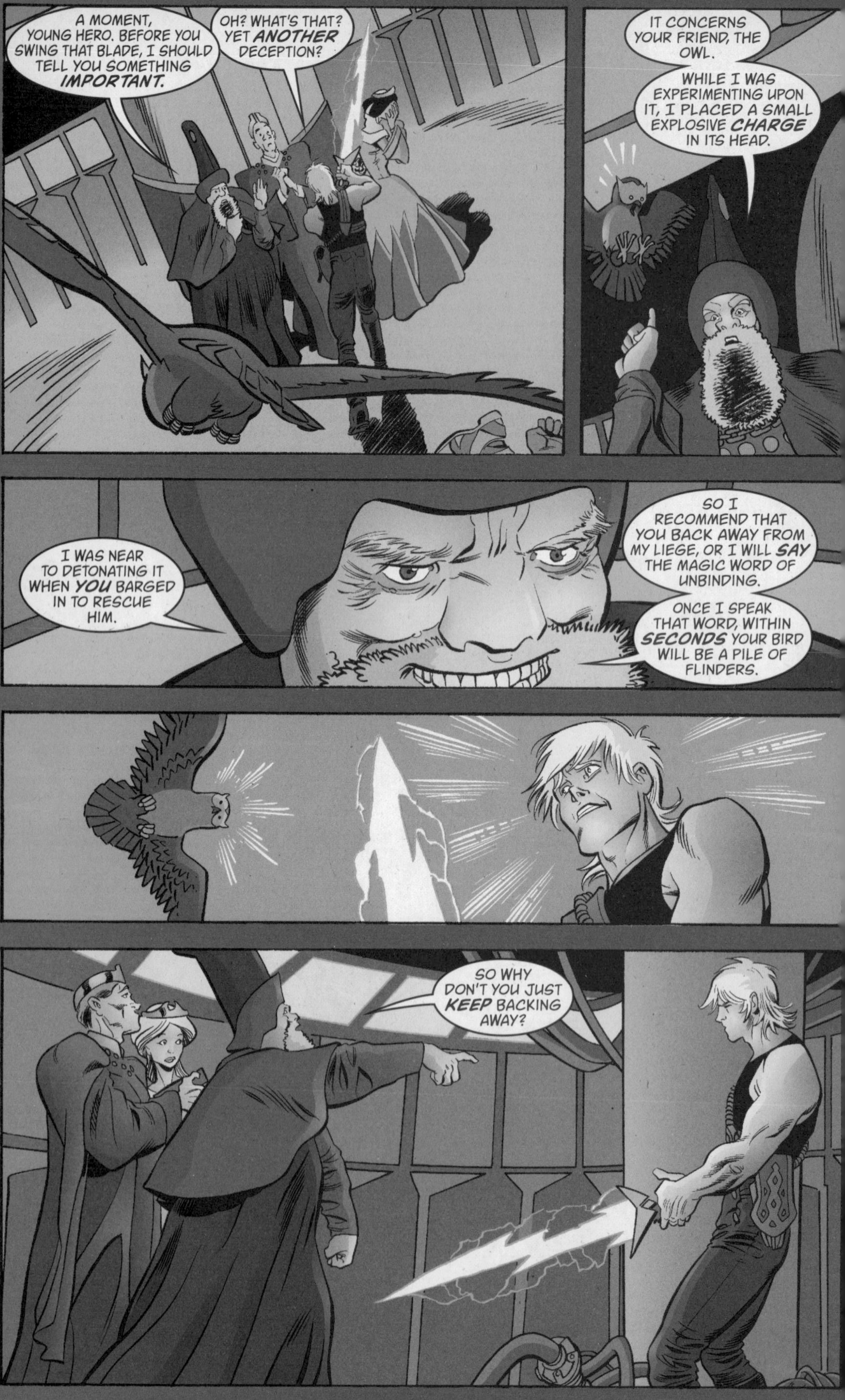

A MOMENT, YOUNG HERO. BEFORE YOU SWING THAT BLADE, I SHOULD TELL YOU SOMETHING IMPORTANT.
OH? WHAT'S THAT? YET ANOTHER DECEPTION?
IT CONCERNS YOUR FRIEND, THE OWL.
WHILE I WAS EXPERIMENTING UPON IT, I PLACED A SMALL EXPLOSIVE CHARGE IN ITS HEAD.
I WAS NEAR TO DETONATING IT WHEN YOU BARGED IN TO RESCUE HIM.
SO I RECOMMEND THAT YOU BACK AWAY FROM MY LIEGE, OR I WILL SAY THE MAGIC WORD OF UNBINDING.
ONCE I SPEAK THAT WORD, WITHIN SECONDS YOUR BIRD WILL BE A PILE OF FLINDERS.
SO WHY DON'T YOU JUST KEEP BACKING AWAY?

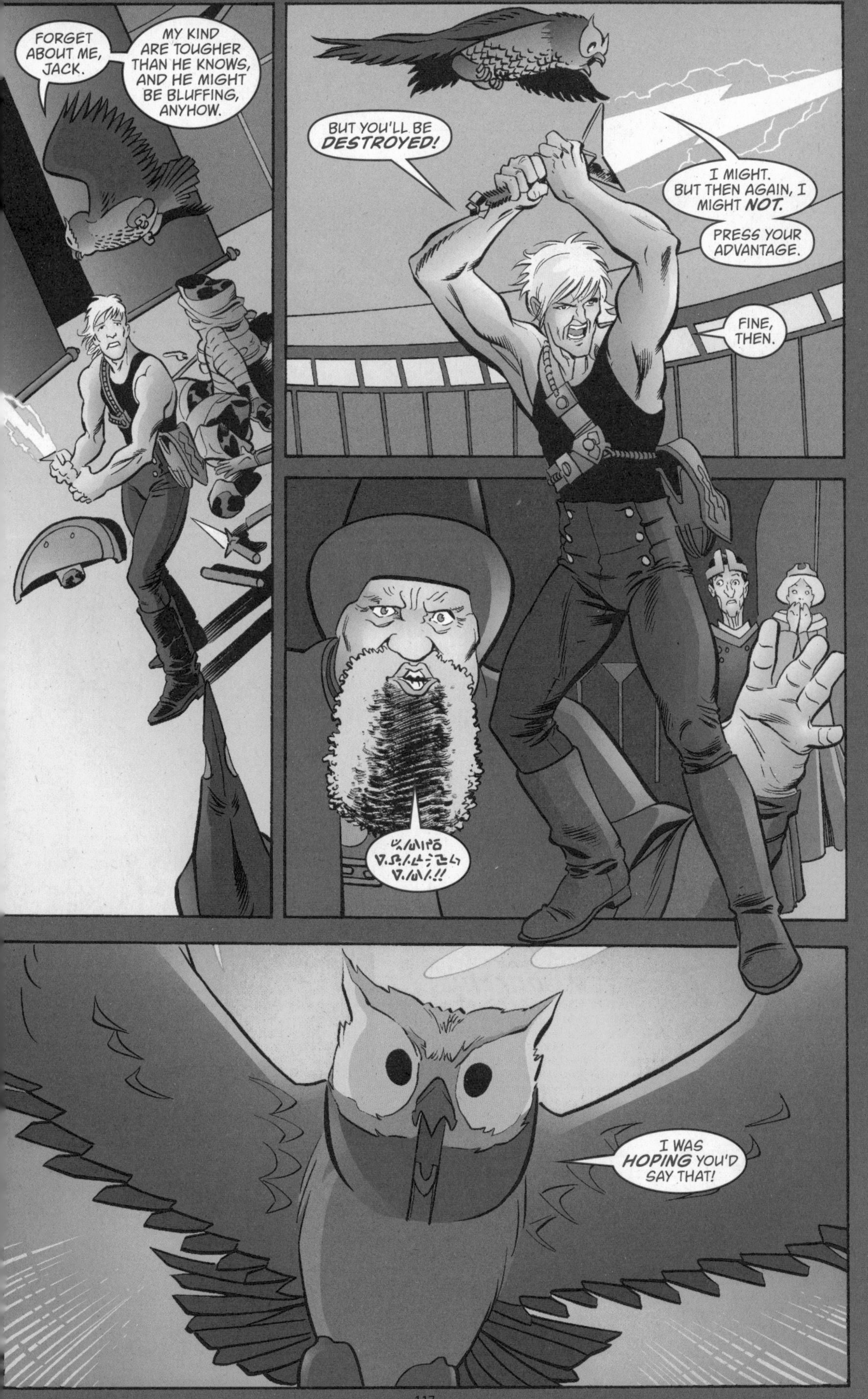

FORGET ABOUT ME, JACK.
MY KIND ARE TOUGHER THAN HE KNOWS, AND HE MIGHT BE BLUFFING, ANYHOW.
BUT YOU'LL BE DESTROYED!
I MIGHT. BUT THEN AGAIN, I MIGHT NOT.
PRESS YOUR ADVANTAGE.
FINE, THEN.
I WAS HOPING YOU'D SAY THAT!

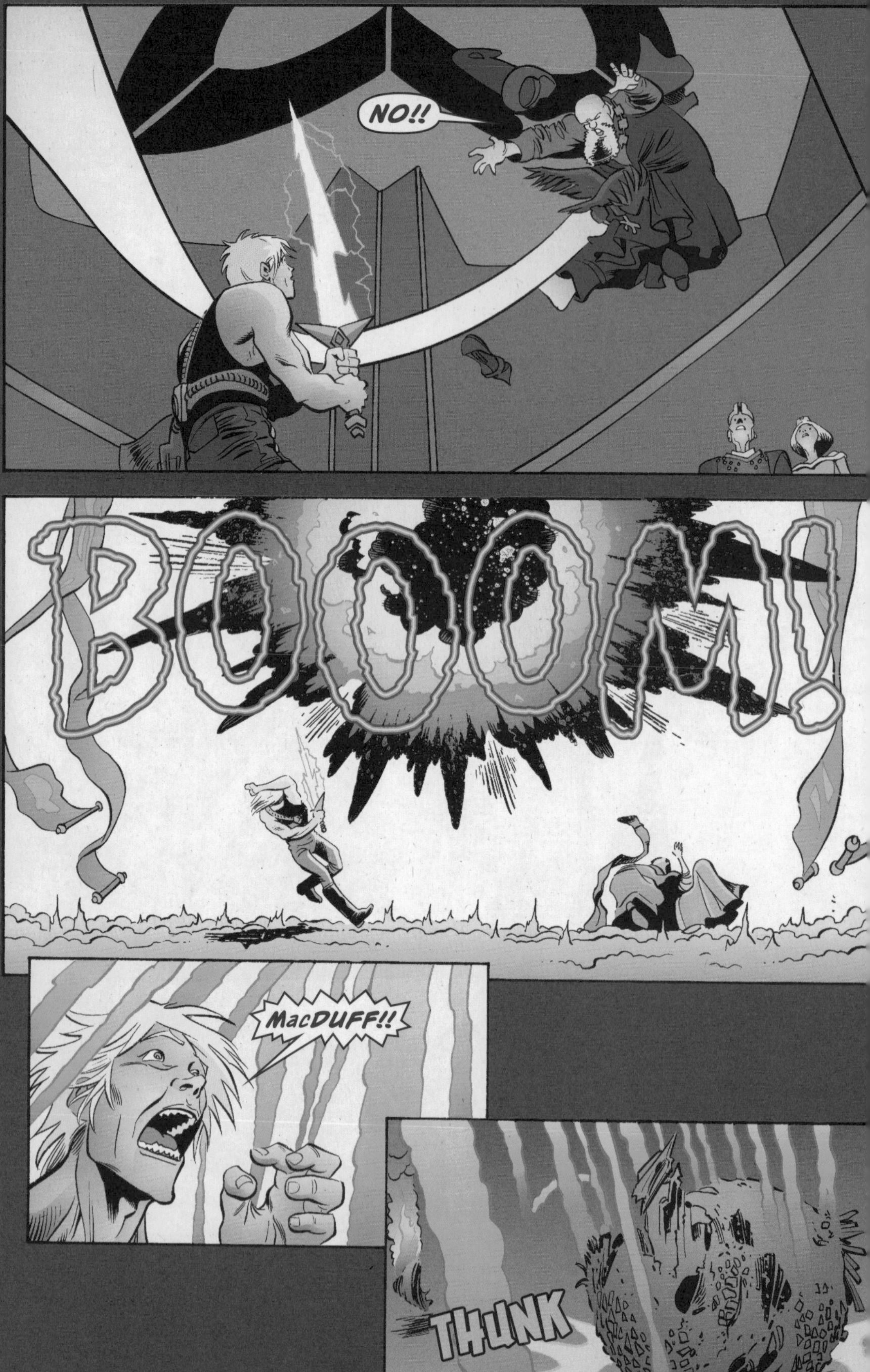
NO!!
BOOOM!
MacDUFF!!
THUNK

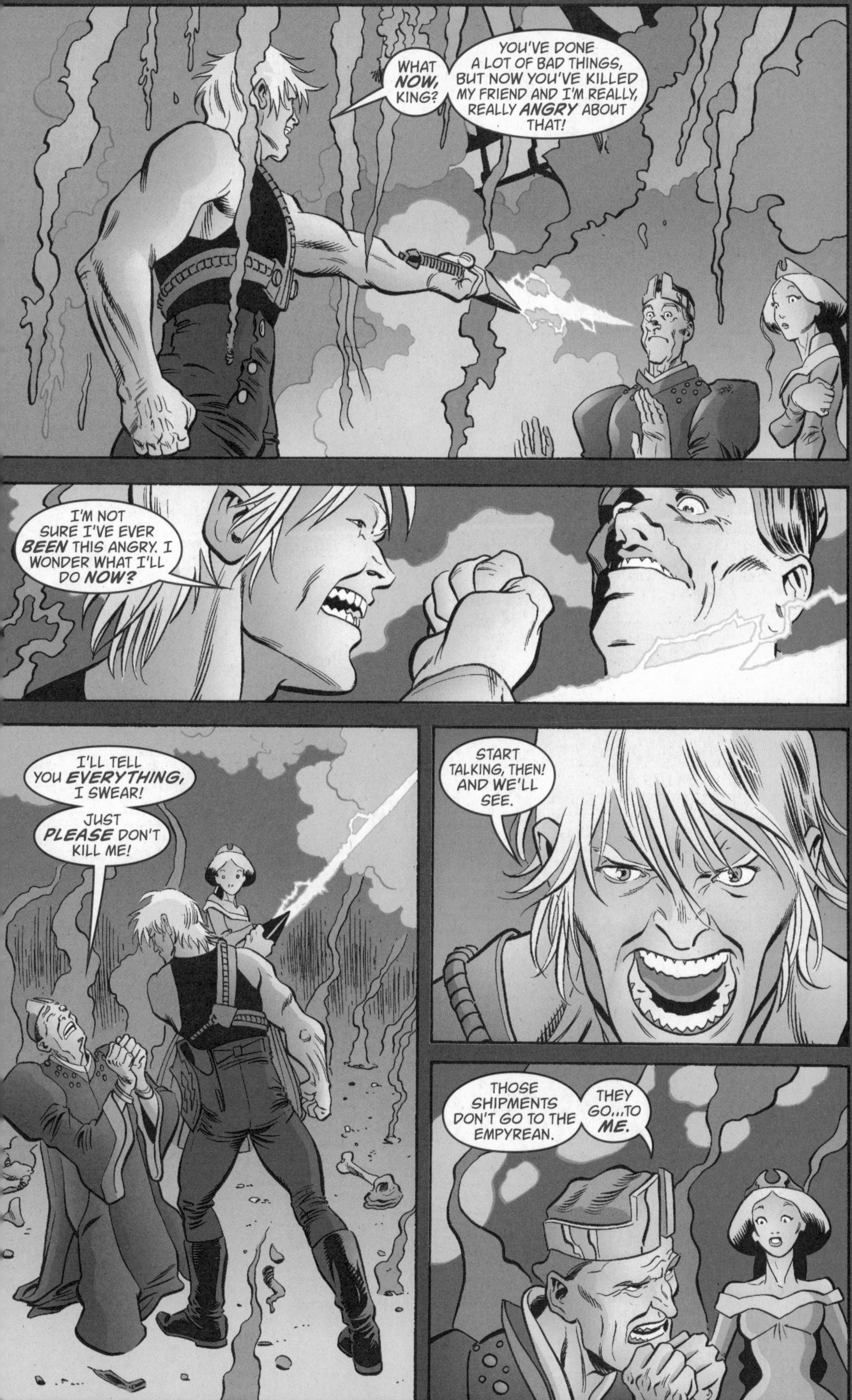

WHAT NOW, KING?
YOU'VE DONE A LOT OF BAD THINGS, BUT NOW YOU'VE KILLED MY FRIEND AND I'M REALLY, REALLY ANGRY ABOUT THAT!
I'M NOT SURE I'VE EVER BEEN THIS ANGRY. I WONDER WHAT I'LL DO NOW?
I'LL TELL YOU EVERYTHING, I SWEAR!
JUST PLEASE DON'T KILL ME!
START TALKING, THEN! AND WE'LL SEE.
THOSE SHIPMENTS DON'T GO TO THE EMPYREAN.
THEY GO...TO ME.

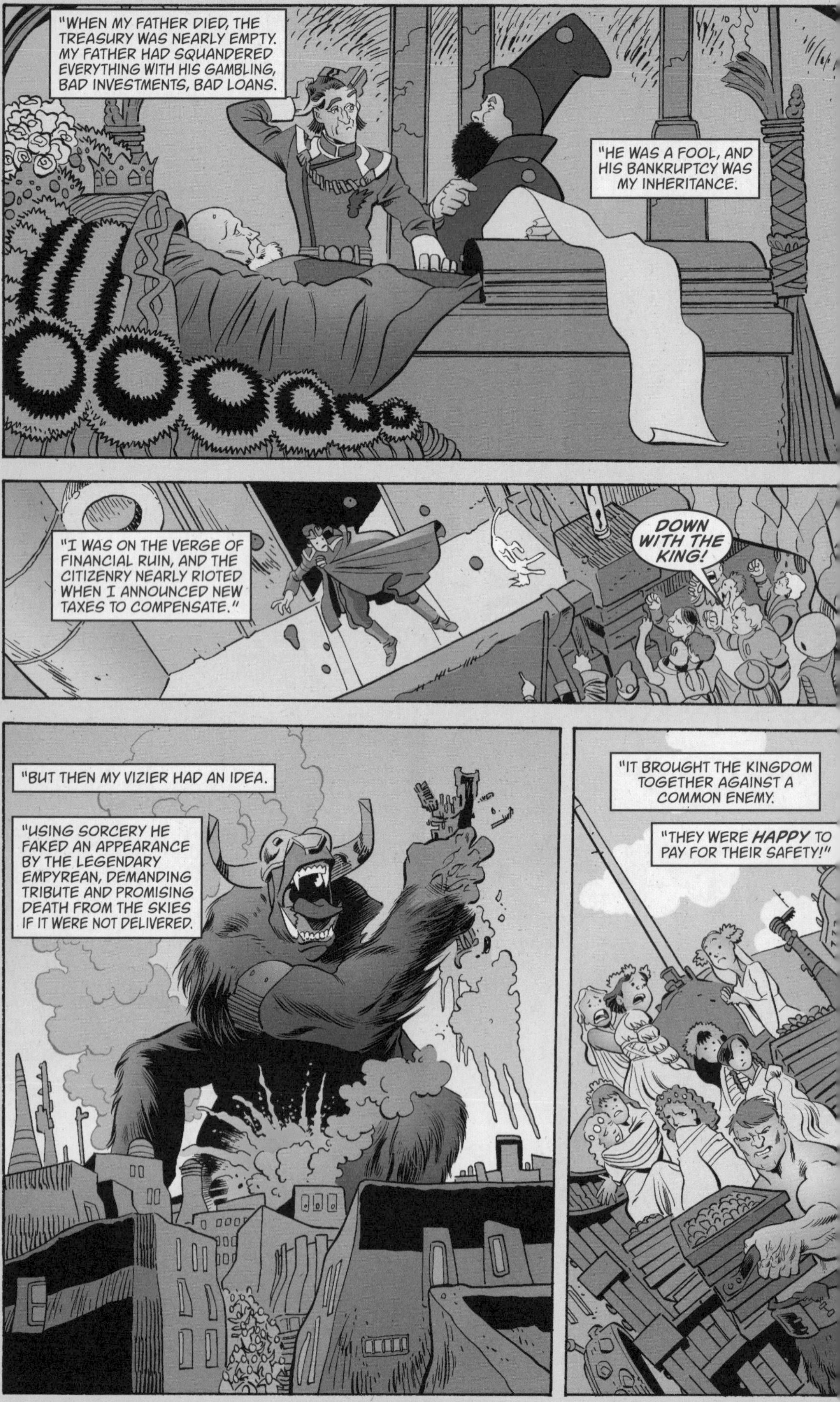
"WHEN MY FATHER DIED, THE TREASURY WAS NEARLY EMPTY. MY FATHER HAD SQUANDERED EVERYTHING WITH HIS GAMBLING, BAD INVESTMENTS, BAD LOANS.
"HE WAS A FOOL, AND HIS BANKRUPTCY WAS MY INHERITANCE.
"I WAS ON THE VERGE OF FINANCIAL RUIN, AND THE CITIZENRY NEARLY RIOTED WHEN I ANNOUNCED NEW TAXES TO COMPENSATE."
DOWN WITH THE KING!
"BUT THEN MY VIZIER HAD AN IDEA.
"USING SORCERY HE FAKED AN APPEARANCE BY THE LEGENDARY EMPYREAN, DEMANDING TRIBUTE AND PROMISING DEATH FROM THE SKIES IF IT WERE NOT DELIVERED.
"IT BROUGHT THE KINGDOM TOGETHER AGAINST A COMMON ENEMY.
"THEY WERE *HAPPY* TO PAY FOR THEIR SAFETY!"

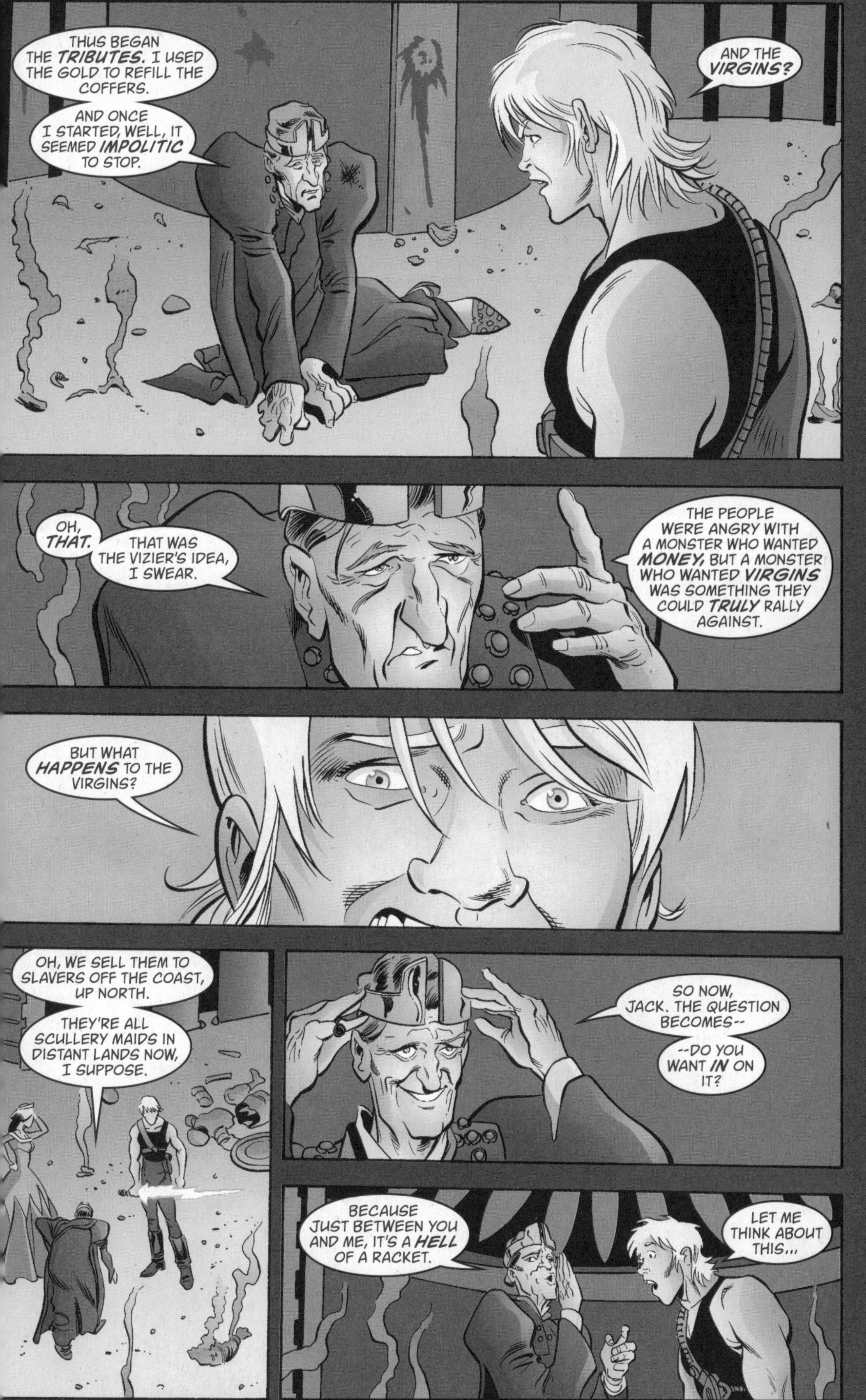
THUS BEGAN THE TRIBUTES. I USED THE GOLD TO REFILL THE COFFERS.
AND ONCE I STARTED, WELL, IT SEEMED IMPOLITIC TO STOP.
AND THE VIRGINS?
OH, THAT.
THAT WAS THE VIZIER'S IDEA, I SWEAR.
THE PEOPLE WERE ANGRY WITH A MONSTER WHO WANTED MONEY, BUT A MONSTER WHO WANTED VIRGINS WAS SOMETHING THEY COULD TRULY RALLY AGAINST.
BUT WHAT HAPPENS TO THE VIRGINS?
OH, WE SELL THEM TO SLAVERS OFF THE COAST, UP NORTH.
THEY'RE ALL SCULLERY MAIDS IN DISTANT LANDS NOW, I SUPPOSE.
SO NOW, JACK. THE QUESTION BECOMES--
--DO YOU WANT IN ON IT?
BECAUSE JUST BETWEEN YOU AND ME, IT'S A HELL OF A RACKET.
LET ME THINK ABOUT THIS...

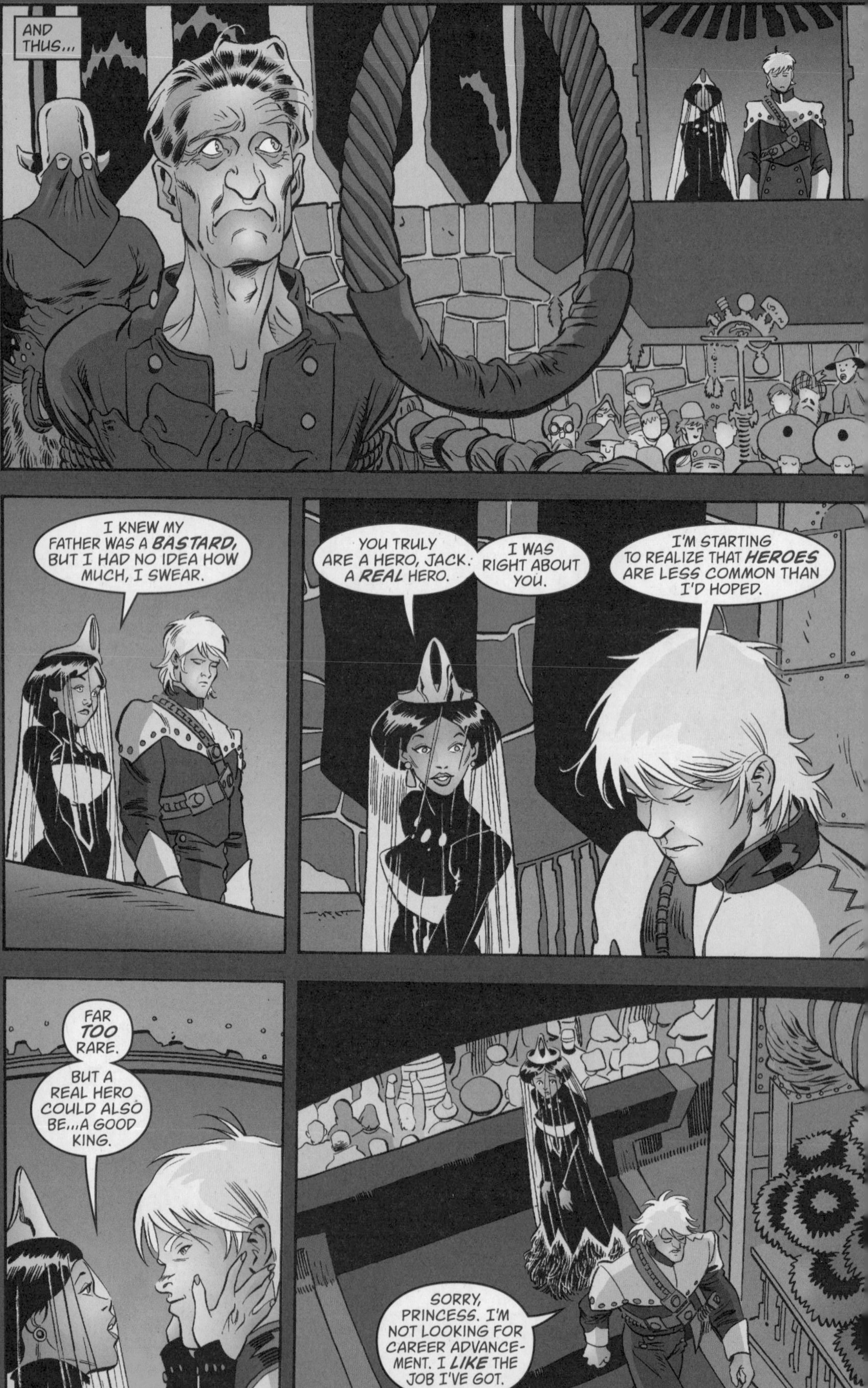

AND THUS...
I KNEW MY FATHER WAS A BASTARD, BUT I HAD NO IDEA HOW MUCH, I SWEAR.
YOU TRULY ARE A HERO, JACK. A REAL HERO.
I WAS RIGHT ABOUT YOU.
I'M STARTING TO REALIZE THAT HEROES ARE LESS COMMON THAN I'D HOPED.
FAR TOO RARE.
BUT A REAL HERO COULD ALSO BE...A GOOD KING.
SORRY, PRINCESS. I'M NOT LOOKING FOR CAREER ADVANCE-MENT. I LIKE THE JOB I'VE GOT.

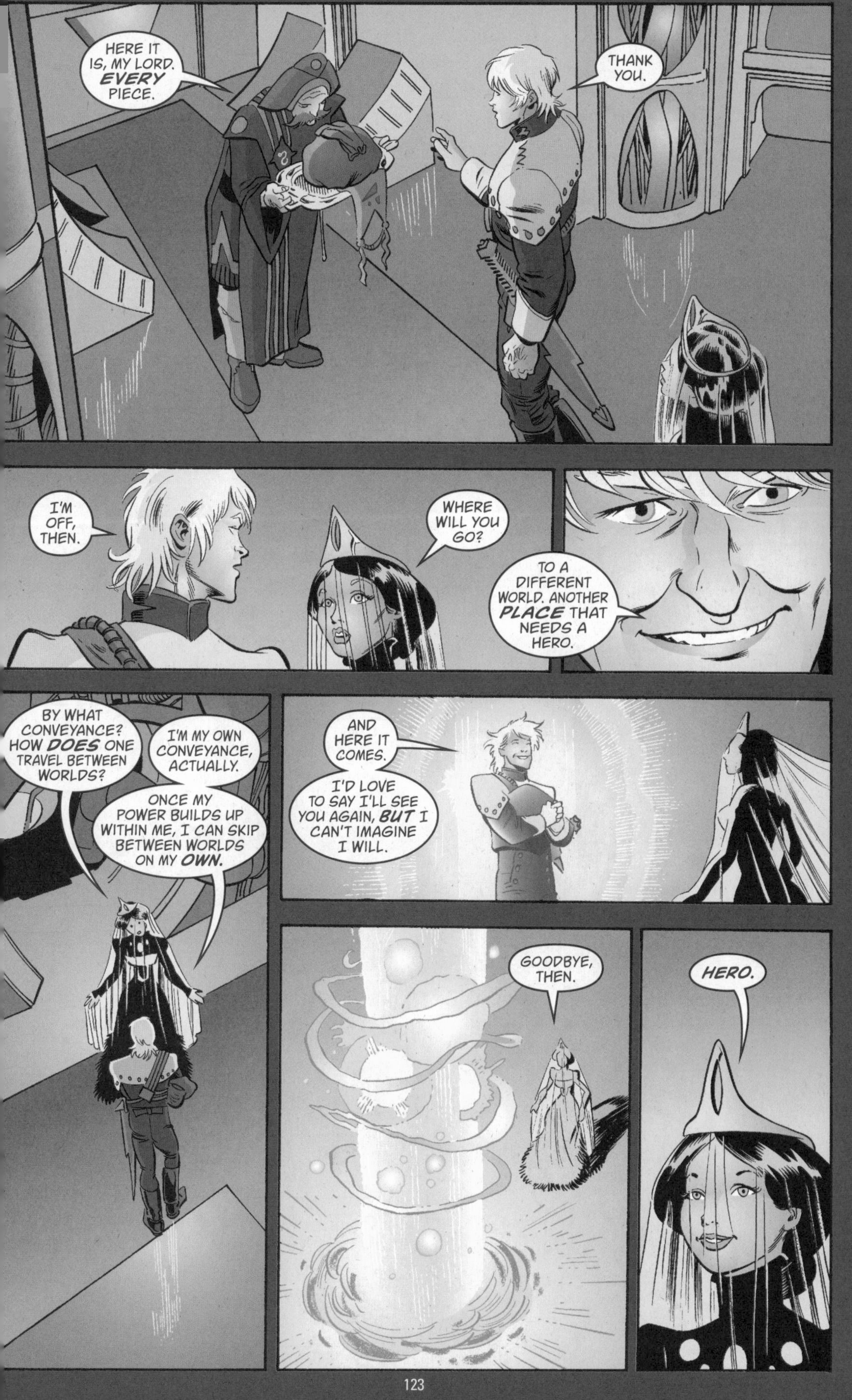
HERE IT IS, MY LORD. EVERY PIECE.
THANK YOU.
I'M OFF, THEN.
WHERE WILL YOU GO?
TO A DIFFERENT WORLD. ANOTHER PLACE THAT NEEDS A HERO.
BY WHAT CONVEYANCE? HOW DOES ONE TRAVEL BETWEEN WORLDS?
I'M MY OWN CONVEYANCE, ACTUALLY.
ONCE MY POWER BUILDS UP WITHIN ME, I CAN SKIP BETWEEN WORLDS ON MY OWN.
AND HERE IT COMES.
I'D LOVE TO SAY I'LL SEE YOU AGAIN, BUT I CAN'T IMAGINE I WILL.
GOODBYE, THEN.
HERO.

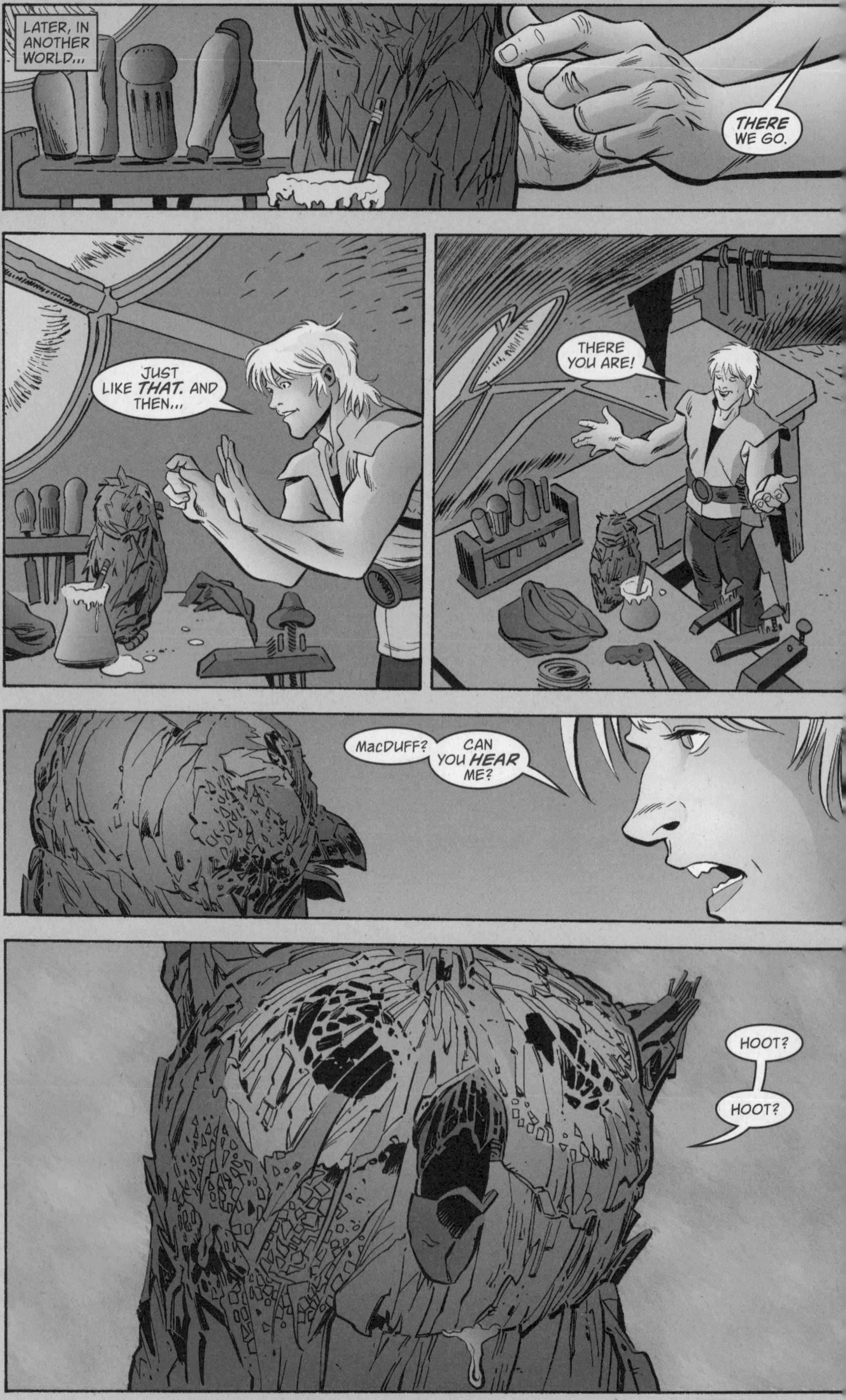
LATER, IN ANOTHER WORLD...
THERE WE GO.
JUST LIKE THAT. AND THEN...
THERE YOU ARE!
MacDUFF?
CAN YOU HEAR ME?
HOOT?
HOOT?

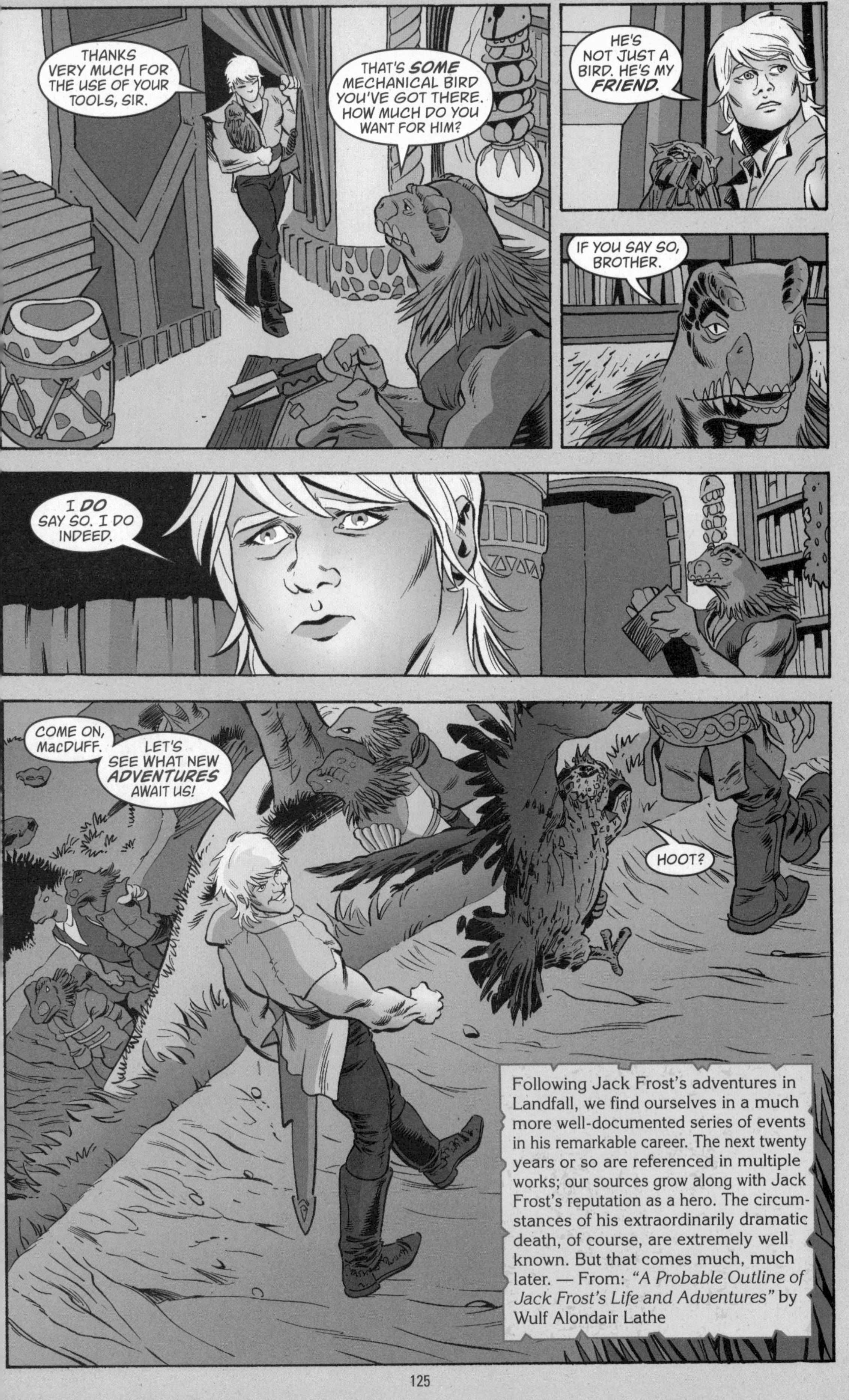
THANKS VERY MUCH FOR THE USE OF YOUR TOOLS, SIR.
THAT'S SOME MECHANICAL BIRD YOU'VE GOT THERE. HOW MUCH DO YOU WANT FOR HIM?
HE'S NOT JUST A BIRD. HE'S MY FRIEND.
IF YOU SAY SO, BROTHER.
I DO SAY SO. I DO INDEED.
COME ON, MacDUFF.
LET'S SEE WHAT NEW ADVENTURES AWAIT US!
HOOT?
Following Jack Frost's adventures in Landfall, we find ourselves in a much more well-documented series of events in his remarkable career. The next twenty years or so are referenced in multiple works; our sources grow along with Jack Frost's reputation as a hero. The circumstances of his extraordinarily dramatic death, of course, are extremely well known. But that comes much, much later. — From: *"A Probable Outline of Jack Frost's Life and Adventures"* by Wulf Alondair Lathe

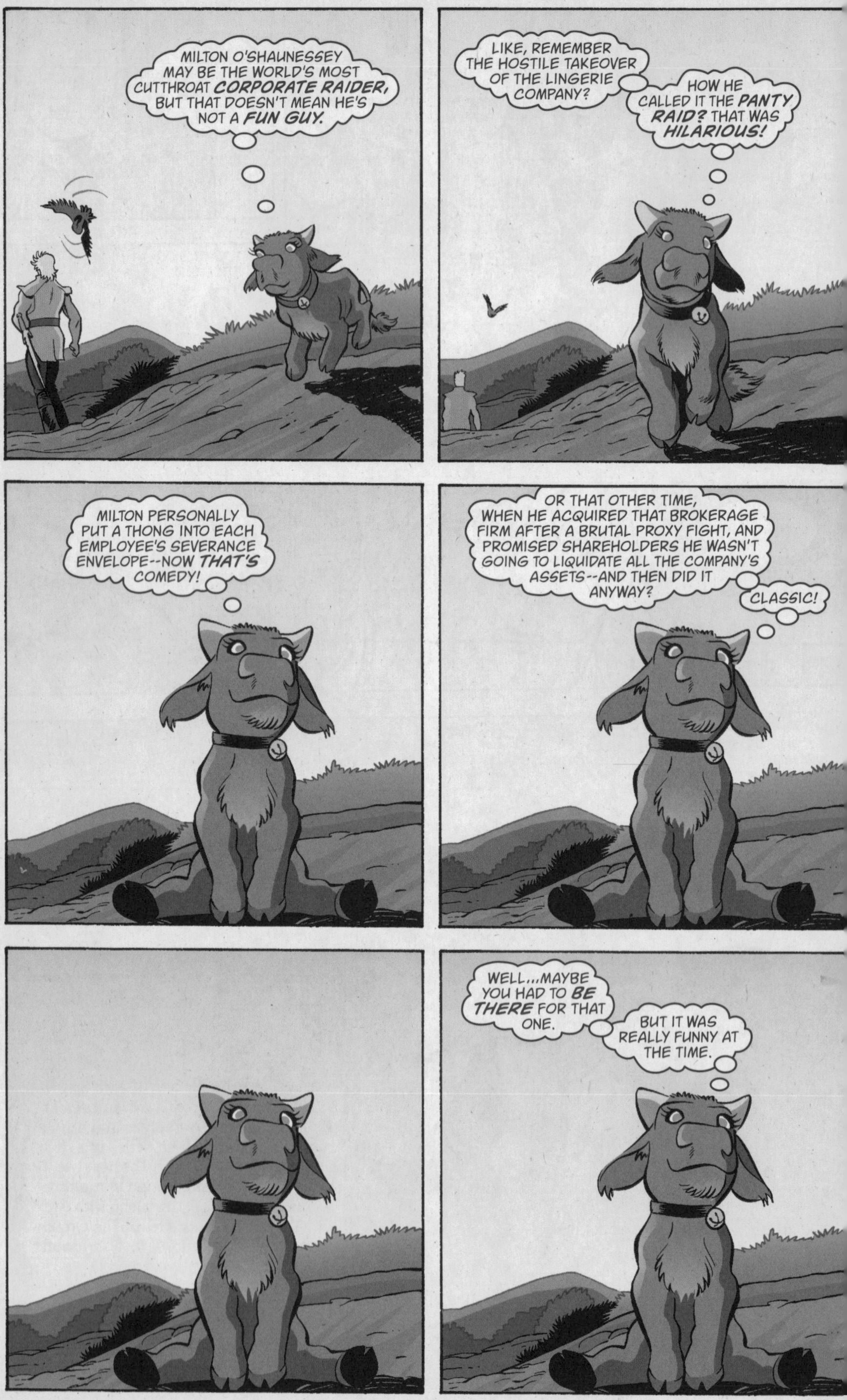

MILTON O'SHAUNESSEY MAY BE THE WORLD'S MOST CUTTHROAT CORPORATE RAIDER, BUT THAT DOESN'T MEAN HE'S NOT A FUN GUY.
LIKE, REMEMBER THE HOSTILE TAKEOVER OF THE LINGERIE COMPANY?
HOW HE CALLED IT THE PANTY RAID? THAT WAS HILARIOUS!
MILTON PERSONALLY PUT A THONG INTO EACH EMPLOYEE'S SEVERANCE ENVELOPE--NOW THAT'S COMEDY!
OR THAT OTHER TIME, WHEN HE ACQUIRED THAT BROKERAGE FIRM AFTER A BRUTAL PROXY FIGHT, AND PROMISED SHAREHOLDERS HE WASN'T GOING TO LIQUIDATE ALL THE COMPANY'S ASSETS--AND THEN DID IT ANYWAY?
CLASSIC!
WELL...MAYBE YOU HAD TO BE THERE FOR THAT ONE.
BUT IT WAS REALLY FUNNY AT THE TIME.

FROM THE PAGES OF
BILL WILLINGHAM'S FABLES

JACK OF FABLES

"It's got a little bit of everything that any sophisticated comics fan will enjoy."
– PUBLISHERS WEEKLY

"An unpredictable romp… it's a lot of fun."
–THE ONION

"Sharp, quick-paced, fun-to-read stuff that is sure to impress."
– METRO TORONTO

"This is fun." **– BOOKLIST**

VOL. 1: THE (NEARLY) GREAT ESCAPE
VOL. 2: JACK OF HEARTS
VOL. 3: THE BAD PRINCE
VOL. 4: AMERICANA
VOL. 5: TURNING PAGES
VOL. 6: THE BIG BOOK OF WAR
VOL. 7: THE NEW ADVENTURES OF JACK AND JACK

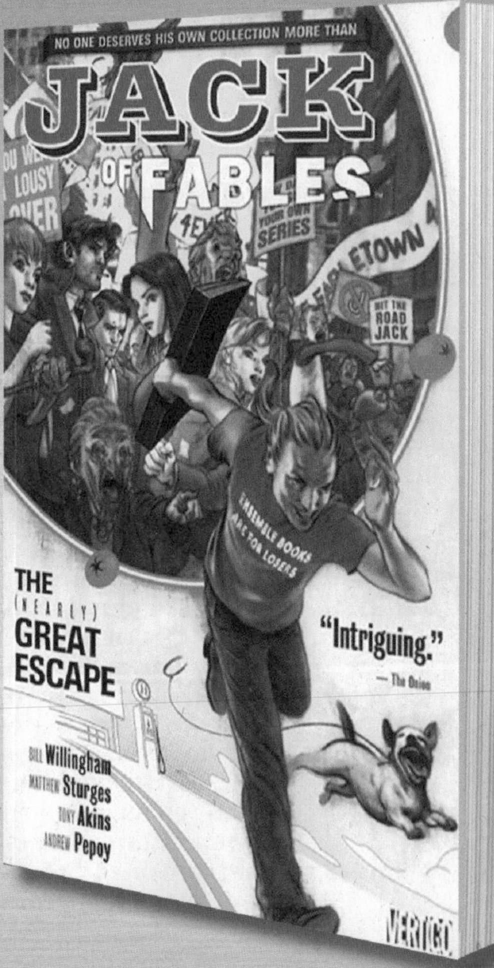
NO ONE DESERVES HIS OWN COLLECTION MORE THAN
JACK OF FABLES
THE (NEARLY) GREAT ESCAPE
"Intriguing."
— The Onion
Bill Willingham
Matthew Sturges
Tony Akins
Andrew Pepoy
VERTIGO

CK OF FABLES VOL. 2: JACK OF HEARTS

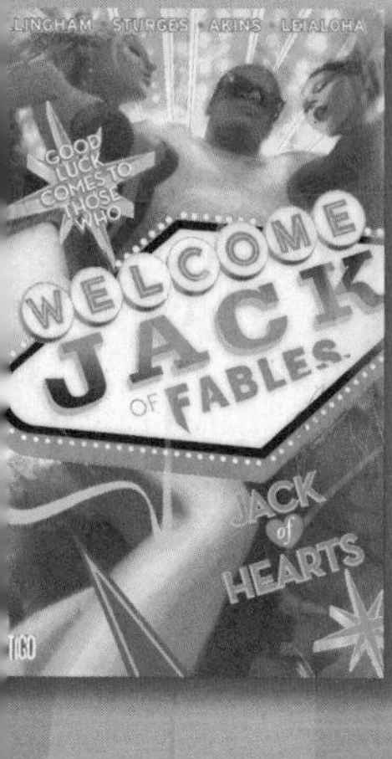
GOOD LUCK COMES TO THOSE WHO
WELCOME
JACK OF FABLES
JACK of HEARTS

JACK OF FABLES VOL. 3: THE BAD PRINCE

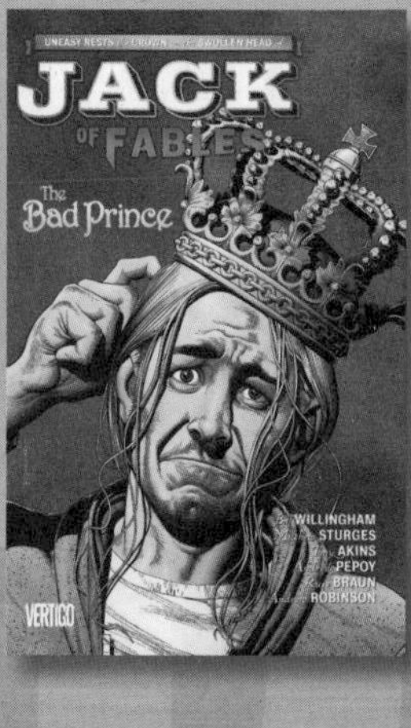
JACK OF FABLES
The Bad Prince
WILLINGHAM
STURGES
AKINS
PEPOY
BRAUN
ROBINSON
VERTIGO

JACK OF FABLES VOL. 4: AMERICANA

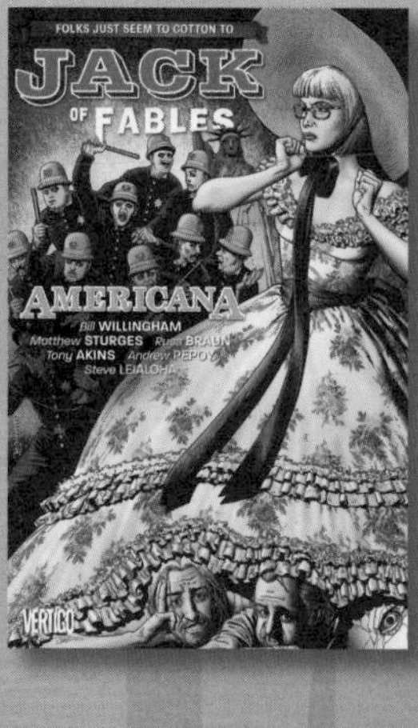
FOLKS JUST SEEM TO COTTON TO
JACK OF FABLES
AMERICANA
Bill WILLINGHAM
Matthew STURGES
Tony AKINS
Andrew PEPOY
Steve LEIALOHA
VERTIGO

JACK OF FABLES VOL. 5: TURNING PAGES

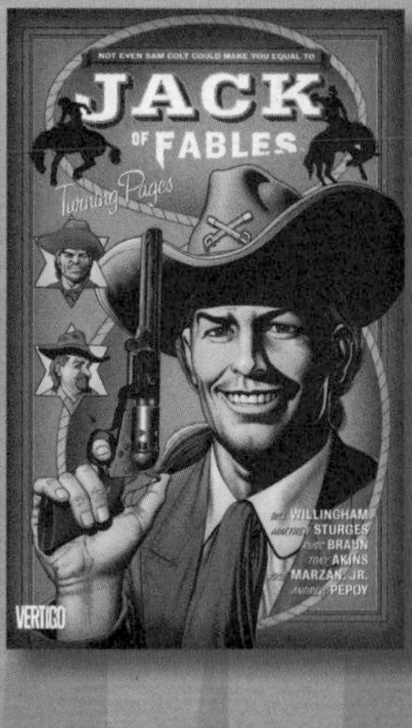
NOT EVEN SAM COLT COULD MAKE YOU EQUAL TO
JACK OF FABLES
Turning Pages
WILLINGHAM
STURGES
BRAUN
AKINS
MARZAN, JR.
PEPOY
VERTIGO

GO TO
VERTIGOBOOKS.COM
FOR FREE SAMPLES OF THE FIRST ISSUES OF OUR GRAPHIC NOVELS

Suggested for Mature Readers